CAMBRIDGE LIBRARY COLLECTION

Books of enduring scholarly value

Archaeology

The discovery of material remains from the recent or the ancient past has always been a source of fascination, but the development of archaeology as an academic discipline which interpreted such finds is relatively recent. It was the work of Winckelmann at Pompeii in the 1760s which first revealed the potential of systematic excavation to scholars and the wider public. Pioneering figures of the nineteenth century such as Schliemann, Layard and Petrie transformed archaeology from a search for ancient artifacts, by means as crude as using gunpowder to break into a tomb, to a science which drew from a wide range of disciplines - ancient languages and literature, geology, chemistry, social history - to increase our understanding of human life and society in the remote past.

Christian Inscriptions in the Irish Language

George Petrie (1790–1866) grew up in Dublin, where he trained as an artist. He became fascinated by Irish antiquities and travelled around the country studying ancient sites while working for the Ordnance Survey of Ireland and the Royal Irish Academy. He won awards for his publications on art and architecture, including the influential *The Ecclesiastical Architecture of Ireland, Anterior to the Anglo-Norman Invasion* (1845), which is also reissued in this series. This collection of Irish-language inscriptions was edited after Petrie's death by Margaret Stokes (1832–1900), the archaeologist daughter of his friend William Stokes, and published in two volumes between 1872 and 1878. Volume 1 is devoted to the important early medieval monastery at Clonmacnoise. It opens with an essay on the historical background, and contains drawings of over 170 inscriptions connected with the monastery. Each is accompanied by notes on its subject, date, script, decoration and linguistic features.

Christian Inscriptions in the Irish Language

Chiefly Collected and Drawn by George Petrie

Volume 1

Edited by Margaret Stokes

CAMBRIDGE
UNIVERSITY PRESS

University Printing House, Cambridge, CB2 8BS, United Kingdom

Cambridge University Press is part of the University of Cambridge.
It furthers the University's mission by disseminating knowledge in the pursuit of education, learning and research at the highest international levels of excellence.

www.cambridge.org
Information on this title: www.cambridge.org/9781108080132

This edition first published 1872
This digitally printed version 2015

ISBN 978-1-108-08013-2 Paperback

CHRISTIAN INSCRIPTIONS

IN THE IRISH LANGUAGE.

CHRISTIAN INSCRIPTIONS

IN THE IRISH LANGUAGE.

Chiefly Collected and Drawn by

GEORGE PETRIE, LL.D.;

AND EDITED BY M. STOKES.

VOL. I.

DUBLIN:

Printed at the University Press,

FOR THE ROYAL HISTORICAL AND ARCHÆOLOGICAL ASSOCIATION OF IRELAND.

1872.

DUBLIN:
PRINTED AT THE UNIVERSITY PRESS,
BY M. H. GILL.

CHRISTIAN INSCRIPTIONS,

&c. &c.

CLONMACNOIS.

THE monastery of Clonmacnois was for a long time the most celebrated religious community in Ireland, and distinguished as the chief school of art and learning in the country.

It is situated on the eastern bank of the River Shannon, in the King's County. The name *Cluain-mic-Nois* (*Cluain maccu-nois* in Old-Irish, Zeuss, G. C., pref. xxxii.) means the Meadow of the son of Nos.

This monastery was founded about the year 544, by St. Ciaran, as we read in the Chronicon Scotorum (p. 44, A. D. 544), "Ciaran the Great, son of the Carpenter, *quievit* in the 33rd year of his age; in the seventh month, also, after he began to build Clonmacnois;" and it is added in the Annals of Clonmacnois that "his body was buried in the Little Church of Clonvicknose."

In the ancient records of this place we find that Diarmaid Mac Cerbhaill, King of Ireland, aided Ciaran with his own hands to raise the humble edifice, and the still humbler cell which adjoined it; the monarch, at the time, being himself actually an outcast, on whose life a price was fixed, and who was seeking shelter from his persecutors in the wilderness to which the saint had come for solitude and repose. After the death of St. Ciaran, in gratitude for some benefit that King Diarmaid deemed he had received miraculously at his touch, he made the monastery a grant of three or four parcels of land in perpetuity; and to this donation his descendants, who chose the cemetery of Clonmacnois for their place of sepulture, added many other gifts of the same kind: thus the wealth of the community accumulated, and its power and influence increased. But it was not to these causes alone that Clonmacnois owed its fame, or the veneration in which it was held. It gradually became the chief school in Ireland; and we have many interesting evidences of its early celebrity as such. In the latter part of the eighth century we find that the fame of one of its lectors, Colcu, had spread to the Continent. He was the author of the *Scuaip Chrabhaidh*, i. e. the Besom of Devotion, transcribed by Colgan from the Book of Clonmacnois, which latter, according to O'Donovan, is probably the manuscript now called *Leabhar na hUidhre*). The high estimation in which Colcu was held is proved by his being called the "Chief Scribe and Master of the Scoti in Ireland," and by a letter to him from Alcuin, then residing at the court of Charlemagne, which is preserved among Archbishop Ussher's *Epistolæ Hibernicæ*, (Epist. xviii., Works, vol. iv., p. 466), beginning "From the humble priest, Alcuin, to the blessed master and pious father Colcu, greeting;" and concluding thus:—"I have sent for thy charity some oil, which at present is scarcely found in Britain; that you may dispense it through the stations of bishops where it is required, for the use of men or the honour of God. I have also sent fifty shekels for the brotherhood, of the alms of king Charles (I adjure you to pray for him); and of my own alms fifty shekels; and to the brothers in the south at Baldhuinega, thirty shekels of the king's alms, and thirty of my own alms; and twenty shekels of the alms of the king to the family of Areides, and twenty of my own alms; and to each of the Anchorites three shekels of pure silver; that they all may pray for me and for our lord king Charles, that God may preserve him for the protection of his holy Church, and for the praise and glory of his name." The death of Colcu is thus given in the Annals, A. D. 789:—"Colgu Ua Duineachda, lector of Cluain-mic-Nois, he who composed the 'Scuaip Chrabhaidh,' died."[a] This work of his is decribed by Colgan as "opus plenum ardentissima devotione et elevatione mentis in Deum" (Acta Sanctorum, p. 379, n. 9).

The next most famous scholar we meet with in the history of this monastery was Suibhine Mac Maelchumai, a drawing of whose tombstone will be found in the following collection. (*See* Pl. xxxi., Fig. 82.) He lived in the ninth century. His death is given by the Four Masters at 887, in Annales Cambriæ under 889, and by Florence of Worcester at 892, by whom he is styled "Doctor Scotorum peritissimus." It is to be regretted that none of his works have come down to us.

Among other names connected with Clonmacnois, it may be allowed to enumerate those of Colman, who, in the early part of the tenth century, erected the great church, and the cross still standing there; Donnchadh O'Braoin; and of Fachtna, the learned professor and priest of Clonmacnois, who became abbot of Iona and "the most distinguished abbot of the Gaeidhil;" and who died at Rome in the year 1024, whither he had gone on a pilgrimage. But the most remarkable of all the scholars of Clonmacnois was Tighernach Ua Braoin, the Annalist of Ireland, and the authority most commonly appealed to by modern writers on Irish history. That his learning was varied and extensive is proved by the examination of his Annals in detail. He quotes Eusebius, Orosius, Sex. Julius Africanus, Josephus, St. Jerome, Bede, and many other learned writers. He also appears to have been familiar with some of the modes of correcting the Calendar. He mentions the Lunar Cycle, and uses the Dominical Letter with the Kalends of several years. He was abbot of both Clonmacnois and Roscommon, and died in the year 1088, as we learn from the following entry in the Annals of the Four Masters: A. D. 1088, "Tighearnach Ua Braoin, chief successor of Ciaran and Coman, died in *imdha Chiarain*[b] [Ciaran's bed]. He was a paragon of learning and history."

The most distinguished ecclesiastic connected with this ancient church in the eleventh century was named Conn na mBocht, that is, Conn of the Poor. The Four Masters contain a notice of this Conn at 1031, which is the earliest passage in which the Céli-dé of Clonmac-

[a] There are two entries of his death in the Four Masters: A. D. 789 (*rectè* 794), "Colgu Ua Duineachda, lector of Cluain-mic-Nois, he who composed the Scuaip Crabhaidh [died]; and A. D. 791 (*rectè* 796), Colca the wise died."

[b] This was a couch covered by the skin of the saint's cow. O'Donovan was wrong in supposing it to be a religious establishment.

nois are mentioned, but from which we may infer that a body so called had been for some time in existence there:—"Conn na mBocht, head of the Céli-Dé, and anchorite of Clonmacnois, the first who invited a company of the poor of Cluain at Iseal-Chiarain, and who presented twenty cows of his own to it." In his essay on the Culdees, Dr. Reeves remarks that the account given in the Annals of this man and his son help to prove the connexion existing between the Céli-Dé and an hospital. A tract of low ground near Clonmacnois, called Iseal-Chiarain, was the site of this institution, and Conn na mBocht was succeeded by his son Maelchiaran in the presidency of it when, in the year 1079, Murchadh O'Melaghlin made a forcible descent upon it, and maltreated the Céli-Dé, and the superintendent of the poor; Maelchiaran was killed on this occasion (*See* Pl. LXIII., Fig. 151.)

The monastery of Clonmacnois seems to have been singularly rich in objects of art. The altar of the great church there was adorned with jewels, which were carried away when it was plundered in the year 1129. The annalists enumerate, among the things stolen, a model of Solomon's Temple; the cup of Donnchadh, son of Flann; the three jewels presented by King Turlough O'Connor—also a silver goblet, a silver cup with a gold cross over it, and a drinking horn of gold; the drinking horn of Ua Riada, King of Aradh; a silver chalice with a burnishing of gold upon it, with an engraving by the daughter of Ruaidri O'Conor; and the silver cup of Ceallach, successor of Patrick. The Crozier of Ciaran also is mentioned in the year 930. The shrine of St. Manchan, at Lemanaghan, within a few miles of Clonmacnois, is another work of this school, which we are told was executed in the year 1166, by "Ruaidhri Ua Conchobhair, and an embroidery of gold was carried over it by him in as good a style as a relic was ever covered in Ireland."[a] This shrine is still in existence,[b] and forms a fine example of late Celtic Christian art.

Many other treasures of this class, beautiful specimens of the goldsmith's and jeweller's art, have from time to time been found in Clonmacnois, and are preserved in the Museum of the Royal Irish Academy, and in the Petrie collection now deposited there, all showing the same high skill and true feeling for art that characterise the sculpture and architecture of this district from the latter part of the ninth to the twelfth century. But many have, we fear, been lost. Dr. Petrie, writing in the year 1821, says: "Some thirty years ago, the tomb of St. Ciaran was searched, in expectation of finding treasure, when a rosary of brass wire was discovered; a hollow ball of the same material, which opened; a chalice and wine vessel for the altar, and the crozier of St. Ciaran, were also found. These curious relics fell into ignorant hands, and were not, probably, deemed worthy of preservation; but there is reason to believe that the last-mentioned—the crozier of St. Ciaran—still exists. It was exhibited to the Society of Antiquaries about the year 1760."[c]

The antiquities still remaining at Clonmacnois may properly be divided into three classes—buildings, stone crosses, and sepulchral slabs. Of the first, there are the remains of

[a] See O'Donovan's Notes to Annals of the Four Masters, vol. ii., p. 843-4.

[b] It is still in fair preservation, and is now kept on a side altar, beneath a glass case, in the modern Roman Catholic Chapel of Boher, not far from Lemanaghan, under the careful guardianship of the Rev. John Dardis, P. P.

[c] Gough's Camden, vol. ii., p. 362.

eight ecclesiastical structures, with two round towers, and an ancient castle ; of the second, there are two large crosses standing, one of which was erected in memory of King Flann, by the Abbot Colman, in the early part of the tenth century ; and of the third class, there were upwards of one hundred and forty when Dr. Petrie visited Clonmacnois in early life. Many of these stones are not forthcoming now, while others have been found in digging graves, and during recent excavations at the Nunnery, since Dr. Petrie was there: drawings of these stones will be added to the collection.

"The value set on this spot as a cemetery is of very early antiquity, and, like that attached to Iona, arose out of a belief in the power which the patron saint's intercession would have with the Deity on the last day. Thus, in the Life of St. Corprius Crom, bishop of Clonmacnois, in the ninth century, the saint asks the unlaid spirit of the king Maelsechlainn, which he encounters on coming from his evening devotions in church, whether prayers had been offered for him, and whether he had any spiritual friends among the clergy in his lifetime, to which the spirit replies: 'My burial at Clonmacnois has availed me more than anything they have done for me, for it will arise on the Day of Judgment, aided by the intercession of St. Ciaran.' The prevalence of this belief is more fully set forth as the cause of the celebrity of Cluain as a place of sepulture, in a translation from an ancient MS. of the thirteenth century, commemorating the erection of its edifices, and enumerating the lands given to this see, for the purchase of places of interment. Thus, in the Life of Ciaran, it is set down that the best blood of Ireland have chosen their bodies to be buried in Cluain, which choice, for that Ciaran had such power—being a holy bishop, through the will of God—that whatever souls, harboured in the bodies, are buried under that dust, may never be adjudged to damnation. Wherefore, those of the said blood have divided the churchyard amongst themselves by the consent of Ciaran and his clerks. (This manuscript is in the British Museum. No. 51 of the Clarendon Collections, 4,796, and appears to have belonged to Sir James Ware).[a] The desire for interment within the precincts of this sacred spot was not confined to the princes of the Hy Neill or Clan Colman race. Those of the Connaught, South Munster, and others, soon followed their examples, and bought their grants at the cost of large donations of land." (Petrie MS.)

To the Hy Niall or Clanna Nèill, to whom, according to the ancient manuscripts, the best part of the cemetery belonged, Dr. Petrie allots several of the inscriptions in the following collection, and he adds other families, such as the O'Kellys, kings of Hy-Many ; the Mac Dermots, of Moyluirg ; the Mac Carthys, kings of South Munster ; the Dálcais family, or kings of North Munster ; besides the many ecclesiastics and learned men of Clonmacnois whose names now live only in the meagre annals of the country and on the simple tombstones, the drawings of which will form the bulk of this collection.

In the Rev. Dr. Todd's list of Irish manuscripts preserved in the Bodleian Library (Rawlinson, B. 486. fol. 29), the following poem, on the tribes and persons interred at Clonmacnois, written by Enoch O'Gillan, who lived on the borders of the River Suck, in the county of Galway, is mentioned.

[a] This interesting MS. has been edited, with copious notes, by Dr. O'Donovan, in the "Journal of the Kilkenny and South-East of Ireland Archæological Society," vol. i., second series, p. 448.

The Editor has to offer her best thanks to Mr. W. D. Macray for his kindness in procuring a tracing of the original MS. for her, and to Mr. Wm. M. Hennessy for the translation and notes with which he has enriched it:—

Caṫír Chíarain Cluain mic Nóis,
baile druċtṡolus dearsróis,
Da ṫíl rigráigi ar buan blaġ,
Sluaig fan riṫbaile sruṫglan.

Ataid ḟuairli cloindi Cuind
Fan reilig leacaid leargduind,
Snaidim no craeb 'os gaċ ċolaind
Agus ainm ċaeṁ ċeart oġaim.

Cland Chairbri fa tuaṫiḃ toir,
Na seaċt tromlaiṫi a Teamraiḋ,
Imḋa dosmeirg ar gort gaiḋ
Ag loċt crosleirg Chiaran.

Fir Theaḟai [is] tuaṫa breag,
Fa uir Cluana docuireaḋ;
Briġ eis feile tall fo tuinn,
Sil Creide is clann Conaill.

Itimdo clainn Cuinn na cath
Gu tur deirg is fod ga falaċ,
Imḋa suil úaine is ball ban
Fa úir uaiḋe ċland Golman.

Imda sa dun fa diaṁair
Fear da cloind Neill Naegiallaiġ,
Fir ra buaiḋ leabaiḋ mar ḃrug.
Fa Cluain lecaiḃ na golluḋ.

"Ciaran's city is Cluain-mic-Nois,
A place dew-bright, red-rosed:
Of a race of chiefs whose fame is lasting
[Are] hosts under the peaceful clear streamed place.

"Nobles of the children of Conn
Are under the flaggy, brown-sloped cemetery;
A knot,[a] or a craebh,[b] over each body,
And a fair, just, Ogham name.

The sons of Cairbre[c] over the eastern territories,
The seven great princes from Tara;—
Many a sheltering standard on a field of battle
[Is] with the people of Ciaran's plain of crosses.

The men of Teffia,[d] the tribes of Bregh,
Were buried under Cluain's clay;
The valiant and hospitable are yonder under thy [sod;
The race of Creide,[e] and the Clan-Conaill.[f]

Numerous are the sons of Conn of the Battles,
With red clay and turf covering them;
Many a blue eye and white limb
Under the earth of Clann-Colman's tomb.

Numerous in the secret stronghold
Are men of the race of Niall of the Nine Hostages;
Men whose fame deserved a bed like the Brugh,[g]
Sleeping under the flags of Cluain.

[a] *Knot*.—Probably this refers to the ornamental designs on the crosses and slabs.

[b] *Craebh*.—The *ogham craebh*, or virgular ogham. *See* O'Donovan's Ir. Gram., Introd., p. xlvii.

[c] *Cairbre*.—Apparently Cairbre Lifechair, son of Cormac Mac Airt.

[d] *Teffia*.—The ancient name of a district, comprising portions of the present counties of Longford and Westmeath.

[e] *Race of Creide*.—The O'Conors of Connacht were sometimes called Sil-Creide, or race of Creide.

[f] *Clann-Conaill*.—Not the Cinel-Conaill, or septs descended from Conall Gulban, son of Niall; but the descendants of his brother, Conall Cremthann, of whom were the Clann-Colman, or O'Melachlainns.

[g] *Brugh*.—The principal cemetery of the pagan Irish kings was at Brugh, which seems to have been situated on the northern bank of the Boyne. A series of tumuli and sepulchral *carns* extends from the neighbourhood of Slane towards Drogheda, beginning with the tumulus of New Grange. (*See* Lays of the Western Gael, p. 240, n. 21, by Dr. S. Ferguson.)

Cland Chonċoḃuir ċnuic in sġáil
Is cland Cheallaiġ na goṁḋáil
Na ḟir anncóni a muiġ
Cona bruiḋ a breaḋ maig.

The Clann-Connor of Cnoc-in-scáil,[a]
And the Clann-Kelly along with them;
The men of valour[b] in the plain
Who brought spoils from the plain of Bregh.

I Maelruanaiġ o ḃuill buig,
Air aiġaiḋ raṫa in ċomraic,
Glan aṁarc on aird a buil
Adarc I Ṫaig in teaglaíg.

The O'Mulronys from the soft Boyle,
In front of Rath-in-chomraic;
Bright is the view from the place where is
The pillow of O'Taidhg-in-teglaigh.[c]

I Lanagan is I Laind,
Ocus I Mael buic ḃrenaind
Craed a saerslat aċ samail,
I Finaċt is I Allaṁain.

The O'Flanagans,[d] and O'Floinns,[e]
And the soft O'Mulrennins;
What but likenesses of a noble branch
Are the O'Finnachtys, and O'Fallons?

I Fiaċraċ ṫís ar tuas,
Is amaille na mor duas
Truaġ age ní cluanar gan cloḋ
Is sluaiġdeaġ e gan impoḋ.

The Hy-Fiachrach, below and above,
Are there together in great esteem,
No misery is heard by him[f] without being subdued;
Powerful is he in reversing them [it].

I Laiṫḟeartaiġ na land ngorm,
Ceinail Aeḋa na nor-ċornd,
Is cian o doċuaig in dream de,
As ferr a Cluain a gumine.

The O'Flahertys of the blue blades,
The Cenel-Aedha[g] of the golden cups;
It is long since the race departed;
Better is their memory in Cluain.

I Diármada ag dul da·Cluain,
Is fir Gaileanga gland sluaig,
Aḃur mar da ċuaiḋ gaċ fear,
Da clas a Cluain ga caeine.

The descendants of Diarmaid[h] going to Cluain,
And the men of Gailenga[i]—a bright host
As each man departed hence,
In Cluain was heard lamenting for him.

Da ċuaiḋ mac Coisi da cluain
O ṫuaim mna go fa mor ḃuaid,
Da gluais craeḃ aenaċ aḃlaċ,
Is Mael meaḋa mall Ḟaḃraċ.

Mac Coise[j] went to Cluain,
From Tumna,[k] in great triumph;
The branch of the apple-tree plain went there,
And Maelmedha the mild, of Fore.

[a] *Cnoc-in-scáil.*—"The hill of the spectre," or of the "champion"—a name for the hill of Rath-Croghan, Co. Roscommon.

[b] *Of valour.*—The text of this line, and the next, is corrupt, and the translation is only conjectural.

[c] *O'Taidhg-in-teglaigh.*—The descendants of Tadhg-in-teglaigh, or Teige of the household. The name is now written *Tighe*.

[d] *O'Flanagans.*—Of Clann-Cahill, Co. Roscommon.

[e] *O'Floinns.*—O'Flynns, of the same county.

[f] *Him.*—i. e. St. Ciaran.

[g] *Cenel-Aedha.*—The tribe name of the O'Shaughnessys, of the Co. Galway.

[h] *Diarmaid.*—Ancestor of the Mac Dermots.

[i] *Gailenga.*—The territory of the O'Garas; now the barony of Gallen, Co. Mayo.

[j] *Mac Coise.*—Erard Mac Coise, a distinguished poet, whose death is entered in the Chron. Scotorum, and Tighernach's Annals, at the year 988. *See* O'Reilly's Irish Writers, pp. lxix and lxxii.

[k] *Tumna.*—Tuaim-mna, in the barony of Boyle, Co. Roscommon.

Ruc mac Lonain ceim craḃaiḋ	Mac Lonain[a] went on a pious journey
Gu Cluain fleadaig fad raṁaiḋ;	To the festive Cluain-Ramhfada;[b]
Noċo nuair int ollaṁ daġ	The good Ollave obtained not
buaig mar ċollud ag Ciaran.	A triumph like sleeping[c] with Ciaran.
Sa relic ḃeandċrosaig ḃain	In the cross-pointed fair cemetery
Da haglaiced corp Ciarain,	Ciaran's body was buried;
Fiu in relig o corp I Chais	The cemetery, from the body of the descendant of Cas,
A heread da ṗort parrṫis.	Is worth its size of the Garden of Paradise.
Atiḃ dḟuil ċorcur claind ui Ḃriain,	It drank of the purple blood of the Clan O'Brian,
Da ċuir caṫo sa seinċriaḋ;	Who fought battles in the old clay;
In ḃrían ḟuil mar ḃu duros,	The O'Brian blood, like to a rose—
Ṅiamaig a sug in senḟod.	Its essence gems the old sod.
Cros i claicaiḋ clog mbind,	The Cross[d] where melodious bells are heard,
D . . . teai . . . deg na déċill,	. . . .
baile dearglan is buan blaḋ;	A clear-bright place of lasting fame—
Cuan fan lergmag is leca.	Under the surface and flags is a host.
Pol easpal aḋḃur go á	Paul the Apostle, source of comfort—
Me lis la na coṁdala,	May I be with him the day of the Assembly;
Daḃí gili is doñ na daṫ	. . . .
Nir miri Cond na cet caṫ. Caṫir Ciarain.	Not more merry Conn of the Hundred Battles. Ciaran's City.
Enog O Gillain da ġaḃ	Enoch O'Gillain uttered
Ar dur in laeiḋ gu leaḃar	This lay broadly at first,
Ata in craeḃ nar ċeil a cra . . .	The scion who concealed not his love,
. . . . re sreiḃ na Suca. Caṫir Cir.	Is . . . . by the stream of the Suck.[e] Ciaran's City.

[a] *Mac Lonain.*—This may have been Flann Mac Lonain, the celebrated writer and chronologer, who was slain near Waterford in the year 891.

[b] *Cluain-Ramhfada.*—Clonrode, near Ennis Co. Clare, one of the residences of the ancient chiefs of Thomond. The writer seems to have understood this name as signifying the Cluan of the long road. Two roads or causeways at Clonmacnois are mentioned in the Annals of the Four Masters, A.D. 1070, viz., "The causeway from the Cross of Bishop Etchen to the Irdom of St. Ciaran, at Clonmacnois, was made by Maolciarain Mac Cuinn na-mbocht; and also the causeway from the Cross of St. Comgall to the Carn of the Three Crosses, and thence westward to the mouth of the street." The Pilgrim's Road—one of the ancient approaches to Clonmacnois—is still traceable for many miles. Another road, called the Long Road, led from Clonburren, opposite Clonmacnois, to Athlone. *See* Ord. Survey Letters, King's County.

[c] *Like sleeping.*—The form of this expression leaves it doubtful whether Flann Mac Lonain was buried in Clonmacnois; but, as he was slain near Waterford, it seems improbable that his remains were conveyed all the way to Cluain. The letters *loan* occur on a broken tombstone at Clonmacnois. *See* Plate v., Fig. 14.

[d] *The Cross.*—The Cross of the Scriptures, which stands close to the great belfry, O'Rourke's Tower, at Clonmacnois. The text of the next line is very obscure.

[e] *Suck.*—The River Suck, Co. Galway. The name of O'Gillain is not found in the general lists of Irish poets.

In the works of the school of Clonmacnois will be included the inscribed stones found at Lemanaghan, Hare Island and Inisbofin (two islands in Lough Ree), Clonburren, Athlone, Gallen Priory, and Calry, near Moate. Situated as these places were, in the neighbourhood of the great Monastery from which some were but mere offshoots, it is not surprising that the same character prevails in all the remains of this class of art which have been found in them. It is noteworthy that, while the standing crosses throughout Ireland are much alike, there is a marked dissimilarity in the sepulchral slabs found in the different ancient burial grounds throughout the country.

LEMANAGHAN.

In the year 645, Diarmaid, King of Ireland, according to the Four Masters, passed through Clonmacnois on his way to Carn Conaill, in the County Galway, where a battle was fought between him and Guaire, King of Connaught, in which the former was victorious. The congregation of St. Ciaran made supplication to God that he might return safe through the merits of their intercession. On his return from victory, he granted the lands of Tuaim Eirc—that is Erc's mound—to Clonmacnois as "altar sod" to God and St. Ciaran, and he gave three maledictions to any king whose people should take even a drink of water there. In 664 we read of the death of Saint Manchan here; from him the place was afterwards named *Liath Manchain*, i. e., according to O'Donovan, St. Manchan's grey land[a]—*liath* (Welsh *llwyd*) meaning grey. This St. Manchan is thus described in the Martyrology of Donegal, p. 27: "Manchân, of Liath, son of Indagh. Mella was the name of his mother, and his two sisters were Grealla and Greillseach. There is a church called Liath Manchâin, or Leth Manchâin, in Dealbhna-Mhec-Cochlâin. His relics are at the same place in a shrine, which is beautifully covered with boards on the inside, and with bronze outside them, and very beautifully carved. It was Manchân of Liath that composed the charming poem, i. e.:—

> 'Would that, O Son of the Living God!
> O Eternal ancient King!' &c.

A very old vellum book states that Manchân of Liath, in habits and life, was like unto "Hieronymus, who was very learned." His day was January 24. Lemanahan is situated in the barony of Garrycastle, King's County.

[a] Archdall, writing in 1786, says of Lemanaghan Church, "Its ruins may yet, though distantly, be seen, being surrounded by a bog at present impassable" (Monast. Hib., p. 402). This bog has since been reclaimed. The cell of St. Manchan, half hidden in trees, and thickly covered with ivy, is still standing. The east window is gone, but the west end remains perfect, with its quaint doorway square-headed and with inclined sides. From this building to the church runs a causeway, at the side of which is a holy well built in a circular form. There remain the ruins of a thirteenth or fourteenth century church, with portions of earlier masonry, and a much injured late twelfth century western doorway: in the graveyard lie the inscribed stones, drawings of which are given among the following Plates.

ISLANDS IN LOUGH REE.

In the lives of the early monks, we often find that towards the close of their lives they left the monastery which had been the scene of their labours, and to which their fame as teachers had attracted students in numbers, to seek some lonely island or mountain solitude, there to pass their latter days in undisturbed communion with God, and resting from all worldly care. Thus, we find that in the end of the ninth century, Caencomrac, of Inis-Endoimh, Bishop and Abbot of Lughmadh (Louth), the tutor of Aenagan and of Dunadach, from whom the family of Conn na-mbocht were descended,[a] "left Cluain in consequence of the veneration in which he was held there, for the neighbours worshipped him as a prophet, so that he went to seek for solitude in Loch Ree afterwards." He died on the island of Inis Endoimh, now Inis-enagh, in Lough Ree, near Lanesboro', in the year 898.

The character of the scenery of Lough Ree—its broad expanse of water studded with islands—is indeed such as might well offer many a quiet place of shelter for those humble and earnest men who thus sought to escape temptations which had reached them even in their schools and monasteries.

Two inscriptions, and one slab on which two crosses are carved, are all that have hitherto been found on these islands. One on Inis Aingin, or Hare Island—*Oraid do Tuathal hua Huarain*—is given by O'Donovan in his notes to the Annals of the Four Masters, (vol. i., p. 553); but this inscription was differently read by Dr. Petrie, who, in his drawing of the slab, gives the words as follows:—*Or̄ ar Tuath Charañ.* It has since disappeared. The other is on Inisbofin, an island a few miles to the north—*Oroit do Cormacan.* That the founder of Clonmacnois was also the founder of a church on Hare Island is stated by Colgan, and Lanigan, and Ware, who says: "Dermid, son of Cervail, Monarch of Ireland, granted to St. Kieran Clonmacnois and Inis Aingin, or the Island of All Saints" (Ware, Monasticon Hib.) He here confuses the Island of All Saints with Hare Island (Inis Aingin). Afterwards speaking of which, he says:—"Saint Kieran founded an abbey of regular canons in a certain island in Lough Ree, called Inis-Aingen."[b] O'Donovan questions the truth of this statement, which, however, seems to be borne out by the account given in the Martyrology of Donegal (at Jan. 7, p. 9) of Donnan, priest of this island, where it is stated that Donnan came to visit Ciaran in Inis Aingin, and that in the year 544 Ciaran left to him the island, and also his Gospel and its bearer, i. e. Maelodhrain.

CLONBURREN.

Clonburren, formerly Cluain Boirenn, is an ancient church on the west side of the Shannon, in the county of Roscommon, not far below Clonmacnois. It was founded in the sixth century by the Virgin Saint Cairech Dergain, who died on the 9th of February, 577. She was a sister of Saint Enna, of Aran.

[a] Annals of the Four Masters. A. D. 898.

[b] Antiquities of Ireland, by Sir James Ware, p. 90.

The following passage occurs in O'Donovan's Letters (Ordnance Survey, vol. f. 1.) from the County Roscommon:—

"Yesterday I visited the old Nunnery of Cloon Burren, from which I had a good view of Clonmacnoise. The following notice of it in the Registry of Clonmacnoise, as translated by Dudley Firbisse for Sir James Ware, excited my curiosity to examine the localities in that neighbourhood.

"'Grany (*rectè* Many) Mor O'Kelly killed a child; the Church forgave him, and he bestowed 12 daies in Relyg-na Keallry in Liosbailemor, in Kylmarusgach, to the cemeterie of O'Kelly in *Cluain*. And Loughlin O'Kelly, from wch are the offspring of the O'Kellys called Sloight Loughlyn, seeing these livings to have been concealed from *Cluaine*, went with this life of St. Kiaran to the Bishop there in *Cluaine*, and delivered it unto the Bishop, for which the Bishop gave unto Loughlyn and to his heirs for ever six quarters of land under this rent, six cows and six fatt hogges at every feast of St. Martin, and to repair the *Togher* or causey of Cluyn Buyrynn from the *Cross* of Carbre Crom westwards to the *Cruaidh* of Failte."

"This *togher* or causeway still exists, and runs across the bog from Cloon Burren to the Cruaidh, or hard ground of *Failte*, and the cross of Carbre Crom, now mutilated, stands nearly in the middle of it. There was a holy well at the foot of this cross, but it removed to the other side of the *togher*, in consequence of an insult offered it by an imprudent woman, who washed her clothes in it, and it has latterly been dried up by drains sunk at both sides of the causeway to keep it dry."

Dr. Petrie does not mention this Cross of Carbre Crom at Clonburren; but in his work on Irish Ecclesiastical Architecture, p. 323, he alludes to a slab at Clonmacnois bearing the inscription—*Or̄ do corbriu chrumm*, which he is inclined to believe was the work of the sculptor that executed the tombstone of Suibine Mac Mailehumai, whose death occurred about the same time as that of Carbre, that is the 6th of March, 899. Unfortunately, Dr. Petrie did not then publish any drawing of this stone, and none such has been found among his collections. The stone itself has since disappeared. This name was borne also by a chieftain of the race of Hy Many[a] in Connaught, who was contemporary with St. Ciaran, of Clonmacnois. The name is written Cairbre Crom, or Cam, which are nearly synonymous terms—*cam* meaning crooked, and *crom* bent or stooped.

In connexion with the subject of the above inscription we have the following passage in the Annals of the Four Masters, with a note by O'Donovan:—"A. D. 899, Cairbre Crom, Bishop of Cluain-mic-Nois, died. It was to him the spirit of Maelsechlainn shewed itself." For a long account of the conversation, which is said to have taken place between this Bishop and the spirit of King Maelsechlainn, or Malachy, see Colgan's Acta Sanctorum, p. 508, and the Martyrology of Donegal, p. 67.

[a] A curious legend connected with Coirpre Crom, chief of Hymany, and a "flag-stone" on the *togher* of Clonburren, is given by O'Donovan amongst his notes to the Registry of Clonmacnois, referred to at p. 4, *supra*. This legend will be referred to more fully in a subsequent page.

ATHLONE.

The Franciscan Monastery at Athlone was founded by Cathal O'Connor, A. D. 1241; in the adjoining churchyard, the inscribed slab (Plate XXII. Fig. 36) was observed by the late Mr. T. L. Cooke in the year 1849. From the ancient character of the cross, and the letters which form the inscription, *Or̄ do Thorpaith*, carved upon this stone, Dr. Petrie was inclined to believe that the site of the monastery must have been previously used for sepulture, if it was not also that of an ecclesiastical establishment more ancient than the house which was founded by Cathal. There was formerly a causeway leading through the bog from Clonmacnois to Athlone, which must have facilitated the intercourse between these places, as we are told by Mr. Cooke in an interesting article published by him upon the above-mentioned stone in the Transactions of the Kilkenny Archæological Society, vol. i., p. 411.

GALLEN PRIORY.

A monastery was erected here by St. Canoc, of Cell Mucraisi, in the year 492. Canoc, sometimes called Mochonóg, was son to the King of the Britons, and grandson of Bracha (meoc). According to the Martyrology of Donegal, p. 342, his mother was daughter of the King of the Saxons. The connexion with Britain appears to have been always preserved; for when we read of the Monastery having been burnt to the ground in the year 820, we find that it was restored by a party of emigrants from Wales, who afterwards founded a celebrated school, whence it acquired its ancient name of *Gailinne na mBretann*, or "Gallen of the Britons." It was successively burnt, or spoiled, in the years 949, 1003, 1519, 1531, and 1548, but was still in existence in the time of Colgan. The ruins of a fifteenth century church, with its flamboyant east window, are still standing in Sir Edmund Armstrong's demesne near the village of Ferbane, in the King's County, at a distance of about two hundred yards from which is a low grassy mound, probably the site of the original foundation. Here a singular group of sculptured slabs, covered with Celtic ornamental design, may be seen half buried in the grassy sod—one fragment, with the letters *Diam*, being the only one with any remains of an inscription. It is not unlikely that were this mound opened many other slabs would be discovered.

CALRAIGHE, OR CALRY.

The inscribed stone *Or̄ do Mailmaire*, now preserved at Shurock, near Moate, was carried thither, as Dr. Petrie learned from an old inhabitant of the place, from Calraighe. This was the ancient name of the M'Gawleys' country in Westmeath — a territory comprising the parish of Ballyloughloe—in which Shurock is situated. There is an old church in the neighbourhood called Culree, from which this stone was taken, and placed on the side of a small moat in the demesne of Shurock House, where it may still be seen. In the Ordnance Survey Letters (County Westmeath, pp. 29, 30), the following passage occurs:— "M'Firbis mentions different tribes in Ireland under the name Calraighe, who belonged to this district. Not far from the site of Ballyloughloe is shown the site of a small abbey, but no remains of any walls; and near the Protestant Church are the remains of a small chapel, said to have been built by the M'Gawleys, chiefs of Culree."

CHRONOLOGICAL LIST;

Being Obituary Notices in the Annals of the Four Masters, the Chronicon Scotorum, and other authorities, respecting persons bearing Names identical with those found on the Ancient Tombstones at Clonmacnois.

A. D.		
628	Colomban, Pl. I., Fig. 3, ...	Abbot of Clonmacnois.
651	Aed, Pl. XXIX., Fig. 74, ...	Abbot of Clonmacnois.
661	Colman, Pl. II., Fig. 4, ...	Abbot of Clonmacnois.
681	Colman, Pl. II., Fig. 6, ...	Abbot of Clonmacnois.
703	Cellach, Pl. IV., Fig. 12, ...	King of Connaught, afterwards Priest.
720	Cuindless, Pl. IV., Fig. 11, ...	Abbot of Clonmacnois.
738	Aedh Allan, son of Ferghil, Pl. XXIX., Fig 74,	King of Ulster.
780	Ruadri, Pl. VIII., Fig. 20, ...	King of Leinster.
783	Maelduin, Pl. I., Fig. 1, ...	Son of Aedh Allan, King of Ulster.
794	Fearghus, Pl. XXVII., Fig. 67, ...	Son of Ailghil, lord of Cinel-Cairbre.
806	Tuathgal, Pl. XII., Fig. 29, ...	Abbot of Clonmacnois.
807	Cobthach, Pl. XIII., Fig. 32, ...	Abbot of Saighir.
809	Orthanach, Pl. XIV., Fig. 34, ...	Abbot of Cill Foibrigh.[a]
809	Tuathal, Pl. XIV., Fig. 35, ...	Scribe of Clonmacnois.
814	Dubinse, Pl. XIV., Fig. 36, ...	Scribe of Clonmacnois.
821	Conaing, Pl. XXX., VII., Fig. 97, ...	Lord of Teffia.
824	Clemens, Pl. XV., Fig. 38, ...	Bishop of Clonard.
826	Uada, Pl. XV., Fig. 39, ...	Lord of Teffia.[b]
826	Artri, Pl. XXVI., Fig. 63, ...	King of Teffia.
834	Cumascach, Pl. XV., Fig. 37, ...	Prior of Clonmacnois.
838	Aed, Pl. XXIX., Fig. 74, ...	Prior of Clonmacnois.
842	Ronan, Pl. XXXVIII., Fig. 99, ...	Abbot of Clonmacnois.
848	Finnachta, Pl. XVII., Fig. 46, ...	King of Connaught.
848	Maelan, Pl. XVIII., Fig. 48, ...	Lord of Ui Briuin.[c]
855	Maeloena, Pl. LXXIII., Fig. 40, ...	Lector of Clonmacnois.
867	Martin, Pl. XV., Fig. 172, ...	Abbot of Clonmacnois and Scribe.
868	Comsudh, Pl. XXII., Fig. 55, ...	Scribe and Bishop of Disertchiarain, in Meath.
870	Ferdomnach, Pl. XX., Fig. 52, ...	Abbot of Clonmacnois.
877	Dublitir, Pl. XXI., Fig. 54, ...	Abbot of Clones.
883	Maelpatric, Pl. XXV., Fig. 61, ...	Abbot of Clonmacnois.
885	Carthac, Pl. XXV., Fig. 58, ...	Abbot of Birr, King's County.
887	Suibine Mac Maeleumha, Pl. XXXI., Fig. 82,	Scribe of Clonmacnois.
888	Maelbrigte, Pl. XXXI., Fig. 81, ...	Abbot of Clonmacnois.
889	Fergus, Pl. XXVII., Fig. 67, ...	Œconomus of Clonmacnois.
889	Tuadhcar, Pl. XXXV., Fig. 91, ...	Bishop of Clonmacnois.

[a] *Cillfoibrigh.*—Probably Kilbrew, in Meath. *See* Ann. Four Mast., vol. i., p. 338, n.

[b] *Teffia.*—In Westmeath.

[c] *Ui-Briuin*, i. e. the Ui-Briuin-Seola—a district lying on the east side of Lough Corrib, in the county of Galway.

A. D.		
891	Blaithmac, Pl. xxviii., Fig. 69, ...	Abbot of Clonmacnois.
895	Toichtech, Pl. xxix., Fig. 75, ...	Anchorite of Inis Ainghin, Lough Ree.
899	Cairbre Crom, Fig. 96, ...	Bishop of Clonmacnois.
914	Flann Mac Maelsechlainn, Pl. xxxiii., Fig. 88,	King of Ireland.
919	Moenach, Pl. xxxvi., Fig. 92, ...	A Culdee.
921	Maeltuile, Pl. xxxix., Fig. 101, ...	Lector of Clonmacnois.
921	Fiachra, Pl. xxxviii., Fig. 95, ...	Of Eaglais Beg,[a] at Clonmacnois.
924	Colman, Pl. xxxiii., Fig. 87, ...	Abbot of Clonmacnois.
925	Maelphetir, Pl. xl., Fig. 102, ...	Abbot of Clonfert.
926	Muirgal, Pl. xlii., Fig. 107, ...	Daughter of King Flann, who died at Clonmacnois.
927	Maelm [och]eirge, Pl. xliii., Fig. 108, .	Œconomus of Clonmacnois.
931	Sechnasach, Pl. xliv., Fig. 113, ...	Priest of Durrow.
932	Uallach, Pl. xliv., Fig. 112, ...	Chief Poetess of Ireland.
942	Guaire, Pl. xlvi., Fig. 117, ...	Priest of Clonmacnois.
948	Rechtar, Pl. xlvii., Fig. 120, ...	Chief Priest of Clonmacnois.
953	Dunadach, Pl. xlviii., Fig. 121, ...	Bishop of Clonmacnois.
961	Fergal, Pl. xlix., Fig. 123, ...	Died at Saighir.
966	Muiredach, Pl. lvi., Fig. 136, ...	Son of Fergus, Bishop of Armagh.
969	Maenach, Pl. xx., Fig. 50, ...	Bishop of Clonmacnois.
991	Maelfinnia, Pl. liii., Fig. 130, ...	Abbot of Clonmacnois.
994	Odran Ua h-Eolais, Pl. liii., Fig. 131, . .	Scribe of Clonmacnois.
1002	Flannchad, Pl. lv., Fig. 134, ...	Abbot of Clonmacnois.
1014	Aed, Pl. lxxii., Fig. 171, ...	Lord of Hy Many.
1017	Muredach, Pl. lvi., Fig. 136, ...	Anmchara[b] of Clonmacnois.
1021	Bran Ua Chain, Pl. lvii., Fig. 138, . . .	Chief of Meath.[c]
1025	Muiredach, Pl. lviii., Fig. 141, ...	Abbot of Clonmacnois.
1028	Maelphatraic, Pl. lviii., Fig. 142, . . .	Priest of Clonmacnois.
1029	Mael Brigte, Pl. lix., Fig. 143, ...	Chief Artificer of Ireland.
1032	Dubinse, Pl. xiv., Fig. 47, ...	Bell-ringer of Clonmacnois.
1036	Angus, Pl. lxxiv., Fig. 176, ... ,	Bishop of Clonfert.
1040	Cosgrach, Pl. lix., Fig. 144, ...	Bishop of Clonfert.
1056	Daighre, Pl. lxi., Fig. 147, ...	Anmchara of Cluain; died at Glendalough.
1056	Maelfinnia, Pl. lxii., Fig. 150, ...	Son of Conn, and Abbot of Clonmacnois.
1059	Conn, Pl. lxii., Fig. 149, ...	The glory and dignity of Clonmacnois.
1066	Fogartach, Pl. lxi., Fig. 148, ...	A wise man, and an Anchorite; died at Clonmacnois.
1079	Maelchiaran, Pl. lxiii., Fig. 151, . . .	Son of Mac Cuinn na mBocht[d], successor of Ciaran.
1080	Muiredach, Pl. lxiii., Fig. 151, ...	Lector of Clonmacnois.
1085	Gillachrist, Pl. lxiii., Fig. 152, ...	Son of Conn na mBocht.
1097	Maelan, Pl. xviii., Fig. 48, ...	Descendant of Conn na mBocht.[e]

[a] *Eaglais Beg*, i.e. The little Church, also called Temple Ciaran.

[b] *Anmchara*, i.e. Soul-friend.—The Irish name for Confessor.

[c] *Chief of Meath.*—Drowned in Loch Ennell, after plundering the Shrine of Ciaran.

[d] *Son of Conn na mBocht.*—The glory and dignity of Clonmacnois. *See* 1127.

[e] *Descendant of Conn na mBocht*.—Airchinnech of Eaglais beg, at Clonmacnois. Dr. Todd believes this word to be the title of the steward, whose duty was to superintend the farms and tenants of the Church. *See* Todd's St. Patrick, Apostle of Ireland, Introduction, p. 160.

A. D.		
1101	Maelciaran, Pl. LXIV., Fig. 153, ...	Senior of Clonmacnois.
1106	Maelmaire, Pl. LXIV., Fig. 154, ...	Son of Conn na mBocht.[a]
1127	Maele[oi]n, Pl. LXV., Fig. 156, ...	Successor of Ciaran.
1128	Cennedig, Pl. LXVI., Fig. 158, ...	Airchinnech of Lis-óiged at Clonmacnois.
1134	Maelchiaran, Pl. XXIX., Pig. 76, ...	Noble head of Clonmacnois.[b]
1172	Maeliohan ep̃s, Pl. LXVIII., Fig. 162, . .	Successor of Ciaran of Clonmacnois.
1278	Thomas, Pl. LXIX., Fig. 165, ...	Bishop of Clonmacnois.

[a] *Son of Conn na mBocht.*—Killed in the stone church.

[b] *Noble head of Clonmacnois.*—Died in the bed of Ciaran.

NOTICES OF THE PLATES.

CLONMACNOIS.

PLATE I.

Fig. 1.

MAELDUIN.

This name is a common one, now anglicised Muldoon. Its genitive singular occurs in an old obituary notice, quoted by Zeuss (Grammatica Celtica, vol. i., Præf. xxxii.): *August ιβ* . . . . *bás muirchatho m. mailedúin hicluain m. cunois. áimdachiarain. x. anno.* The death of Muirchad, son of Maeldúin in Clonmacnois, from Ciaran's Bed, in the tenth year. It is also found in the Book of Armagh, fo. 18. *b*, 2; Muirgus m̄ Mailduin. In an ancient poem found by O'Curry among the MSS. in the Burgundian Library at Brussels, a copy of which is now preserved in the Catholic University, Dublin, on the Kings and Chieftains buried at Clonmacnois, we read that Mailduin, son of Aedh Allan, was there interred, and the Four Masters record his death in the year 783. He is mentioned by the same Annalists in a previous passage:—"A. D. 781. A victory was gained by Mailduin, son of Aedh Allan, over Domhnall, son of Aedh Muin-dearg."

The design of a cross within a parallelogram—a fragment of which is seen on this stone—occurs on several of the oldest sepulchral slabs at Clonmacnois, where this stone was first drawn by Dr. Petrie, in the year 1822. It is no longer to be found.

Fig. 2.

COM . . .

The termination of this name being lost, the word may have been any of those beginning with the syllable Com, such as Comgan, Comman, Commaigh, the last two of which belonged to persons connected with Clonmacnois, as we learn from the following entry in the Annals of the Four Masters, A. D. 742: "Comman of Ross, Abbot of Clonmacnois, died;" and, in the Martyrology of Donegal, Commaigh, virgin, daughter of Ciaran, is named, whose day was the 19th of December.

Fig. 3.

OR̄ DO CHOLUMBON.

(Pray for Colomban.)

Or̄ is the abbreviated form of Oroit [i. e. orait, borrowed from the Latin *orate*, and sometimes, like *oremus*, used as a substantive].

Columbon is the dative sing. of Colomban, latinised Columbanus, diminutive of Colomb. Columbanus Colomb. (*See* Reeves's Adamnan, p. 5.)

This inscription was found at Clonmacnois by Dr. Petrie, in the year 1822, on a stone then used in stopping a hole in a wall at the east end of the churchyard. It has since been placed as a headstone to a grave of recent date.

The form of the cross and character of the letters belong to the earliest period of Christian art in Ireland. The circle, crossed by lines of equal length, seems to have preceded the cross with a prolonged shaft, which became more common in the eighth century; and the occurrence of the diamond-shaped ◇ among the letters points to the seventh century, and before it. It occurs, for instance, on the stones of Dufthach, at Killeen Cormac, and of Joseph, at Roscommon—both being remains of the earliest period, illustrations of which will be given in a subsequent portion of this work.

The identification of the name upon this slab with that of some person connected with Clonmacnois in the seventh century is thus rendered probable; and we find the death of an Abbot of this place, named Columbanus, or Colman, recorded by the Annalists as having occurred at this period. He is called Colman Mac ua Bardani, and his death is placed at the year 623 by the Four Masters; but in the Annals of Ulster, at 627, we find recorded the "*Pausa* Columbani, filii Barddaeni, *Abbatis* Clono." *See* the Annals of Clonmacnois at the year 624.

It was about this time (the first half of the seventh century) that the following events took place. A. D. 601—Pope Gregory sent Justus to help the mission of St. Augustine in England. A. D. 615—Columbanus died at Bobbio in Italy. A. D. 627—The church of Lindisfarne was founded by Aidan. A. D. 635—St. Gall died in Switzerland. A. D. 650—St. Fursae died, and was buried in Peronne.

A drawing of this stone is given by Mr. O'Neill in his Ancient Crosses of Ireland, and a larger one by Mr. George Victor Du Noyer may be seen in vol. vii. of his Antiquarian Sketches presented to the Royal Irish Academy.

PLATE II.

Fig. 4.

COLMAN >ııı⊥ıııı‖┬

(Colman the Poor.)

The name Colmán is an abbreviated form of Colombân, and is often given as an equivalent for Columbanus (*see* Reeves's Adamnan, p. 29, n.). This is one of the only three stones which have yet been found in Ireland where the Ogham character is used with the Roman. Drawn at Clonmacnois by Dr. Petrie, in the year 1822. It is no longer to be found.

A. D. 661. Colmán Cas, Abbot of Clonmacnois (son of Fulascach; his tribe was of the Corca Mogha; one year and three days only he held government); and Cumine, Abbot of Clonmacnois, whose tribe was of the Gregraighe, of Loch Teched, dormierunt (Chron. Scot.).

A. D. 664. Colmán Cas, Abbot of Cluain mic Nois, died of the great mortality called the *Buidhe Connaill* (the yellow plague). Four Masters.

A small cross prefixed to the name is the only ornament on this stone. The Ogham >ııı⊥ıııı‖┬ answers to the Irish word Bocht, or Poor.

Fig. 5.

FORCOS.

Fergus Mac Eirc is called Forcus by Adamnan (Vit. S. Columba, ed. Reeves, p. 33). The name Forcus occurs in the inscription on the St. Vigean's Cross. *See* "Sculp. Stones of Scotland," vol. ii., Notices of the Plates, p. 70.

Here is the first example we have met with of the circle crossed by prolonged shaft and arms. It seems an early development of the Irish Cross.

Drawn by Dr. Petrie in 1822. It is no longer to be found.

Fig. 6.

COLMAN.

This is a very common name. There are ninety-four saints so called in the Martyrology of Donegal.

"A. D. 681. Colman, Abbot of Cluain-mic-Nois, died." (Four Masters.) He was twelfth Abbot of Clonmacnois. He was from Airtech, between the rivers Lung and Brideóg, in the old barony of Boyle, in the county of Roscommon.

This slab was drawn at Clonmacnois by Dr. Petrie in 1822. It still exists; but the lettering is indistinct.

Fig. 7.

MAICHTECH.

This name has not been identified. But that it may be referred to an ancient date appears from the fact that the family name, Ui Maightecháin, or descendants of Maightechán, a diminutive of Maightech (*Maichtech*), is noticed in the Annals of the Four Masters, and Chron. Scotorum, at the year 1021. The sept was situated in the present county of Westmeath.

The Irish Cross, with looped terminations, was a common form about the seventh and eighth centuries.

Drawn by Dr. Petrie at Clonmacnois, in 1822. The stone which bears this inscription is not now to be found.

PLATE III.

Fig. 8.

FERCHOMUS.

This name occurs as a surname in the form Ua Fercubhais. The Four Masters record, at 1152, the death of Ferghal Ua Fercubhais, Lector of Armagh; and, at 1189, the death of Ua Fearcomais, Lector of Derry. The name cannot be identified with that of any person connected with Clonmacnois.

This drawing was made by Miss Boxwell from a rubbing taken of the stone at Clonmacnois by the Rev. James Graves and Mr. William M. Hennessy, in the year 1869.

Fig. 9.

DITHRAID.

This name has not been identified. It would be pronounced Diraid; and this is the name of a Bishop of Ferns, who died in 690, and of an ecclesiastic, who founded the church at Edardruim, in the diocese of Elphin. *See* Colgan's Acta SS., pp. 312, 313.

The small stone thus inscribed is built into the wall of Temple Dowling, at Clonmacnois.

Drawn by M. S. from a rubbing made of the stone at Clonmacnois by the Rev. James Graves and Mr. William M. Hennessy, in the year 1869.

Fig. 10.

CONLARAT.

The name has not been identified.

This stone was found in the churchyard of Lemanaghan, in the Clonmacnois district.

Drawn by Miss Boxwell from a rubbing made of the stone by the Rev. James Graves and Mr. William M. Hennessy, in the year 1869.

PLATE IV.

Fig. 11.

OR̄ AR CHUINDLESS.

(Pray for Cuindless.)

In this inscription we have the less common form *Oroit ar*, instead of *Oroit do*. *Ar* is a preposition signifying 'for.'

The above inscription is quoted by O'Donovan (*vide* Grammar, p. 43) as an example of the aspiration of the initial consonant C in ancient Irish. Thus we have also Cholumbon, Cholman.

This Cuindless was Abbot of Clonmacnois, and died, according to the Annals of Tighernach, in the year 724.

On this stone we meet with the first perfect example of the Irish cross—the Latin engrafted on the so-called Greek cross, or cross within the circle, which was the earlier form in Italy, as well as here.

This stone is described by the Rev. James Graves, in his list of Irish Monumental Stones, in the Journal of the Kilkenny South-East of Ireland Archæological Society, vol. iii., 1st series, p. 293. It was also drawn by Colonel Burton Conyngham for Dr. Petrie, on a smaller scale, and a sketch of it has been given by Mr. O'Neill in the Sculptured Crosses of Ancient Ireland.

Fig. 12.

DO CELLACH.

It is probable that the usual abbreviated form *Or̄* was on the upper portion of the stone, which has been broken off.

The modern name 'Kelly' represents *Cellaigh* (the gen. sing. of *Cellach*), which occurs in the inscription quoted by O'Donovan in his Irish Grammar, p. 398: "*Oroit do thadg ó ceallaig do ri o maini*—a prayer for Tadhg O'Kelly for the King of Hy-Many."

Cellach, son of Sechda, of the family of the Conmaicne, was Abbot of Clonmacnois, and died A D. 735. (Four Masters, p. 337.) Ceallach, son of Ragallach, was buried at Clonmacnois, as we learn from the ancient Irish poem on the Interments at this place, before referred to, p. 15. Of him we have the following records:—"A. D. 704. Ceallach Mac Ragallaigh, Rex Connacht, post clericatum, obiit." (Ann. Clon.) "A. D. 703. Ceallach, son of Raghallach, King of Connaught, died, after having gone under the yoke of priesthood." (Ann. Four Mast.)

The Irish cross is carved on this stone, without any ornamental detail.

Drawn by Dr. Petrie at Clonmacnois, in the year 1822.

PLATE V.

Fig. 13.

OR̄ DO COMGÁN.

(Pray for Comgán.)

This is the same name as Comdhan, as Dr. Reeves has pointed out in his edition of Adamnan's Life of Columba, p. 421, note, col. 1. This identity is still further proved by the fact that the name which is written Comdhan, of Glenn-Uissen (or Killeshin, Queen's County), in the Martyrologies, is written *Comgán* in the Book of Leinster, fol. 126, *a* 2. But still the identity of the Comgan, interred at Clonmacnois, is not well established. He was, perhaps, either the Comghan Maccuthenne (written *Comgan* Mac Cuitheine in the Chron. Scotorum), who died in the great plague of 663 (Four Masters, and other Annals), or the person called Comdhan, the Céledé mentioned in the Martyr. of Donegal, under August 2.

The plain Irish cross is carved on this stone.

Drawn by Dr. Petrie at Clonmacnois, in the year 1822.

Fig. 14.

OR̄ DO LŌÁN.

This name may be an abbreviated form of Lomán or Lonán; but it is more likely to be *Londán,* as the abbreviation for *m* is not common in early Irish inscriptions.

There are three Lommáns in the Martyrology—one of Ath-truim (Trim), in Meath, son of St. Patrick's sister; and another at Port-Loman, on the west bank of Lough Owel, county Westmeath; and a third of Lochgile (Loch Gill).

This cross is interesting as containing the first example of ornamental detail in this collection. The existence of the triquetra knot might lead to the belief that it was work of the ninth or tenth century, although the general form of the cross resembles that commonly used in the eighth.

Drawn by Dr. Petrie at Clonmacnois, in the year 1822. It cannot now be found.

Fig. 15.

R̄OEIN̄.

It is hard to say how this inscription should be read. Some letters may have been broken away at the beginning, so the inscription might have been [*Or̄ a*]*r Oein.* The name Oenu or Aenna occurs in the Martyrology of Donegal, January 20, p. 25. He was Abbot of Clonmacnois; and his death is entered in Chron. Scotorum, Four Masters, &c., under the year 569.

An Irish cross, with looped terminations to the arms and top of the shaft, is carved on this stone.

Drawn by Dr. Petrie in 1822. It cannot now be found.

PLATE VI.

Fig. 16.

THUTGUS.

No such name as Thutgus is known, although *gus* is a very common termination of Irish names.

The drawing of these letters may possibly be incorrect, and the true reading may perhaps be Tnutgal.

We find there was an Abbot of Seirkieran who bore that name, and who died A. D. 771. (Four Masters.)

The design on this stone—an oblong space divided into four compartments—is the second example of a series of fourteen of these designs which are found belonging to the eighth and ninth centuries in Clonmacnois. It may be called a cross within a parallelogram.

This stone was drawn by Dr. Petrie at Clonmacnois, in the year 1822. It is not now to be found there.

Fig. 17.

O . . . A C .

Dr. Petrie found the inscription on this stone illegible, and, as the stone has disappeared, there is now no possibility of deciphering it.

The design belongs to the same class as those fourteen mentioned in the note on Fig. 16, but the execution is much ruder.

This drawing was made at Clonmacnois by Dr. Petrie, in 1822.

PLATE VII.

Fig. 18.

OR̄ D . . . B . D .

This stone is marked with a well-preserved and perfectly formed Irish cross, although the principal part of the inscription has unfortunately been broken away.

Drawn by Dr. Petrie at Clonmacnois, in 1822.

Fig. 19.

OR̄ DO HUACAN.

(Pray for Ua Acan.)

This reading of the inscription was first given by Mr. Hennessy. Dr. Petrie read it Riacán. However, the letter H was very visible when Mr. Hennessy saw the stone, in 1869, in the churchyard of Clonmacnois, where it still stands at the head of a grave. The letters are very rudely cut, and the cross is of the oldest type, the arms and shaft of equal length, and bound by a circular band, the circle being so imperfectly drawn that it is more an oval than a circle.

The name Mael-*acain*, i. e. the servant of *Acan*, occurs in the Chronicon Scotorum, as that of the father of Guaire, Priest of Clonmacnois, who died A. D. 943.

Drawn by Dr. Petrie at Clonmacnois, in the year 1822.

PLATE VIII.

Fig. 20.

RUADRI.

This was a common name among the lords of Connaught; and the same as the Rhodri of the Welsh.

The name belonged to an abbot of Clonard, and tanist-abbot of Clonmacnois, as we learn from the following entry in the Chronicon Scotorum, p. 143 :— "A. D. 838. Ruaidhri, son of Donchadh, Vice Abbot of Cluain-Iraird, and tanist-abbot of Cluain-Muc-Nois, quievit."

We have here a form of cross—the cross within the circle—older than those that have hitherto occurred on the stones of the ninth century.

This stone was drawn by Dr. Petrie in the year 1822. It cannot now be found.

Fig. 21.

OROIT AR REMI[D].

(Pray for Remid.)

This is the first example we have yet found of the word *Oroit* being written in full; and we again meet with the use of the preposition *Ar* instead of *Do*.

The name Remid, which may be the same as Rimidh, occurs in the Four Masters, A. D. 781, as borne by a chieftain in Ulster. No other person is mentioned in the Annals as bearing this name. In the Martyrology of Donegal, p. 11, we have a Rimhidh, father to Finan, who was a Bishop, A. D. 659.

"A. D. 656. Fynian Mac Rivea, Bushop, died." Annals of Clonmacnois. "A. D. 659. Obitus Finnani Episcopi, filii Rimedo." Annals of Ulster. His name is recorded also in the Chronicon Scotorum.

This stone was drawn by Dr. Petrie in 1822. It is no longer to be found.

Fig. 22.

CONASSAC[H].

This name is perfect, with the exception of the last letter, which must have been an *h*, so that it read Conassach.

A Conassach is mentioned in the Annals of the Four Masters as the father of the Abbot Cudinaisc, of Armagh, who died A. D. 790.

This cross may have been a Latin one; but it is impossible to decide the form, as the stone is so much mutilated. It has already been described by the Rev. James Graves. *Vide* Journal of Kilk. and S.-E. of Ireland Archæol. Soc., vol. iii., p. 293.

Drawn by Dr. Petrie at Clonmacnois, in 1822.

PLATE IX.

Fig. 23.

OR̄ DO BOISSE.

(Pray for Boisse.)

The name of Boisse does not occur in the Annals or Martyrologies.

An Irish cross, with looped terminations, marks this stone. It cannot be older than the eleventh century, otherwise we should have had the dative ending in *in*, or *i*.

It was drawn by Dr. Petrie in 1821; and is not now to be found.

Fig. 24.

OR̄ DO BROTUR.

(Pray for Brótar.)

Brotur is the dat. sing. of Brótar, which was the name of the Danish chief who slew King Brian Boroimhe. It is probably not, however, originally a Danish name; although, like Niall, Cormac, &c., it was very probably borrowed from the Irish by the Danes. *See* Todd's Danish Wars, Introd., p. 169. It is the same as Bruadar, from which comes O'Brodair; and in the Annals of the Four Masters, A. D. 895, we read that Rían, son of Bruadar, i. e. Brodar, was slain by the Galls. This shows that Bruadar was Irish; and in the years 955 and 990, the Four Masters have the names Cairbre Finn Ua Bruadair, and Dubhlitir Ua Bruadair.

The design, now mutilated, is a portion of an Irish cross, with looped terminations to the arms and shaft.

Drawn by Dr. Petrie at Clonmacnois, in 1822.

PLATE X.

Fig. 25.

MARTINI.

(Of Martin.)

The employment of the genitive case, without a governing word, is common in inscriptions. It occurs in the Apostles' names on the Chalice found at Ardagh, in the county of Limerick, now deposited in the Museum of the Royal Irish Academy. For examples of inscriptions with names in the genitive case, see Lluyd's Archæologia Britannica, p. 227, halfway down the middle column.

Three stones bearing the name of Martin—one Martini, another Marthine, and a third, the diminutive form Martanan—are found at Clonmacnois; while only one ecclesiastic of the name of Martin is mentioned in the Annals as connected with this place:—"Martin, Abbot of Clonmacnois, died A. D. 867."

No cross is sculptured on this stone.

This drawing was made by Mr. R. Callwell, from a rubbing taken from the stone at Clonmacnois by the Rev. Charles Graves, D. D., now Bishop of Limerick.

Fig. 26.

EPSCOP DATHAL.

(Bishop Dathal.)

It is possible that this inscription has been wrongly read, as this name Dathal, which seems cognate with Dathi, has not been found in any of the Annals or Martyrologies; while that of Cathal is very common. There was a Bishop Cathal of Clonfert, whose death, in the year 961, is recorded in the Annals of the Four Masters.

The form of cross which accompanies this inscription is the Greek cross, enclosed in a parallelogram.

Drawn by Dr. Petrie at Clonmacnois, in the year 1822. It is no longer to be found.

PLATE XI.

Fig. 27.

[O R̄] AR LIA . . .

This fragment was drawn from a rubbing made by Mr. William M. Hennessy, at Clonmacnois, in the year 1869.

Fig. 28.

TOICTHECH.

Mr. Hennessy is inclined to believe that the broken fragments of the letters remaining in the inscription may have formed the ancient Irish name Toicthech, which is found on another stone at Clonmacnois.

This drawing was made from a rubbing of the stone at Clonmacnois.

PLATE XII.

Fig. 29.

TUATHGAL.

This name may be allied to that of Tuathal.

Tuathgal is the seventh Abbot of Clonmacnois whose name has been found among these inscriptions. "A. D. 806. Tuathghal, Abbot of the religious seniors of Cluain, died." In the old English version of the Annals of Ulster, in Cod. Clarend., tom. 49, the death of this Abbot is noticed thus:—"A. D. 810 Tuahgall, Abbas Sapiens Clona, moritur;" but in Dr. O'Conor's Edition, p. 107, the reading is:— "Tuathgal, Ab. Sruithe Cluana, moritur."

This inscription is accompanied by a highly decorated cross within a parallelogram; a border composed of the gammadion or Greek pattern surrounds it.

It may seem doubtful whether the art of sculpture in Ireland was so far advanced in the year 809 as to render the date assigned to this tombstone probable. However, it is certain that the arts were much cultivated here in the eighth and beginning of the ninth century. The following allusions to works of art in the Annals help to prove this fact:—

A. D. 784. The Bachall-Isu, or Crozier of St. Patrick, is mentioned. However, this may have been only a *holly stick*, which was enshrined afterwards.

A. D. 790. The Shrine of Rechra (Lambay, off the coast of Dublin) broken and plundered.

A. D. 793. The Shrine of Dochonna was borne away by foreigners from Inis Padraig, now Holm Peel, in the Isle of Man.

A. D. 796. The relics of Ronan, son of Berach, were placed in a shrine formed of gold and silver.

A. D. 804. The Shrine of Patrick is mentioned, and in such a way as shows the high esteem in which its contents were held; for King Aedh Mac Neil invaded Ulster in revenge for dishonour done to the shrine.

This drawing was made by Dr. Petrie, at Clonmacnois in 1822.

Fig. 30.

OROIT AR LIAT . . .

(Pray for Liat . . .)

This may be the beginning of the name Liathan, whence comes O'Liathan.

An Irish cross is sculptured on this stone, enclosed in a parallelogram, with a rich border composed of the gammadion, or Greek fret.

Drawn by Dr. Petrie at Clonmacnois, in 1822.

PLATE XIII.

Fig. 31.

. . . DO . . . .

This fragment is of interest, as being one of the few yet found on which is any representation of an animal. It is, therefore, placed on the same plate with the representation of the first example of a stone containing such a form.

This drawing is a reduction from a rubbing of Mr. O'Neill's.

Fig. 32.

OR̄ DO CHOBTHAC[H].

(Pray for Cobthach.)

This name, now represented by O'Coffey, or Coffey (without the O), has not been identified.

We learn from the Registry of Clonmacnois that the family of O'Cobthy, or Coffey, gave alms to the church of Clonmacnois, when they obtained a burial ground. O'Donovan adds in a note:—"This family was seated in the barony of Barryroe, in the county of Cork." *Vide* Journal of Kilk. and S. E. of Ireland Archæol. Soc., vol. iii., p. 459.

In the year 807 we read of a Cobthach, Abbot of Seirkieran, in the King's County, who may possibly have been the subject of the inscription, though the cross and ornamental design upon this stone seem to belong to the tenth or eleventh century. In the lizards, which form part of the ornament on this stone, is seen the second example of the use of animal forms that we have met with in sculptures of this class.

This drawing was made by Dr. Petrie at Clonmacnois, in the year 1822. The stone is now so much mutilated, that only half of the inscription remains.

PLATE XIV.

Fig. 33.

ORTHANACH.

Orthanach was the name of an Abbot of Cill Foibrigh, or Kilbrew, near Ashbourne, in Meath, who died in the year 809. There was also a Bishop of Kildare of this name, who died in the year 839. Subsequently it became a Christian name, and Dr. Todd mentions a poet called Orthanach O'Caellama, of the Curragh of Kildare. (Proceedings Royal Irish Academy, vol. v., p. 171.)

Fig. 34.

IRAL

There is no name commencing with these letters in the Annals. The name Irial occurs A. M. 3519.

Since the drawing of this stone was made another has been found at Clonmacnois, with a cross of exactly the same design; and we may from this form some conclusion as to its probable date. The tombstone referred to is that of Muirgel, daughter of King Flann, who died A. D. 926.

Drawn by Dr. Petrie at Clonmacnois, in 1822.

Fig. 35.

OR̄ DO THUATHAL.

(Pray for Tuathal.)

Tuathal is the Old Celtic Teutalus, as Pictet was the first to point out.

This inscription is quoted by O'Donovan as an example of the aspiration of the initial consonant T in ancient Irish. (Irish Gram., p. 43.)

The death of Tuathal, son of Dubhtach, scribe, wise man, and doctor, of Clonmacnois, is recorded by the Four Masters, at the year 809.

A. D. 969. Tuathal, Comarb of Ciaran, and a Bishop, died a sudden death after a three days' fast. (Chron. Scotorum.)

Fig. 36.

DUBINSE.

This name appears four times in the Annals of the Four Masters, twice in connexion with Clonmacnois.

A scribe of Clonmacnois, called Duibhinnsi, died in the year 814; and the great similarity in design of the crosses on the tombs of Tuathal and Duibinnse is a good argument for fixing the dates of these stones respectively at the years 809 and 814, being the years at which two officials of this monastery, bearing these names, are recorded as having died within an interval of only five years.

A Lector of Clonmacnois, named Duibhinnsi, died in the year 1032.

This stone was drawn at Clonmacnois, on a scale of an inch to a foot, by Colonel Burton Conyngham, and given to Dr. Petrie by Mr. Cooper.

PLATE XV.

Fig. 37.

CŪMASA.

Cūmasa should be read Cummascach. The genitive singular of this name, which was a very common one in the North of Ireland, and means literally "confuser," is represented by the modern surname of Comiskey, or Cumisky.

A. D. 834. Cumasgach, son of Aenghus, Prior of Cluain-mic-Nois, died. (Four Masters.)

A. D. 834. Cumuscach Mac Oengusa, Secnas Cluana-mic-Nois, *moritur*. (Ann. Ult.)

A. D. 832. Comasgagh Mac Enos, Abbot of Clonvicknose, died. (Ann. Clon.)

Drawn by Dr. Petrie at Clonmacnois, in the year 1822.

Fig. 38.

ORIT AR CLE[MENS].

These three letters may be the first syllable of the name Clemens, which occurs four times in the Annals of the Four Masters. It is a Latin name, and was borne by a native of Ireland, who was employed as a teacher of youth in France by the Emperor Charlemagne. The Irish correlatives for it may be *Cainnech, Caemhan*, or *Maithmech*. We read in the Annals of a Clemens, who died in the year 824, and was Abbot of Clonard; but it is not likely that an Abbot of Clonard would be interred at Clonmacnois. There was also a Clemens, Abbot of Tír-dá-glas, who died A. D. 797. (Four Masters.)

Drawn by Dr. Petrie at Clonmacnois, in the year 1822.

Fig. 39.

OR̄ DO UADA.

(Pray for Uada.)

The Four Masters record the death of an Uada, lord of Teffia, a district not far from Clonmacnois, at the year 826. In the poem above referred to (see page 15), the name Uatha Eochran occurs in the list given there of Kings and Chieftains buried at Clonmacnois.

This inscription is drawn from a rubbing made by the Rev. James Graves and Mr. Hennessy, at Clonmacnois, in 1869.

Fig. 40.

MARTHINE

This is the second of the four forms of the name Martin, alluded to in the notice of Fig. 25.

Martin is not a name of Irish origin; but, like Patrick and others, was introduced with Christianity, and, as we may suppose, adopted in honour of St. Martin of Tours, uncle of our great Apostle by the mother's side. Thus we meet with Mael-Martin, i. e. the reputed servant of Martin, among the saints who are interred with St. Gormgal in Ard-Oilen. This stone was probably the tomb of Martin, Abbot of Clonmacnois and Devenish, and scribe, of the sept of Dartraighe, or Dartry, in the west of the county of Monaghan, who died in the year 867.

Drawn by Dr. Petrie at Clonmacnois, in the year 1822.

PLATE XVI.

Fig. 41.

MA . . . .

The second character seems to be an A.

This fragment was drawn by Dr. Petrie at Clonmacnois, in the year 1822.

Fig. 42.

OR̄ AR FINDAN.

(Pray for Findán.)

Findán is a diminutive from the adj. *find* 'fair;' Welsh *gwynn*. It cannot be identified with that of any person connected with Clonmacnois.

There was a St. Findan of Reichenau, whose bowl is still preserved in the sacristy of the Abbey. He is commemorated at Nov. 16 in the Irish Calendar, and in the Necrologium of Reichenau. He is called Findán of Lemchoill in the Martyrology of Donegal. (*See* Reeves' Columba, p. 389.)

This stone was drawn by Dr. Petrie at Clonmacnois, in the year 1822.

PLATE XVII.

Fig. 43.

COLLÁN.

This appears to have been the name of a saint who belonged to Meath, as the name of an old church in that county was Tech Colláin, or the house of Collán. It is mentioned in the Chronicon Scotorum, A. D. 1045, and the Annals of the Four Masters, A. D. 1047. "Cethernach, Bishop from Teach-Collain, died at Hí on pilgrimage." The name of this place is now anglicized Stackallan. It is situated nearly midway between Navan and Slane.

A Collán lived at Durrow, as we learn from an ancient Irish poem, professing to have been composed by St. Columba. When speaking of the early inmates of the monastery there, the poet says :—"And Collán of pure heart, who has joined himself to them."

This stone was found by Dr. Petrie in the year 1822, lying loose at the east end of the churchyard at Clonmacnois; and a rubbing of it was made by Dr. Todd in August, 1847.

Fig. 44.

RARCEN.

. . R AR CEN . . . . . .

It has been suggested by Mr. Hennessy that this fragment may contain the first syllable of the name Cennetig, and that, when perfect, the inscription may have been *Or̄ ar Cennedig*. Another stone bearing the name of Cennetig is found in Clonmacnois. The name occurs three times in the Annals.

A. D. 1128. Ceinneidigh Ua Conghail, archinneach of Lisaeigheadh at Clonmacnois, died. (Four Mast.)

This appears to be a fragment of an altar stone, from the small crosses seen above the name. There are several instances of altar stones found at Clonmacnois. The stone is interesting, as showing the first perfect example of the plain Latin cross.

Drawn by Dr. Petrie at Clonmacnois, in the year 1822.

Fig. 45.

OR̄ DO FINNACHTU.

(Pray for Finnachta.)

Finnachtu is the dat. sing. of *Finnachta*, and may be cognate with the name Fiannachtach, i. e. *fian-gnimach*, 'hero-deedful,' *gnim fian lais*, 'the Fians' deed with him,' anciently a man's name. Still preserved in the surname O'Fiannachtaigh, *anglicé* Finaghty, or Finnerty. (Cormac's Glossary, p. 80; translated by O'Donovan.) In the poem (page 6) on the tribes and persons interred at Clonmacnois, it is stated that the O'Finnaghtys were one of the families who possessed burial-grounds there; and in the poem on the Kings and Chieftains interred there (*see* page 15), we find the name of Finnachta occurs as borne by one of them.

In the Chronicon Scotorum we read, A. D. 848, "Finnachda, son of Tomaltach, the saint of Luimnech, latterly an anchorite, and previously King of Connaught, quievit." Dr. O'Donovan, in his note (Four Masters, 864), says that Luibneach was "a place on the borders of ancient Meath and Munster, where it is probable he was fostered."

The Latin cross is seen on this stone.

Drawn by Dr. Petrie at Clonmacnois, in the year 1832.

PLATE XVIII.

Fig. 46.

O R Ō A [R . . . . . .] T H I N .

The abbreviation here used for Oroit is singular. As only three and a half of the final letters of the name exist, it is difficult to conjecture what it was, unless some name which ends in *thin*, such as Cairrthin.

The stone, when perfect, must have been a fine example of the Irish cross, framed by a border, enriched with an Etruscan design.

Drawn by Dr. Petrie at Clonmacnois, in the year 1822.

Fig. 47.

O R O I T A R M A E L A N .]

The name Maelan occurs three times in the Annals of the Four Masters. The word signifies one tonsured. Maelan is a diminutive of Mael, and is anglicized Moylan or Mullen.

This stone may have been the tomb of Maelan, a Connaught lord, whose death is thus given in the Annals of the Four Masters, p. 479:—"A. D. 848. Maelan, son of Cathmogha, lord of the Ui Briuin, of South Connaught, was slain by the foreigners."

This cross is much the same in design as the previous one on this Plate, but that a spiral ornament is seen at the end of the shaft. The way in which the form of the border, is made to yield to, and follow the outline of the stone, is very remarkable and characteristic.

Drawn by Dr. Petrie at Clonmacnois, in the year 1822.

PLATE XIX.

Fig. 48.

M A E L O E N A .

This name is compounded of Mael and Oena. Oenna was the name of a Saint and Abbot of Clonmacnois, who lived in the sixth century, and who has been already mentioned in the remarks on Fig. 15, page 19.

The name Maeloena is not to be confounded with that of Malone, which was adopted as a surname by a branch of the royal house of O'Conor in the eleventh century, and which is derived from the name Mael-Eoin, or 'Servant of John.'

The tombstone represented in this drawing may be that of Maeloena, son of Olbrann, one of the Luigni of Connaught, who was Lector of Clonmacnois, and died in the year 855. That it may be attributed to the ninth century is rendered still more probable by the appearance of the small Latin cross after the inscription, such as has been hitherto observed on stones held to belong to this century. Otherwise the rude form of the letters would lead to the belief in its still greater antiquity.

This stone was drawn by Dr. Petrie at Clonmacnois in 1821, but cannot now be found.

Fig. 49.

ŌR DO BRAN U CAILLEN.

(Pray for Bran O'Caillén.)

This name has not been identified with that of any one connected with Clonmacnois, although Bran is a common name among the Irish. There is a peculiar interest about this inscription, as being the first example of the use of surnames that has yet appeared in this collection; and it may, therefore, be objected by some, who hold that the formation of surnames did not take place till the eleventh century, that it is a mistake to suppose this stone to belong to so early a period as the ninth or tenth century. However, O'Donovan, in his Essay on Ancient Names of Irish Tribes (Irish Top. Poems, Dublin, 1862), has refuted the statement made by Ware, Keating, and Lynch, that family surnames did not become fixed in Ireland till A. D. 1002, and proved that they were in use at a much earlier date—as, for instance, the family name, Ua Dubhda (anglicised O'Dowda), first applied to Aedh, the grandson of Dubhda, who flourished A. D. 876; and Ua Ceallaigh, or O'Kelly, of Hy Many, first applied to the grandsons of Cellach, who lived in the year 874. In general the ancestors of the most distinguished Irish families, whose names have been preserved in the surnames of their descendants, flourished from the year 900 to 950. (*See* Irish Top. Poems, Introd., pp. 9, 11.) We learn from the Registry of Clonmacnois that the family of Ua Caillen, anglicised O'Killen, had a burial-ground there; and the ruins of a church, called Tempull O'Killen, are still standing. This church is said to have been built by Cormac O'Killen (or O'Cillene), successor of St. Ciarán, who died in 964, according to the Chronicon Scotorum, and who is also stated in that chronicle to have erected the Round Tower of Tomgraney, county Clare. (*See* Journal of the Kilk. and S. E. of Ireland Archæol. Soc., 2nd Series, vol. i., p. 459.) The Four Masters also record the death of a Conall O'Cillene at A. D. 1026. He was Bishop of Tomgraney. The surname of Caillén is found to belong to one person who was connected with Clonmacnois in the twelfth century. Under the year 1106 these Annalists record the death of Cormac Ua Caillén, who was airchinnech, or steward, of the Teach-aeigheadh, 'the house of the guests,' or 'hospital,' at Clonmacnois.

The small Latin cross marked on this stone, so closely resembling those in Figs. 40, 46, and 54, the period of which is held to be from the year 855 to 877, has led us to place this stone in a group with those, all of which seem to belong to the middle or end of the ninth century.

Drawn from a rubbing made of the stone by the Rev. James Graves and Mr. William M. Hennessy, in the year 1869.

PLATE XX.

Fig. 50.

OR̄ AR MAINA..

(Pray for Maina . .)

This may be a fragment of the name Mainach (a derivative from *máin, móin,* 'treasure'?), which was given to ecclesiastics and laymen indiscriminately.

The Chronicon Scotorum, at the year 969, which is the year 971 according to O'Flaherty's computation, records the death of a Maenach, son of Maelmichil, "Bishop of Cluain-muc-Nois." The Four Masters, at A. D. 866, have the obit of a person named Maenach, who was a chieftain of the septs O'Conor, of Connaught; and it appears from the registry of Clonmacnois that this family had purchased a burial-ground in that place. (*See* Journal of Kilk. and S. E. of Ireland Archæol. Soc., 2nd Series, vol. i., p. 451). The same fact may be inferred from the passage on the Clann Conor, in the seventh verse of the poem on the tribes interred at Clonmacnois. (*See* p. 5, *supra.*) But the inscription is more likely to be intended for Bishop Maenach than for the chief referred to.

This drawing was made at Clonmacnois by Dr. Petrie, in the year 1822.

Fig. 51.

OROIT AR FERDAMNACH.

(Pray for Ferdamnach.)

There are but eleven instances occurring in this collection of the word *Oroit* being written in full. The name Ferdamnach, better Ferdomnach, would be in Old Celtic *Verdumnâcos* ('very lordly'?). Cf. *Dumnacus.*

There was an Abbot of Clonmacnois, in the latter part of the ninth century, who bore this name, as we learn from the following entries:—"A. D. 870. Feardomnach, Abbot of Clonmacnois, died." (Four Masters.) "A. D. 871. Ferdomnach, Superior of Clonmacnois, dormivit." (Ann. Ult.) "A. D. 872. Feardomnach, i. e., of the Mughdorna, Abbot of Cluain-muc-Nois, quievit." (Chron. Scot.) We may gather something of his extraction in this last passage, as Mughdorna was the name of a sept seated in the present Barony of Cremorne, in the County of Monaghan, from whom sprang also Gorman, the ancestor of the family of Conn na mBocht. The writer of the Book of Armagh was named Ferdomnach. This inscription was noticed by Dr. Petrie in the year 1846, when an illustration of it from his collection was also given by Dr. Graves. (*See* Proceedings of the Royal Irish Academy, vol. iii., p. 322.)

An Irish cross, quadrate at the centre, and with spiral terminations to the shaft, is carved beneath this inscription.

Drawn by M. S., from a rubbing of the stone, taken in 1869, by Kyran Molloy, for the Rev. James Graves.

PLATE XXI.

Fig. 52.

OR̄ DO MAELMAIRE.

(Pray for Maelmaire.)

Maelmaire, more recently written Maelmuire, signifies 'tonsured servant of Mary.' This name occurs upon a stone of apparently later date, found in the Nunnery Church of Clonmacnois, and was given both to men and women. Its Latin correlative is *Marianus*. This name cannot be identified with any one on record as connected with Clonmacnois before the twelfth century; but the Four Masters record the deaths of two women of this name; one at least of whom would very likely be interred in Clonmacnois. "A. D. 964. Mailmaire, daughter of Niall, son of Aed, died." This Niall, son of Aed, was probably the lord of Ailech, mentioned by the Four Masters at A.D. 913. The second, and probably the person referred to, is Maelmaire, wife of King Malachi the Second, and sister of Sitric, the Dane, who died A. D. 1021.

This stone is now lying in a gentleman's demesne at Shurog, near Moate, about fifteen miles from Clonmacnois. It was carried from the old churchyard of Calraighe (Calry), in Westmeath, as Dr. Petrie learned from some old persons in the neighbourhood, to its present resting-place on the side of a mound.

The small Latin cross at the beginning of the inscription is interesting, as resembling those seen on many of the shrine inscriptions, and is precisely the same in form as that on the inscribed stone found in the Catacombs of Rome, which presents the most ancient example of the representation of the cross in dated epitaphs—belonging, as it also does, to the early part of the fifth century.

This drawing was made by Dr. Petrie, in the year 1822.

Fig. 53.

$\overline{\text{OR}}$ DO DUBLITIR.

(Pray for Dublitir.)

The gen. sing. *Duiblitrech* occurs in the Félire at May 15: *feil duiblitrech dermair* 'the feast of vast Dublitir,' Abbot of Findglas Caindech, near Dublin, who died A. D. 791.

This inscription may possibly belong to Dublitir, Abbot of Cluain Eois (Clones), and of Tech Airindan, or Tech Farannain, anglicised Tifarnham (County Westmeath), whose death is given in the Annals as occurring in the year 877. There was also a celebrated scribe and poet of the name, who flourished about the year 900, some of whose compositions are preserved in the MS. Rawlinson, 502, in the Bodleian Library, and who may not improbably have ended his days, like so many others of his class, under the hospitable roof of the "guest-house" of Clonmacnois. (*See* Dr. Todd's Paper on the Irish MSS. in the Bodleian Library. Proceed. R. I. Acad., vol. v., pp. 169, 179.)

The inscription was published without an illustration by the Rev. James Graves in March, 1855. (*See* Jour. of Kilkenny and South East of Ireland Archæol. Soc., 1st Series, vol. iii., p. 298.)

Drawn by Dr. Petrie at Clonmacnois, in the year 1822.

PLATE XXII.

Fig. 54.

$\overline{\text{OR}}$ DO CUMSI . .

(Pray for Cumsi . .)

This inscription is so much obliterated that it is difficult to read. The first and second syllable of this name are much separated by a fissure in the stone; but no trace of an intervening letter can be found, such as would occur were the name Cumascach. It may have been Cumsud. And the Four Masters record the deaths of several of this name in the ninth century; amongst them an Abbot Comsudh, of Disert Ciarain, in the Barony of Upper Kells, County of Meath, who died in 868, and who was "a scribe and bishop;" a Comsudh, Bishop of Clonard, in Meath, ob. A. D. 856; and a Cumsudh, son of Derero, a bishop, ob. A. D. 842. The name seems to be peculiarly a ninth century one.

Fig. 55.

ŌR DO THORPAITH.

(Pray for Thorpaith.)

Many forms of this name are given by ancient Irish writers—Torpaith, Tairpaithe, Torbath, &c. It is pronounced Torpa, anglicised Torpey or Tarpey. The aspiration in this inscription of the initial *t* of Torpaith is due to the vowel of the preposition *do*. (*See* Zeuss' Grammatica Celtica, ed. Ebel, p. 182.)

This name has not been identified with any one connected with Clonmacnois, or its neighbourhood. It occurs once in the Annals of the Four Masters, at A. D. 872; and Torptha, which may be the genitive singular of the same name, occurs in the same Annals, at 760; and in the Martyrology of Donegal, p. 376.

Mr. T. L. Cooke has already published this inscription, and described this stone as lying in the grave-yard of the Franciscan Monastery at Athlone. This monastery, which was founded by Cathal O'Conor, A. D. 1241, was probably built on the site of an ancient place of sepulture, to which the stone originally belonged. (*See* Journal of Kilkenny and South East of Ireland Archæol. Soc., 1st Series, vol. i., p. 409.)

The drawing was made by M. S. from a rubbing found in Dr. Petrie's collection. This stone is not now to be found.

PLATE XXIII.

Fig. 56.

MAELTUILE.

This name is formed by the union of the prefix Mael, 'servant,' and *tuile*, which seems the genitive case of *tol*, signifying 'will,' or 'desire;' *scil.*, perhaps, of God.

Two Abbots of Clonmacnois were so called; and it is interesting to observe that another fragment has been found at this place, bearing a portion of the same name. "A. D. 874. Eoghan and Maeltuile Ua Cuana, two Abbots of Cluain-mac-Nois, died." (Four Mast.) "A. D. 877. Maeltuile ua Cuana, Abbot of Clonmacnois, quievit." (Chronicon Scotorum.) The death of the second Maeltuile is given in the Chronicon Scotorum, A. D. 922:—"Maeltuile, son of Colman, Lector of Cluain-mac-Nois, quievit."

Drawn by Dr. Petrie at Clonmacnois, in the year 1822.

Fig. 57.

ŌT AR HUIDRINE.

(Pray for Uidríne.)

The abbreviation *Ōt* for *oroit* is a very peculiar form, no other instance of which occurs in this collection.

This name, Huidríne (apparently a diminutive from *odar*), has not been identified with any one connected with Clonmacnois; but it occurs, though at a date too early to be associated with this inscription, in the Annals of Ulster, where we read:—"A. D. 693. Huidren Campi Bile, Magh-Bile, or Moville, quievit;" and in the parallel passage in the Annals of the Four Masters, at 691.

A drawing of this stone, on a small scale, is given in Mr. O'Neill's work on the Sculptured Crosses of Ancient Ireland, where the inscription is read—"Ōt ar Huelrine;" and another drawing of the same stone, by Mr. Du Noyer, may be seen in vol. vi., No. 53, of the Antiquarian Sketches, presented by that artist to the Royal Irish Academy.

Fig. 58.

ŌR DO [C]HARTHAC.

(Pray for Carthach.)

This name is a common one—the same as Carataue, Caradawg in Welsh, and Caratâcos in Old Celtic.

The Mac Carthys, of Desmond, derive their name from Carthach, son of Saerbrethach or *Justinus*, who died A. D. 1045; and this family purchased a burial-ground in Clonmacnois, as we learn from the Registry of Clonmacnois. (*See* Journal of Kilk. and S. E. of Ireland Archæol. Soc., 2nd Series, vol. i., p. 457.)

Drawn by Dr. Petrie at Clonmacnois, in the year 1822.

PLATE XXIV.

Fig. 59.

TET....

These letters appear to have formed the first syllable of some such name as Tetghal, which appears in the Martyrology of Donegal, April 16; and as the name of a bishop of Lann-Ela (Lynally, King's County), in the Four Masters, at the year 709.

The cross beneath the name is a curious one, being a Latin cross sharpened at the end of the shaft. This form was afterwards termed in heraldry the cross fitchée, so called because, being sharpened at the end, it could be fixed upright in the ground, and was probably copied from the pilgrim's staff.

This stone was drawn by Dr. Petrie at Clonmacnois, in the year 1822.

Fig. 60.

ŌR DO FERAGAN.

(Pray for Feragan.)

This name is derived from *Fer*, 'a man,' by adding *-agan*—a very usual affix in proper names. It is probably equivalent to the Old Irish *-ucán*, in *Dubucán*, *Flanducán*, *Echucán*, &c. The name cannot be found in the Annals or Martyrologies; and, as the stone has disappeared, it is not possible now to verify the writing.

A large Latin cross accompanies this inscription. This form came into use in Italy about the beginning of the fifth century, and by the end of the sixth had grown more common. (De Rossi, de Titul. Carthag. apud Spic. Solesm. iv. Roma Sotteranea, J. S. Northcote, D. D., p. 232.)

Drawn by Dr. Petrie at Clonmacnois, in the year 1822.

PLATE XXV.

Fig. 61.

ŌR DO MAELPATRIC.

(Pray for Maelpatric.)

This name was a common one in Ireland; it signifies 'tonsured servant of Patrick;' and is latinised *Calvus Patricii* in the St. Gall Codex Priscian. 157*a*. (Zeuss' G. C., ed. Ebel, pref., p. xi.) That, as our annalists testify, there were many ecclesiastics of the name in the early ages of the Church, is only to be expected, and might be advanced as a proof, if proof were wanting, of the belief in the existence of the Apostle in honour of whom so many devoted to religion received their name, at the time this one was first used. One Abbot of Clonmacnois, in the ninth century, was so called. His death is thus recorded by the Four Masters:—"A. D. 883. The seventh year of Flann Mael-padraig, Abbot of Cluain-mic-Nois, of the race of the Ui Maine, died;" and in the Chronicon Scotorum his death is entered as occurring in the year 885; and we not only learn that he was from Hy-Many, the territory of the O'Kellys, in Galway and Roscommon, but also (Chronicon Scotorum) that he came from Tech inghine Lingaig, "the House of Lingach's daughter," which place has not been identified. That this clan had their burial-ground at Clonmacnois is stated not only in the Registry of that place, but also in the poem on the tribes and persons buried at Clonmacnois, given at page 5, *supra*, verse 7.

Drawn by Dr. Petrie at Clonmacnois, in the year 1822. In Mr. Du Noyer's Antiquarian Sketches, vol. vii., No. 69, a copy of this inscription may be seen, with a slight variation of the reading of the first syllable of the name, Mr. Du Noyer making it *Moel*, instead of *Mail*. He adds in a note, that the form of the letters indicates an early date.

PLATE XXVI.

Fig. 62.

SNEDGUS.

It is possible that this may be the tombstone of Snedgus, of Disert Diarmarta (now Castledermot), County Kildare, the tutor of the celebrated Cormac, the reputed author of the *Sanas Chormaic*, or Glossary of Cormac. His death is thus recorded:—"A. D. 888. Snedgus, wise man of Disert Diarmada, tutor of Cormac Mac Cuilennain, quievit." (Chronicon Scotorum.) His death is also recorded by the Four Masters at 885.

Drawn by Dr. Petrie at Clonmacnois, in the year 1822.

Fig. 63.

ARTRI.

This may be the tomb of Artri, King of Teffia, whose name is thus recorded in the Chronicon Scotorum:—"A. D. 826. Mortal wounding of Artri, son of Muirghes, King of Teffia." The name Artri, or Airtri, occurs in the Annals of the Four Masters, at the dates 797, 817, 822, 824, 832, and 850.

The inscription on this stone has been published by the Rev. James Graves; (*see* Journal of Kilk. and S. E. of Ireland Archæol. Soc., 1st Series, vol. iii.); and a drawing of it is given by Mr. Henry O'Neill. (*See* Sculptured Crosses of Ireland, Pl. xxiv.)

Drawn by Dr. Petrie at Clonmacnois, in the year 1822.

Fig. 64.

ECTBR . .

This may be the beginning of the name Ectbran, an Old Irish name, which, however, does not occur in the Annals.

The names Ectbrict and Ectbrit occur in the Martyrology of Donegal. To the first, at May 5, a more recent hand has added:—"Saxo, Mart. Taml. et Marian." And Dr. Todd believes him to be S. Eadbert, Bishop of Lindisfarne; while to the second, Ecbrit, or Icbrit, a later hand has added:—"He seems English." From the prefix *Ect* (yet the prefix *Ect* occurs in undoubted Irish names—*see Echtgus*, Four Masters)—it seems to be a Teutonic name. For examples of such, beginning with "Ect," *see* the Index to Kemble's Charters. There is also a Low German Ecdbrat in Förstemann's *Altdeutsches Namenbuch*, p. 14, col. 2. The name Ecbricht is written Ecgberht, or Ecbyrt, in Anglo-Saxon. An Eicbericht Christi Miles (i. e. 'Soldier of Christ') is mentioned in Reeves' Columba, p. 383; and in the Félire of Oengus, at December 8, we have the same name, with the diminutival *án* affixed:—

"Búaid Ichtbrictáin umail
donarlaid tar romuir
do Christ cachain figil,
hi curchán cen chodail (leg. choduil)."

i. e. (The) 'victory of humble Egbert, who came over a great sea. To Christ he sang vigil in a little boat without a skin (round it).' (*See* Martyr. Donegal, at December 8.)

Drawn by Dr. Petrie at Clonmacnois, in the year 1822.

Fig. 65.

+ AND . . . . .

This inscription is so much mutilated, it is impossible to suggest what the name may have been. The small cross preceding the inscription is an interesting feature.

Drawn by Dr. Petrie at Clonmacnois, in the year 1822.

Fig. 66.

CIRINI.

This is the Irish form of Hieronymus, or Jerome. *Cirini* is the genitive singular of *Cirine* (= *Cyrenaeus ?*), the name by which the Irish called St. Jerome.

The design of the crosses on all the stones on this plate, being a cross within a parallelogram, bears so strong a resemblance in character to that on the stone of Snedgus, that we may well believe that they belong to the same period of art.

PLATE XXVII.

Fig. 67.

FERGUS.

The name Fergus occurs on two tombstones of apparently different dates at Clonmacnois. (*See* Fig. 5, Pl. ii.)

In the Irish poem quoted above, copied by Professor O'Curry from a manuscript in the Burgundian Library, Brussels, we read that Fergus the Great, son of Ailgill, was one among "the illustrious chieftains and kings" who were buried there; and the Four Masters tell us that, in the year 794, this Fergus, son of Ailgil, was slain at the battle of Finnabhair (now Fennor, in Westmeath). He was lord of Cinél Cairbri, or Clann-Cairbri, a tribe who possessed a burial-ground at Clonmacnois, as we learn from the Registry of that place, as well as from the third verse of the poem of Enoch O'Gillan, p. 5, *supra*, where it is said, that "the sons of Cairbre over the eastern territories," were interred under the flags of Clonmacnois. Fergus is again mentioned in the Annals, at the year 786, as having slain, in the battle of Ard-abhla (or Lissardowlin, in Longford) the lord of Teffia, Diarmaid, son of Bec.

This is more probably the tomb of the Fergus, whose death is thus recorded in the Annals of Ulster, "A. D. 893. Fergus Mac Mailmichil, oeconomus of Clonmacnois, dormivit;" and at 889 in the Annals of the Four Masters.

Fig. 68.

LATICEN.

This name has not been identified.

In both the figures on this plate the form of cross is the same, the only difference being that one is accompanied by the circle, and the other is not. Possibly they may have belonged to about the same period.

Drawn by Dr. Petrie at Clonmacnois, in the year 1846.

PLATE XXVIII.

Fig. 69.

BLAIMAC.

This is fo Blaithmac, possibly the same name as Blathmac, from *blath*, 'a flower,' and *mac*, 'son.' Its latinised form is Florentius or Florentinus.

The name Blathmac was borne by an Abbot of Clonmacnois, whose death is thus recorded:—"A. D. 891. Blathmac, son of Taircellach, one of the people of Breaghmaine [Brawney, County Westmeath], Abbot of Cluain-mhic-Nois, died." (Ann. Four Mast.) "A. D. 895. Blamack, Superior of Clon-mic-Nois, mortuus est." (Ann. Ult.) And the same event is given in the Chronicon Scotorum, at the year 896.

Figs. 70 and 71.

ANGE . . ILL . . .

So little of these inscriptions is legible, that it would be difficult to conjecture what the names may have been.

Drawn by Dr. Petrie at Clonmacnois, in the year 1822.

FIGS. 72 AND 73.

Neither of these inscriptions has been read. More than one drawing of the first was made by Dr. Petrie without success, and in the autumn of the year 1869, Mr. Hennessy examined this stone very carefully, but found the letters in such an obliterated condition, that it was impossible to decipher it. The following have been suggested as possible readings:—

. . . . . [F]ERDOMNAC[H] DO MOER IND . . . .
. . . . . Ferdomnach, for (the) steward of the . . . . .
[OR] ER DUNALAD MOER IN G . . . . .
Pray for Donnalad, steward of the G . . . . .

Moer here is a corrupt form of *máer*, borrowed from the Latin *major*, and the latter part of the well-known compound *mór-máer*, the title of the Grand Stewards of Buchan and Mar.

With reference to the design on this stone, Mr. Du Noyer observes, that it bears a resemblance to the ornamentation on some of our small Cumdachs (*see* Antiquarian Sketches, Royal Irish Academy, vol. vi.). The figures grouped together in this plate all belong to the same class of pattern as those in Plate xxvi., called, for want of a better term, crosses within a parallelogram, sometimes with and sometimes without, a circle at intersection. About sixteen such crosses have been found at Clonmacnois; and it is interesting to note that the only two which can be identified—those of Snedgus and Blaithmac—mark the tombs of men who died within eight years of one another.

Drawn by Dr. Petrie at Clonmacnois, in the year 1822.

PLATE XXIX.

FIG. 74.

AED.

This name occurs on two monuments found at Clonmacnois. According to Cormac's Glossary, it signifies 'fire:' it is cognate with Welsh *aidd*, Greek *αἶθος*, Latin *aedes*, and, probably, the Gaulish tribe-name *Aedui*. The gen. sing. is *Áido*, *Áedo*, or *Áeda*.

The Chronicon Scotorum records the death of Aedh, son of Colca, King of the Airthera, in pilgrimage at Clonmacnois, at the year 610; but it is not likely that this inscription belongs to so early a date.

Aedh Allan, son of Fergal, was buried at Clonmacnois, as we learn from the poem already referred to (*see* p. 5, *supra*) on the kings and nobles interred in that place. He was king of Ireland in the year 730, and fell in battle near Kells, in the year 738.

Drawn by M. S. from a rubbing taken of the stone by the Rev. James Graves and Mr. W. M. Hennessy, in the year 1869.

FIG. 75.

TOICTHEG.

This is probably the same as Toicthech, the name of an ecclesiastic connected with Inis Ainghin, or Hare Island—a place which, as we have already shown, was affiliated to Clonmacnois. In the Annals of the Four Masters we read—"A. D. 895. Toicthiuch, of Inis Aingin, died."

A small Irish cross is carved on this stone, and the letters which form the inscription are arranged so as to add to the ornamental effect of the whole, by following the outline of the circle.

Drawn by Dr. Petrie at Clonmacnois, in the year 1822.

Fig. 76.

ŌR AR MAELQUIARAIN.

(Pray for Maelquiaráin).

Four stones have been drawn by Dr. Petrie at Clonmacnois, all of which bear this name, though spelt in different ways—Maelquiarain, Mailciaran, Maelciaran, Maelchiaran, 'the tonsured (servant) of Ciarán.' The name is anglicised Mulhern. Erard Mac Coisi, in his Elegy on the death of Fearghal O'Ruairc, refers to the house of O'Maelchiarain as being not far from the grave of Fearghal, at Clonmacnois; and adds, that it was a habitation which admitted no guests in the evening. (*See* Note by O'Donovan, Ann. Four Mast., vol. i., p. 878). Ciarán being the patron saint of Clonmacnois, it is but natural to suppose that a name thus expressive of devotion to his memory would be a common one amongst the ecclesiastics of that place. However, no one of this name is mentioned in the Annals of the Four Masters, as connected with Clonmacnois, till the close of the eleventh century; and this type of cross seems to have been more commonly used in the ninth century.

The use of *qu* for *c* is remarkable. We find it also in the latinised name Quiaranus, gen. Ciarani, Lib. Hymn. fo. 31, *a;* Queranus Coloniensis, Cummian's letter, A. D. 634 (Ussher, Works, iv., p. 442); and cf. *sequtus* for *secutus* (Reeves' Columba, xviii).

Drawn by Dr. Petrie at Clonmacnois, in the year 1822. Mr. O'Neill has already published an illustration of this stone in his Sculptured Crosses of Ancient Ireland (Pl. xxiv., Fig. 15), and a drawing of it is given in Mr. Du Noyer's Antiquarian Sketches (vol. vi., No. 84), in the Royal Irish Academy.

PLATE XXX.

Fig. 77.

. . . NNGENI . . .

It is impossible to say what name these letters may form part of, as the stone has been so much mutilated. Mr. Hennessy suggests that it may have been Finngeni. There was a *tipra Fingine* (or 'well of Finngen'), at Clonmacnois. (*See* Chron. Scotorum, at A. D. 615).

This fragment, along with the other three represented on this plate, come from Clonburren (Cluain-boireann), near Clonmacnois, and was drawn by Miss Boxwell from rubbings made by the Rev. James Graves.

The design on this stone appears to have been a cross within a circle.

Fig. 78.

GORM . . . .

Gorm is explained in O'Clery's Glossary by *dearg*, 'red,' and *rí oirdheirc*, 'conspicuous king.'

Two stones thus inscribed are found in this collection. This syllable may have been the beginning of such names as Gorman, Gormflaith, Gormghal, &c.; but it would be vain to attempt to identify a name of which a mere fragment remains.

Fig. 79.

ŌR DO ANGUS.

(Pray for Angus).

The name Angus, better Aenghus or Oenghus, is so common that in this instance it is not possible to identify it with any certainty. There was a bishop of Clonfert so called, whose death is thus recorded by the Annalists :—"A.D. 1036. Aenghus Mac Flainn, Coarb of Brenainn Cluona, mortuus est." (Ann. Ult.) "A. D. 1036. Aenghus Ua Flainn, successor of Brenainn of Cluain-fearta, died." (Ann. Four Mast.) "A. D. 1034. Oenghus Ua Flainn, Comarb of Brenainn of Cluain-ferta, quievit." (Chronicon Scotorum.)

Drawn by M. S. from a rubbing taken of the stone by the Rev. James Graves and Mr. W. M. Hennessy, 1869.

Fig. 80.

ANNOC.

This word may be a diminutive in *-óc*; but the name has not been identified.

Drawn by M. S. from a rubbing made at Clonmacnois by the Rev. James Graves and Mr. W. M. Hennessy.

PLATE XXXI.

Fig. 81.

ŌR DO MAELBRIGTE.

(Pray for Máelbrigte).

This name occurs three times on tombstones at Clonmacnois. It signifies the 'tonsured servant of Brigit,' the patron saint of Kildare. This is probably the tombstone of Maelbrigte, Abbot of Clonmacnois, whose obit is given A. D. 888. (*Vide* Four Masters, p. 541; and Chronicon Scotorum, A. D. 892). Maelbrighte-na-Gamhnaide, from Gabhar, i. e. Cell Ula, who was of the men of Umhall, Abbot of Cluain-mac-Nois, quievit. The name is written *Máelbrigtæ* in a marginal gloss in the St. Gall Priscian (Zeuss' G. C., præf. xiii). The Old Welsh form is *Máelbrigit* (Zeuss' G. C., 121).

Drawn by Dr. Petrie at Clonmacnois, in the year 1822.

Fig. 82.

SUIBINE MAC MAELÆ HUMAI.

(Suibine, son of Maelhumai).

This drawing is of more than usual interest, representing, as it does, the tombstone of a learned member of the community at Clonmacnois, whose fame in England was so great that his death was recorded by the ancient chroniclers and annalists of that country, as well as by those of Ireland. Thus Florence of Worcester, at the year 892, has—"Eodem anno Swifneh doctor Scottorum peritissimus obiit." (Florentii Wigorniensis Chronicon, Tom. i., p. 109. Ed. Thorpe).

In the Saxon Chronicle the same event is recorded at A. D. 891:—"7 Swifneh se betsta lareow þe on Scottom wæs. gefor," i. e. "S. etiam, præcipuus doctor qui inter Scotos fuit, decessit."

889. "CCCCXLV. Subin Scotorum sapientissimus obiit." Annales Cambriæ (ed. J. Williams ab Ithel), p. 15.

Amongst Irish chroniclers the Annals of Ulster and Chronicon Scotorum have given the same event as happening four years later; while in the Annals of the Four Masters we read:—"A. D. 887. Suibhne, son of Maelumha, anchorite and scribe of Cluain-mic-Nois, died."

The English annalists above quoted relate that, in the same year in which Suibine Mac Maelehumai died, the Court of King Alfred was visited by three remarkable Irishmen, one of whom appears to have been skilled in the arts; and the story of this visit is thus given by them, and by Æthelwerd in his chronicle:—

"DCCCXCII. Tres Scotici viri, Dusblan, Mahbethu, Malmumin, peregrinam ducere vitam pro Domino cupientes, assumpto secum unius hebdomadæ viatico, occulte de Hibernia fugerunt carabumque qui ex duobus tantum coriis et dimidio factus erat, intraverunt, mirumque in modum sine velo et armamentis post septem dies in Cornubia applicuerunt; et postmodum regem Alfredum adierunt. Eodem anno Swifneh doctor Scotorum peritissimus obiit." Florentii Wigorniensis Chron. (Monumentă Hist. Brit.), p. 564.

"An. 892. And three Scots came to King Ælfred in a boat without any oars from Ireland, whence they had stolen away, because they desired for the love of God to be in a state of pilgrimage, they recked not where. The boat in which they came was made of two hides and a half; and they took with them provisions sufficient for seven days; and then about the seventh day they came on shore in Cornwall, and soon after went to King Ælfred. Thus they were named—Dubslane, and Macbeth, and Maelnimuin And Swifneh, the best teacher among the Scots, died." (Saxon Chron., Eng. translation, in Monumenta Hist. Brit., p. 362.)

"An. 891, vel 892. Abstrahuntur tum feruentes fide anno in eodem Hybernia stirpe tres viri lecti, furtim consuunt lembum taurinis byrsis, alimentum sibi hebdomadarium supplent, elevant dies per vela septem totidemque noctes, aduehuntur in primna [πρύμνα] Cornuualias partes relicta classe non armis ductam [leg. ducta?] nec copiosis scilicet lacertis, nutu potiùs sed cuncta tuentis. *Aelfredum* adeunt regem Anglorum in quorum aduectum cum rege pariter sinclitus [i. e. σύγκλητος] ouat. Deinde Romam vestigia legunt, vt soliti crebro Christi magistri petitum: mentes ab inde Hierosolymis ire prætendunt. Protinus eorum migrat eminentior via; vnus quippe frater custodia cernit reliquias sui compagi socii: nec non miracula quidem non minima facta breuiario in hoc fas esset prædicere tota. Namque alter domi vertitur, puluerem concutiens calo [leg. talo?] absentiumque infert nomina sic. *Dufflan* primus, *Macheathath*que secundus, *Magilmumen* tertius,[a] artibus frondens, littera doctus magister insignis Scottorum." Chron. Ethelwerdi, lib. iv., cap. 3. (Rer. Anglicar. Script. post Bedam, Francofurti, 1601, p. 846).

That this was a period of great proficiency in the arts, and of great intellectual activity in Ireland, we have ample proof. Among other facts bearing on this subject, the existence of this inscribed stone is one of the most important, for it is remarkable, not only as being the first example to which we can assign a certain date (since the unusual addition of the father's name makes the identification of that of Suibine the more certain), but as being a perfect type of the highly ornamental Irish cross; for here the circle and semicircles in the centre and extremities of the cross are filled in with details, offering fine examples of the divergent spiral and diagonal patterns peculiar to the early Celtic art of these islands. This stone helps then to confirm all that has been already written by Dr. Petrie as to the progress of the art of sculpture at this period in Ireland, and the dates he has assigned to the great crosses of Clonmacnois and Monasterboice—both, according to him, erected at the beginning of the tenth century. The records of the annalists of Ireland, as well as the literary remains of that period, all combine in confirming the correctness of his views. The deaths of forty celebrated scribes and learned men of Ireland, four of whom belonged to Clonmacnois—namely, Dubinnse, Luchairne, Martin and Suibine,

[a] These names are given thus in the various MSS. of the A. S. Chronicle, ed. Thorpe:—*Dubslane*, *Dubslâne*, *Dublasne*; *Maccbethu*, *Macbethath*, *Machbethu*; *Maelinmun*, *Maelinmum*, *Malmumin*, *Maelinmumin*.

are related by the Four Masters as taking place in the ninth century. At the opening of this century died Oengus the Culdee, whose writings, the Félire, the Martyrology, and Saltair na rann, are preserved to us, along with the hymns and historical poems of many others, such as Fingin, author of the Hymn to the Holy Trinity ; and Fothadh, the poet and adviser of King Aed, who issued the decree exempting the clergy from attendance on military expeditions; Maelmaire, the author of various historical poems ; as well as Flann Mac Lonain, and his mother Laitheog, the poetess. The arts seem to have flourished in and before this century, although few examples of metal work remain to which so early a date can be assigned ; yet we read of the Shrine of Patrick, A. D. 804 ; the Shrine of Comgall, A. D. 822 ; the Shrine of Columba, A. D. 828 ; the Shrine of Adamnán, A. D. 830 ; and the Croziers of Fedhlimidh, A. D. 840 ; and of Ciarán, A. D. 884 ; while Mac Riaguil, who wrote the finely illuminated Gospels, now in the Bodleian Library, Oxford, died in 820. Maelinmun, who is mentioned above as devoted to the arts, in the quotation from Æthelwerd, may possibly have been the same person as the Maelinmain, wise man and anchorite, who died at Glendalough, in the year 953.

The history of Ireland in this century is altogether a strange one, opening with a tale of rapine, and bloodshed, and war; but closing in the peace that ensued after the defeat of Turgesius, the Dane, by Malachy, and the accession of this monarch to the throne of Ireland. Then Clonmacnois was allowed to enjoy an interval of repose, during which her ancient edifices were restored, and many new ones erected; while throughout Ireland—"Tout rentra alors dans l'ordre naturel ; on rétablit la religion ; on rebâtit les églises et monastères ; on remit les loix en vigueur pour défendre l'innocent et punir le coupable ; les anciens proprietaires furent mis en possession des terres et seigneuries perdues pendant l'usurpation." (Ma-Geogegan, Histoire de l'Irlande, tom. i., p. 386).

PLATE XXXII.

Fig. 83.

OR̄ DO FECHTNACH.

(Pray for Fechtnach).

Fechtnach is explained *firenta*, in O'Clery's Glossary. But, when used as a name, its Latin correlative is *Felix*, and this is the meaning of the word in a gloss in the Milan Codex : *is fechtnach an andach*, 'felix est eorum malitia.' Two stones on which this name is inscribed are still to be seen at Clonmacnois.

Fechtnach was the name of a learned reader, scribe, and priest of Clonmacnois, and of the Island of Iona; but he died in Rome in the year 1024, whither he had gone on a pilgrimage. There was a Fechtnach, Abbot of Fore, in Westmeath, who died in 776 (*see* Four Masters), whose tombstone this may be; for it is not unlikely that an Abbot of Fore should have been buried at Clonmacnois, as a very close connexion seems to have existed between the two places. Cormac, Abbot of Fore, who died in 887, was also tanist Abbot of Clonmacnois; and Maelpóil, Bishop of Clonmacnois, in 1000, was likewise styled successor of Feichin of Fore.

Drawn by Dr. Petrie in 1822. A representation of it may also be seen in Mr. Du Noyer's Antiquarian Sketches, vol. iv., in the Royal Irish Academy.

This stone was found near St. Ciaran's Well, at Clonmacnois.

Fig. 84.

OROIT AR MAELBRITE.

(Pray for Máelbrite).

Maelbrite is another and corrupt form of the name Máel-Brigte. (*See* Fig. 81). The Four Masters record the death of an abbot of this name in the following passage :—" A. D. 929. Maelbrigde, son of Feadacan, Abbot of Lann-mic-Luachain [in the County Westmeath], died."

The form of this cross is interesting and uncommon, having a diamond-shaped space in the centre, and semicircles at the terminations, filled with Celtic ornamental patterns.

Drawn by Dr. Petrie at Clonmacnois, in the year 1822.

Fig. 85.

. . . . . . GGÁN.

This fragment is possibly the last syllable of the name Tadgán, which name occurs on two other stones found at Clonmacnois. One of these may have belonged to Tadgan, Prince of Teffia, who died in the end of the ninth, or beginning of the tenth century; or Tadgan, father of Duḃcen. (*See* notice of Fig. 99, *infra*).

The design of this cross is the same in character as No. 84; but, in addition to the other ornamental work, the diamond-shaped central space is filled with interlaced patterns.

Drawn by Dr. Petrie at Clonmacnois, in the year 1822.

PLATE XXXIII.

Fig. 86.

Fig. 87.

Fig. 88.

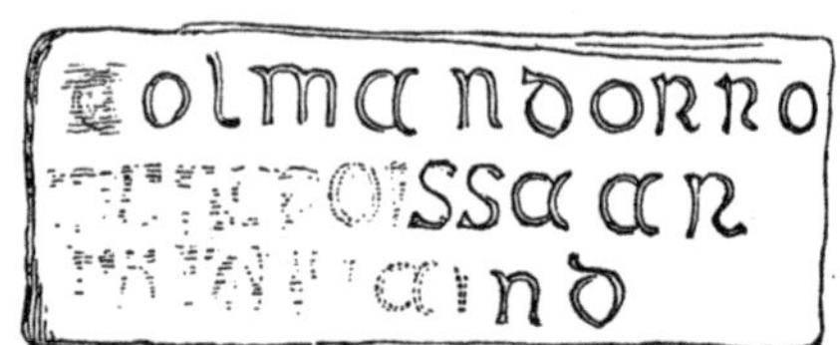

OR̄ DO FLAVND MAC MAELSECHLAIND.

C]OLMAN DORRO[INI IN CROI]SSA AR IN RI [FL]AND.[a]

(Pray for Fland, son of Maelsechlaind).

(Colman, who made this Cross for the King Fland).

The king, to whose memory this cross was raised by his friend Colman, Abbot of Clonmacnois, was the son of the good King Malachy, who died in the year 863. He was named Fland Sinna, and suc-

[a] The letters represented by dots in the wood-cuts are very faint in the original drawings, and therefore doubtful.

ceeded Aed Finnliath in the supreme government of the island. This monarch's reign was long, and filled with troubles; the Danes, who had remained quiet at the close of King Malachy's reign, having resumed their hostilities, while the princes of Ireland forgot the union established between them at the same time, and the rights of the monarchy were violated.

In the years 902 and 903, Fland went to war with Cormac, King of Cashel, the reputed author of the ancient Irish glossary called *Sanas Chormaic,* who fell in battle at Ballaghmoon, in the south of the County of Kildare. (*See* Annals of the Four Masters, vol. ii., p. 564, *n.*).

The close of King Fland Sinna's reign was comparatively tranquil. He devoted himself to the restoration of churches and public schools, and he assisted Colman, Bishop of Clonmacnois, in building his stone church at that place. His death is thus recorded by the Four Masters :—" A. D. 914. After Flann, the son of Maelsechlainn, had been thirty-eight years in the sovereignty of Ireland, he died at Tailltin ;" and in the Chronicon Scotorum, at 915, it is said he died in the thirty-seventh year of his reign, at Cenneich (Kinneigh), of the family of Cluain. Colman, who raised this cross in memory of King Flann was the Abbot of Clonmacnois during part of his reign, of whom we have the following records :—" A. D. 901 [recte 908]. King Flann and Colman Connellagh this year founded the church in Clonvicknose, called the Church of the Kings." (Ann. Clon.) The same event is given at 904 by the Four Masters ; and 908 in the Chronicon Scotorum.

Colman's death is thus recorded by the Four Masters:—" A. D. 924. Colman, son of Ailill, Abbot of Cluain Iraird and Cluain-mic-Nois, a bishop and wise doctor, died." It was by him the Daimhliag of Cluain-mic-Nois was built. He was of the tribe of the Conaill Muirtheimhne.

" The tenth year, a just decree, joy and sorrow reigned :
Colman of Cluain, the joy of every tower, died."

The Annals of Ulster and Chronicon Scotorum have his death at 925.

Little doubt can be entertained of the date of this cross, when the evidence afforded by the above inscription is supported, as it is, by occasional notices of such a cross in the Annals of the Four Masters. Dr. Petrie's reading of this inscription was verified by Mr. Hennessy, who indeed in some places could trace remains of letters, suggested merely, and not drawn by Dr. Petrie; and evidence is afforded of the existence of a cross such as this one about thirty years after the period assigned for its erection. " A. D. 957. The Termon of Ciaran was burned this year from the 'high cross' to the Sinainn [Shannon], both corn and mills." The Munstermen were the depredators on this occasion, as we learn from the Chronicon Scotorum and the Annals of Ulster and Clonmacnois, at the years 953, 957, and 958. Again, in the eleventh century, mention is made of this cross, under the title Cros-na-Screptra; or, the ' Cross of the Scriptures' :—

" A. D. 1060. The Eli and Ui Forgga came upon a predatory excursion to Cluain-mic-Nois, and they took prisoners from Cros-na-Screaptra, and killed two persons, i. e., a student and a layman."

This cross has been described, not only by Dr. Petrie in his Ecclesiastical Architecture of Ireland (pp. 269, 270), but also by Ledwich (Ant. Ireland, pp. 5, 6). Mr. O'Neill, in his Sculptured Crosses of Ireland, has given a large drawing of both the east and west sides, besides twenty-four carefully executed drawings of the details on the north and south sides. The material is silicious sandstone.

Two illustrations of the sculpturings on this cross are given by Mr. Du Noyer (Ant. Sketches R. I. A., vol. vii., Nos. 16 to 25), who, however, does not attempt to read the inscriptions on the lower part of the shaft. In the first compartment King Flann and the Abbot Colman Conaillech, who founded the Church of the Kings in A. D. 909, are represented making a compact by swearing on the cross or pastoral staff of the saint. A broad strap is suspended over the right shoulder of the king, and joins on to a waist belt, into which is thrust a broad and short sword, with a plain cross-guard, and a very massive semicircular pommel, quite resembling those iron swords said to be Danish, found in the old burial-ground at Bully's Acre, near Island-bridge, Dublin. St. Colman wears a short cloak, with a large hood hanging behind.

The next compartment seems to contain the figure of King Flann again, who may be recognised by the long plaited beard, standing beside another figure. A large fibula, pierced with four circles, so as to form a cross, is represented as fastening his mantle on his right breast below the shoulder. The beard of the second figure is bifurcated.

The group in the third and uppermost compartment of this side of the cross is difficult to explain. It calls to mind the early representations of Moses standing with his arms upheld in prayer: also, an illumination in the Book of Kells, where Christ is represented between two disciples, to whom he says—" All ye shall be offended because of me this night."

Drawn by Dr. Petrie at Clonmacnois, in the year 1822.

PLATE XXXIV.

Fig. 89.

O̅R̅ DV ETICH.

(Pray for Etech).

The ancient form DU, instead of DO, for the preposition here, is curious, and occurs on only two other inscriptions, Or. du Doraid, Fig. 118, and O̅r̅, du Ruarcan, at Monasterboice. It is found in the Book of Armagh (a MS. of the beginning of the ninth century), and in the Milan Codex, and is identical with the Goth. *du*, Nhg. *zu*, and probably the Latin *du* in in-*du*-perator, in-*du*-pedio.

The Four Masters, at the year 967, record the death of Echtighern, son of Eitech, or Etech, lord of the Comanns, a district in Ossory, extending as far as Slieve Bloom, or the borders of the King's County. The name Etech was also in use amongst the Clann-Uadach (ancestors of the O'Fallamhains, or O'Fallons, who are referred to in the poem above printed, as having a place of sepulture in Clonmacnois); for as early as the year 1021, the name of Mac Etigh, or son of Etech, occurs as that of a chief of Clann-Uadach, whose territory was situated in the barony of Athlone, nearly on the opposite side of the Shannon to Clonmacnois.

The appearance of the cable-moulding, which forms the outline of this cross, induces us to believe it may belong to the same period as that assigned to the Cross of Colman. The triquetra knot may be seen at the foot of the shaft, and that knot is certainly characteristic of crosses of the tenth century.

Drawn by Dr. Petrie at Clonmacnois, in the year 1822.

PLATE XXXV.

Fig. 90.

O̅R̅ DO DAINÉIL.

(Pray for Daniel).

This name has not been identified with any one at Clonmacnois. It is just possible that this may be the tombstone of the person whose death is recorded in the following passage:—" A. D. 916. Daniel of Cluain-Coirpthe, a celebrated historian, died."

In a note to the Félire of Oengus at the 15th of February, Cluain Cairpthe is described as in the desert or wilderness of Cenél Dobtha, in Connaught. This church, now known as Kilbarry, County Roscommon, of which the ruins are still remaining, was founded by St. Berach, or Barry, in the end of the sixth century. (Annals of Four Masters, note, A. D. 916).

An illustration of this stone is given by Mr. Du Noyer (*see* Antiquarian Sketches, R. I. A., vol. vi., No. 70), who suggests that it may have marked the grave of Daniel, who was Abbot of Glendalough, and died A. D. 866; but this is most unlikely to be correct, judging from the character of the art, which belongs to a later date, and the improbability of an Abbot of Glendalough having been interred in Clonmacnois.

Drawn by Dr. Petrie in 1822.

Fig. 91.

OR̄ AR TUATHCHARÁN.

(Pray for Tuathcharán).

The form Tuathcharán is a diminutive of Tuathchar, which was the name of a Bishop of Clonmacnois, whose death is thus recorded in the Chronicon Scotorum:—"A. D. 889. Tuadhcar, Bishop of Cluain-mic-Nois, quievit."

Dr. Petrie drew this inscription and cross in the year 1822. The stone he found lying in the burial-ground of an old church dedicated to St. Ciaran on Inis Ainghin, or Hare Island, Lough Ree.

Dr. O'Donovan, when engaged on the Ordnance Survey some years afterwards, saw this tombstone. He gives another reading of the inscription differing from Dr. Petrie's, and one which does not seem so likely to be correct. His version is—

ORAID DO TUATHAL HUAHUARAIN.

(A prayer for Tuathal Hua Huarain).

This was published by Dr. O'Donovan in his notes on Inis Ainginn, Four Masters, vol. i., p. 553. This stone is not now to be found.

PLATE XXXVI.

Fig. 92.

MOEN . . . .

This fragment may be the first syllable of either of the names Moenach, or Moengal, or Moenan.

It is probable that it may be the tombstone of Moengal, or Maengal, who was Prior of Clonmacnois in the latter part of the ninth century, and died A. D. 873.

Drawn by Dr. Petrie at Clonmacnois, in the year 1822.

Fig. 93.

MAELCIR GG.

This name is compounded of the name Cirig, with the epithet Mael, meaning tonsured servant of Ciric. The boy-saint Ciric (Quiricus) is mentioned in the Félire of Oenghus, Prol. 137: *nimtá ciric macán*, 'not so is Ciric the child.' He was martyred at Tarsus, in Cilicia, and is commemorated, at June 16, along with 'S. Julia vidua.'

The Four Masters, and the Annals of Lough-Cé, at the year 1088, record the death of a Maelisa O'Maelciric, or O'Maelgiric, "chief poet of Ireland," possibly the descendant of the very person whose name occurs on this stone.

Drawn by M. S. from a rubbing taken by the Rev. James Graves and Mr. Hennessy.

Fig. 94.

E C H T . . . . . .

We have spoken before of words commencing with *Echt* in our notice of Fig. 64, Pl. xxvi.

Drawn by M. S. from the stone, which is now in the Royal Irish Academy. It was found some years ago in the River Shannon, close to Clonmacnois, and presented by the Rev. C. A. Vignoles,

---

PLATE XXXVII.

Fig. 95.

O̅R̅ DO FIACHRAICH.

(Pray for Fiachra).

Fiachraich is the dative case of Fiachra, a masc. *c*-stem.

This is probably the tomb of Fiachra, of Eaglais Beg, or the Little Church, whose death is thus recorded :— "A. D. 921. Fiachra, of Eaglas beag [at Cluain-mic-Nois], died."

The name "Fiachra" has given rise to the French *fiacre*, 'hackney-coach.' "So genannt," says Diez (Etym. Wörterbuch, 2te ausg. ii., 294), "weil der unternehmer in einem haus zu Paris *à l'enseigne de St. Fiacre* wohnte."[a]

The design on this stone is very peculiar—four hexagons arranged in the form of a cross, surrounded with a broad circular band, and all the interstices filled in with rich ornaments of interlaced bands, spirals, and the diagonal form of the Greek fret.

Drawn by M. S. from the stone at Clonmacnois in 1869. A sketch of this stone has been published by Mr. O'Neill in his work on the Sculptured Crosses of Ireland, Pl. 23.

[a] *See* Du Plessis, tom. i., p. 683, note 29; Menage, Dict. Etymol., voc. *Fiacre*, tom. i., p. 589; *apud* Proceedings R. I. A., vol. vii., p. 290.

"Fiachrach [i. e. (the festival) of Fiachra], an Eremite, and he blessed (administered his religious blessings) also in France. (Mart. Doneg., Aug. 30, p. 229.)

St. Fiacre (anciently called *Fefre*) died on the 30 Aug. circ. 670. His hermitage was at Breüil, in the province of Brie, about two leagues distant from Meaux. His shrine became celebrated for miracles performed in the cure of various diseases, and was frequented by pilgrims from all parts of France.

The name Fiacre is explained by Richelet thus:— "*Fiacre.*—Carosse de loüage, auquel on a donné ce nom à cause de l'enseigne d'un logis de la rue S. Antoine de Paris, où l'on a prémièrement loüé ces sortes de carosses. Ce logis avoit pour enseigne un Saint Fiacre."

Du Plessis shows that the name *Fiacre* was first given to hackney coaches, because hired coaches were first made use of for the convenience of pilgrims who went from Paris to visit the shrine of this saint, and because the inn where these coaches were hired was known by the sign of St. Fiaker.

St. Fiacra was also venerated at Kilfiacra (now Killfera), on the west bank of the River Nore, two miles below Kilkenny, where the foundation of a very small cell remained until a few years since. "St. Fiacra's Well" is close by.

Fig. 96.

OR̄ DO CORBRIVCRVM.

(Pray for Corbre, the Bent.)

Corbriu is the dative singular of the masculine ia-stem *Corbre.* There are only two other inscriptions found at Clonmacnois, in which the name of the person is accompanied by an epithet—these are, Colman Bocht, or Colman the Poor, and Murgus deicola. Corbre, Corpre, or Carbre, is the same name as Cairbre, now Carbury, and *crom* (dat. sing. masc. *crum*) means 'stooped' or 'bent,' Welsh *crwm,* 'bending.'

This name and epithet were borne by two persons connected with Clonmacnois; the first a chieftain of the Ui Maine, in Connaught, who was the contemporary of St. Ciaran, of Clonmacnois, and seems to have had some physical defect, which gave rise to the epithet; the second who was probably the subject of this inscription, and is mentioned by the annalists and martyrologists as follows:—"March 6. Cairpre Crom, son of Feradhach, son of Lughaidh, son of Dallan, son of Bresal, son of Maine Mór, from whom descend the Ui Maine, of the race of Colla-da-Chrioch, who was of the posterity of Heremon, Bishop of Cluain-mic-Nois, head of the religion of the greater part of Erinn in his time." (Mart. Donegal). "A. D. 894. The profanation of Inis Ainghin; and a man was wounded in the middle of it: and the Shrine of Ciaran there, and a synod of seniors, along with Cairbre Crom, Bishop of Cluain-muc-Nois." Four Masters.) "A. D. 904. Cairbr Cam, Bishop of Cluain muc-Nois, quievit. It was to him the spirit of Maelechlain, son of Maelruanaidh, showed itself." (Chron. Scotorum). Here the epithet *Cam,* 'crooked' (Welsh *cam,* Gaulish *cambos,* Greek σκαμβός), is used instead of *Crom,* 'bent.' His death is recorded by the Four Masters at A. D. 899, who also refer to the apparition of King Malachi, whose death occurred on Tuesday, the 30th of November, A. D. 863. (*See* O'Flaherty's Ogyg., pp. 434–436). Colgan in his Acta Sanctorum, p. 509, gives a life of this saint, and after relating the legend of the apparition of King Malachi, he adds: "Our annals also record a certain visitation divinely sent on the army of the men of Connaught, who heedlessly violated the sacred place over which he was a holy president [antistes], which visitation is believed to have been justly attributable to the merits both of himself and St. Ciaran. For the Connaught men, in the year 894, with a strong band invaded West Meath [Midhe]; nor did the soldiers restrain themselves from plunder and rapine, until at length they even invaded a certain island in Loch Ree, named Inis Ainghin, in which, together with the holy shrine of St. Ciaran, there was St. Corprius, bishop and clerk of the church of Cluain, before whose eyes they slew some men, no respect being shown to the bishop, or to the holy relics. But God, punishing the injury done, and sacrilege perpetrated on his own people, that same army, on the same day, at the town of Athlone, suffered a great destruction, and was put to flight. But this man, renowned for his merit in the eyes of God, and for his virtues, yielded up his spirit to heaven in the year of our Lord 899, on the 6th day of March, on which day the festologies of the house relate his natal rites were celebrated in the church of Cluain."

The cross which accompanies this inscription, Dr. Petrie says (Ecclesiastical Architecture of Ireland, p. 325), was in its form and ornamental detail exactly the same as that of Suibine Mac Maelehumai, who died A. D. 887, and Dubcenn Mac Tadgán (*see* Fig. 98, Pl. xxxviii.); and as only twelve years elapsed between the death of Suibine and that of Bishop Cairbre, the slabs were probably cut by the same hand.

Drawn by Dr. Petrie at Clonmacnois, in the year 1822.

Fig. 97.

OR DO THADGAN.

(Pray for Tadgan.)

Dr. Petrie supposes that this inscription probably belonged to Tadgan, chief of Teffia, at the close of the ninth century, the particulars respecting whose life he goes on to notice, in connexion with that of his son Dubcenn, whose tombstone we have next to consider.

Drawn by Dr. Petrie at Clonmacnois, in the year 1822.

PLATE XXXVIII.

Fig. 98.

OROIT DO CONAING MAC CONGHAIL.

OROIT DO DUBCEN MAC THADGGAN.

(Pray for Conaing, son of Conghal).

(Pray for Dubcen, son of Tadggan).

The family of O'Duigenan derived their name and origin from Dubhcenn, the second son of Tadhgán, chief of Teffia at the close of the ninth century, from whose eldest son the ancient family of Fox have descended. Dr. Petrie observes:—"The tomb of this Dubhcenn is also at Clonmacnois; and as it exhibits a good specimen of Irish monumental carving . . . . . . , and at the same time furnishes a remarkable evidence of the truth of the Irish genealogies, I have been induced to insert a copy of it in this place. . . . . .

"I have not been able to find in the Irish Annals an entry of the death of Dubcen, the son of Tadgan, whose name occurs in the second of these inscriptions, nor of his father Tadgan; but the periods at which they flourished may be determined with tolerable accuracy from the records of the deaths of Agda, the son of Dubcenn, Prince of Teffia, who, it is stated in the Annals of the Four Masters, died in the chair of St. Kieran, after having spent a good life, in the year 979; or, according to Tighernach, in the year 980; and of his grandson, Gilla Enain, the son of Agda, who was slain in the year 977. The other inscription, which is less perfectly preserved, is obviously older, and contemporaneous with the carvings; and, as it is in the highest degree improbable that Dubcen would have been interred in a grave appropriated to any but a predecessor of the same family, we should naturally expect to find the name in the upper inscription in the Irish Annals at an earlier period, and among the Princes of Teffia. Accordingly, on a reference to these Annals, we find the death of Conaing, son of Congal, King of Teffia, recorded at the year 822 in the Annals of Ulster, and at 821 in the Annals of the Four Masters." (The Ecclesiastical Architecture of Ireland, p. 326.)

The names above given also occur in the Chronicon Scotorum in the following passage:—

"A. D. 823. Conaing, i. e. son of Congal, King of Teathbha, [obiit]. A. D. 978. Aghda, son of Dubhcenn, King of Teabhtha, after penance, mortuus est."

The Annals of Ulster, A. D. 973, again mention Aghda, son of Dubhcenn, as having put to death Donchadh Finn; and in the Annals of the Four Masters we read :—"A. D. 972. Donnchadh Finn, son of Aedh, lord of Meath, was killed by Aghda, son of Duibhcenn, son of Tadhgan, lord of Teathbha."

The style of this cross, and the art with which it is decorated, bear so close a resemblance to that of Suibine Mac Maelæhumai, that it is, in all probability, a work of the same period—that is, about the close of the ninth century.

The second, third, and fourth letters of the name read "Congail," are very doubtful, and it is impossible that the GH could have occurred for an aspirated G on so ancient a stone. Can the true reading be *Cathail* (as Dr. Petrie himself conjectured), the gen. sing. of *Cathal*?

The letters which form both inscriptions must have been carved after the cross was cut upon the stone, as they are so divided as to leave the exact space for the shaft of the cross; therefore, the cross could not have been of a later date than the period at which the first inscription was cut.

This drawing was made by Dr. Petrie in the year 1822; and a wood engraving of it appears in the Ecclesiastical Architecture of Ireland, p. 326.

Fig. 99.

RONAIN.

(Of Ronan.)

There were three Abbots of Clonmacnois of this name. The death of the first is recorded in the Annals of the Four Masters as having occurred in the year 759. And, in the Chronicon Scotorum, we learn that, in the year 823, being the same year in which Conaing, King of Teathbha, died, an Abbot of Clonmacnois, named Ronan, left his abbacy. The same fact is recorded in the Annals of Ulster, under the year 822. Then in the Annals of the Four Masters, p. 465, we read.—"A. D. 842. Ronan, Abbot of Clonmacnois [one of the tribe of the Luaighni, of Ros Teamhrach], died." This tribe were a people in Meath, near Donaghmore.

The cross is the same in character as that of Maelquiaran, who died at the close of the ninth century.

PLATE XXXIX.

Fig. 100.

O̅R̅ DO CHO . . . IN GORMAI . .

The names on this stone are so much mutilated as to be very difficult to decipher. They seem, however, to be portions of the names Colmán and Gormán, both common names in Ireland, and both of which occur on other tombstones in Clonmacnois.

The only Colmán connected with Clonmacnois, whose death is mentioned in the Annals, is Colmán Conaillech, who has been already spoken of as the person who erected the cross to the name of King Flann, son of Malachi, and who died A. D. 924.

In the ornamental details on this and the following slab may be seen the divergent spiral or trumpet pattern, and the diagonal patterns, carved with the same skill and care, as they are seen in the great standing crosses of the tenth century.

Drawn by Dr. Petrie at Clonmacnois, in the year 1822.

Fig. 101.

[M A E L] T U I [L E].

Although only the three letters *tui* of this inscription remain, it is not improbable that the proposed restoration of the name may be correct, as the space on each side of the shaft of the cross would just allow room for the missing letters; and the name Maeltuile, the most probable in the composition of which the letters *tui* would be found, was borne by two ecclesiastics connected with Clonmacnois—namely, the Abbot Maeltuile, who died in 874, and Maeltuile, the Lector, son of Colmán, whose obit is given by the Four Masters, and also in the Chronicon Scotorum, under 921.

In the year 921, in the Chronicon Scotorum, we read that "Maeltuile, son of Colman, Lector of Cluan-mac-Nois, quievit."

Drawn by M. S. from a rubbing made in 1869 by the Rev. James Graves.

PLATE XL.

Fig. 102.

T A D G G . . . .

This fragment is so much mutilated, it is impossible to say what the name may have been. It might, perhaps, have been Tadggán—a name which has been already discussed in the notice of Fig. 98 (*see* page 48).

Tadg, anglicised Teague, signifies a 'poet.' (*See* O'Dav. Gl.)

Drawn by Dr. Petrie at Clonmacnois, in 1822.

Fig. 103.

O R O I T M A R M A E L C I A R A I N .

The name Maelciarain has been already discussed. (*See* page 38). There appears to be a letter *m* between the *Oroit* and the AR, for the existence of which it is impossible to account, unless the sculptor may have forgotten the preposition *ar*, and carved the first letter of the word Mael, which he afterwards omitted to erase.

Found while digging a grave in Temple M'Dermot at Clonmacnois in 1781, and drawn from a rubbing made by Kyran Molloy.

Fig. 103*a*.

O̅R̅ D O M A R T A N Á N .

(Pray for Martanán).

This name is the diminutive of Martán, formed by progressive assimilation from the Latin Martinus, of which the gen. sing. occurs in Fig. 25, Pl. x. The Irish added the diminutival ending to the names of saints as a mark of affection. The suffix ÁN occurs also in Aedán, Brecán, Colmán, Ciarán, Cathalán, Gormán, Columbán, Findan, Maelán, Odrán, Ronán, Tadgán, Tuathcharán, &c. For numerous examples of masc. and neut. diminutives in ÁN (latinised -anus), *see* Zeuss, G. C., ed. Ebel, pp. 273, 274.

PLATE XLI.

Fig. 104.

ŌR DO CHOLMÁN.

(Pray for Colman.)

This name occurs on four mortuary inscriptions in Clonmacnois (*see* Figs. 4, 6, 100), besides appearing in the inscription on the great Cross of the Scriptures, as the name of the man who erected that monument to the memory of King Flann. The annalists record the death of four ecclesiastics of Clonmacnois so called who bore this name ; and it is probable that the name now under consideration may be identified with the last and most remarkable of these four Colmans—the Abbot of Clonmacnois and Clonard, Colmán Conailleach. He was the friend of King Maelsechlainn, who, with his assistance, built the great stone church of Clonmacnois, in the year 904, as we learn from the following entries:—

"A. D. 904. The Daimhliag of Cluain-mic-Nois was erected by the king, Flann Sinna, and by Colmán Conailleach."

"A. D. 901, *recte* 908. King Flann and Colmán Conellagh founded the church in Clonvicnose this year, called the Church of the Kings." [*Teampoll na riogh*]. Annals of Clonmacnois.

"A. D. 908. The stone church of Cluan-muc-Nois was built by Flann, son of Maelechlainn, and Colmán Conaillech." (Chronicon Scotorum.)

The Cross of the Scriptures at Clonmacnois was another monument raised by this Abbot, of whom we may learn more particulars in the various notices of his death given by the annalists. He belonged to the tribe of the Conaille Muirthemne, whose territory lay in the present county of Louth, extending from the River Boyne to the mountains of Carlingford; they sprang from Conall Cremthann, of whom were the Clann-Colmán or O'Melachlainns.

A. D. 924. Colmán, son of Ailill, Abbot of Cluain-Iraird and Cluain-mic-Nois, a bishop and wise doctor, died. It was by him the Daimhliag of Cluain-mic-Nois was built; and the same event is recorded in the Chronicon Scotorum at the year 926. As this bishop Colmán seems to have been remarkable for his holiness and learning, it is probable that he is identical with the St. Colman of Clonard (Cluain Iraird), whose day was February the 9th. Rioghnach, sister of Finnen, of Cluain Iraird, was his mother." (*See* Mart. Donegal, p. 43.)

Drawn by Dr. Petrie at Clonmacnois, in the year 1822.

Fig. 105.

ŌR AR GILLAGIARAIN.

(Pray for Gillaciarain.)

This name is compounded of *gilla* (meaning 'youth' or 'servant') and the gen. sing. of the name Ciarán. The change of *c* to *g* is due to the lost *n* of the acc. sing. *gilla*(*n*), here governed by the preposition *ar*. As Irish history does not exhibit any name beginning with *Gilla* before the invasion of the Northmen in 792, some are of opinion that it was borrowed from the Scandinavians, who postfixed it to the names of their gods to form names of men, as in Thorgils. However, the name of Gilla, or Gildas, uncompounded, is certainly more ancient than the Danish invasion. (*See* Irish Top. Poems, Introd., p. 55.)

There was a Gilla-ciarain, son of Gluniarain, son of Olaf, who is mentioned in the Wars of the Gaidhil with the Gaill, p. 165, as one of the leaders of the Dublin Danes at Clontarf; and again, p. 207, as having been slain in that battle in the year 1014.

Drawn by Dr. Petrie at Clonmacnois, in the year 1822.

PLATE XLII.

Fig. 106.

[F E R] D O M N A [C H.]

The letters forming the first syllable of this name being destroyed, it is not possible to say with certainty what it may have been. When the stone was complete there was sufficient room for the additional letters which would have formed the name Ferdomnach (*see* Nos. 54 and 72, pp. 30-37). Dr. Petrie, however, thought it should be read Domna[ch] (= Dumnâcos)—a name which occurs amongst the princes of North Munster, and which was also borne by one member of the ancient house of O'Neill.

There was also a St. Domnauc, a disciple of St. David, in Wales.

Drawn by Dr. Petrie at Clonmacnoise, in 1822.

Fig. 107.

M U I R G A L A E.

(Of Muirgal.)

This is the genitive singular of *Muirgal*, which seems a compound of *muir*, 'sea,' and the feminine noun *gal*, which means 'valour.'

Drawn by M. S. from a rubbing taken off the stone by the Rev. James Graves, at Clonmacnois, in 1869.

PLATE XLIII.

Fig. 108.

$\overline{\text{OR}}$ D O M A E L M [O I C H] E I R G [E].

(Pray for Maelmoicheirge).

If the fragment containing the remaining portion of this cross were recovered, the space would exactly contain the letters required for the proposed reading of this inscription, Maelmoicheirge.

In the Annals of the Four Masters, we find at A. D. 927, "Maelmoicheirghe Œconomus of Cluainmic-nois, died."

The ornamental design on this stone, and the composition and arrangement of the lines, recall some of the greater illuminated pages of the Book of Kells more than any sculptured slab we have yet seen. This is now the third instance we have met with of the use of animal forms in the ornament of the stones of the Clonmacnois school.

This tombstone was found at Clonburn, near Clonmacnois (*see* page 9), and a small sketch of it was made by Dr. Petrie in the year 1822. The above drawing by M. S. is from a rubbing made in the year 1869, by Kyran Molloy, at Clonburn.

Figs. 109, 110, 111.

In the first of these figures the inscription is so much mutilated as to be quite illegible. This fragment, along with the stones drawn in figs. 110 and 111, were found at Clonburn.

Drawn by M. S. from rubbings taken by Kyran Molloy, in 1869.

PLATE XLIV.

Fig. 112.

OR DO UALLAIG.

(Pray for Uallach.)

The word *Uallaig* is the dative singular of *Uallach*, a woman's name, signifying 'superba,' cf. *huallach* (gl. arrogans), Z. 2[a] 809, a derivative from *uall* (superbia), Z[2]. 55, 241, gen. *uailbe. ib.*

In the Annals of the Four Masters we read, "A. D. 932. Uallach, daughter of Muimhneachan, chief poetess of Ireland, died."

This tombstone was found buried in the churchyard of the Relig-na-Cailleach, now called the Nunnery Church at Clonmacnois, in 1868, by the Rev. James Graves. It was first read and identified by the Rev. Dr. Todd.

Drawn from a rubbing made by the Rev. James Graves.

Fig. 113.

[OR] DO SECHNASACH

(Pray for Sechnasach.)

The name *Sechnassach* occurs in the Book of Armagh, "fo. Sechnassach filius segeni." fol. 16 *bb*, and from the gen. sing. *Sechnasaig* the name O'Shaughnessy is formed. This family, seated in the county of Galway, belonged to the tribe of Cenel-Aedha, one of those enumerated among the possessors of burial ground at Clonmacnois, in the poem quoted at p. 6:—

"The Cinél Aeda of the golden cups.
It is long since the race departed.
Bitter is their memory in Cluain."

This drawing has been already published by Dr. Petrie, in his Ecclesiastical Architecture, p. 339, where he describes it as a quern, or hand millstone, afterwards used as a tombstone in the cemetery of Clonmacnois. It now forms part of the Petrie collection deposited in the Museum of the Royal Irish Academy.

PLATE XLV.

Fig. 114.

. . . . [D]ELLACH.

This inscription has been so much mutilated that it is impossible to read it. The name may have been probably some such as Foircellach, or Foendellach. In the Annals of the Four Masters we read: "A. D. 809, Foircheallach, of Fobhar, Abbot of Cluain-mic-nois, one of the Gailenga Mora (i. e. the inhabitants of the barony of Morgallion, in the county of Meath), died."

This is the first example as yet given of the altar-stones, which came into use in Italy in the fourth or fifth century, when it was the custom to make temporary altars, by placing a flag on a wooden frame, or table, for convenience of carriage or removal. It was required that this stone should be large enough to hold the paten and chalice, with five crosses engraved on its surface. On this fragment only three crosses can now be seen; the others may have been on the part of the stone which has been broken away.

The use of such stones was introduced into Ireland at an early period, as may be inferred from the following passage in the Life of St. Patrick:—"Portavit Patricius per Sininn secum l. clocos l. patinos l. calices *altaria* libros legis ævanguelii libros et reliquit illos in locis novis." (Book of Armagh, fol. 8, *bb.*)

Drawn by Dr. Petrie, at Clonmacnois, in the year 1822.

Fig. 115.

O̅R̅ DO FOGARTACH M̅ BROENAIN.

(Pray for Fogartach, son of Broenan.)

Fogartach, the genitive singular of which, *Fogartaigh*, is anglicised Fogarty. The name Fogartach is a common one, and occurs again in this collection. (*See* Fig. 115.) This is one of the eleven inscriptions found at Clonmacnois, in which the father's name is also given, but it has not been identified with any one connected with Clonmacnois.

This stone appears to belong to the class above mentioned, called "Altar Stones."

Drawn by Dr. Petrie, at Clonmacnois, in 1822, and by Mr. Du Noyer, in the year 1854, between which dates the portion containing the letters O̅R̅ was broken off. (*See* Antiquarian Sketches, Royal Irish Academy, vol. v., No. 78.) A sketch of it is also given by Mr. O'Neill in his work on the Sculptured Crosses of Ireland, Plate 25; and it has been described by the Rev. James Graves. (Journal of Kilk. and S. E. of Ireland Archæological Society, vol. iii., 1st Series, p. 299.)

PLATE XLVI.

Fig. 116.

O̅R̅ DO CATHUL U . . . UC.

O̅R̅ DO BENE[DI]CHT.

(Pray for Cathal O . . . . Pray for Benedicht.)

The family name, or patronymic, is lost here.

Three chieftains of the name of Cathal, of which *Cathul* is the dative singular, were interred at Clonmacnois, as we learn from the poem above alluded to on interments at that place. 1st. Cathal, son of Fiachra, whose death is thus recorded by the Four Masters:—"A. D. 805. Cathal, son of Fiachra, lord of Rath Airthir and Feara-Cul, died;" and Cathal, son of Ailill, lord of the Ui-Fiachrach, who died A. D. 812, and Cathal the Beautiful, son of Muirghius, son of Tomaltach, king of Connaught, whose death occurred shortly after a victory gained over the men of Munster, who died in the year 836.

No person called Benedicht is mentioned in the Annals or Martyrologies except the Benedictus, one of the disciples of Palladius (Book of Armagh, fol. 2, *a. b*), to whom, with three others, Palladius entrusted the care of his churches in Ireland.

Drawn by Dr. Petrie, at Clonmacnois, in 1822.

Fig. 117.

ŌR DO GUARIU.

(Pray for Guare.)

This word is thus explained in Cormac's Glossary, Codex B., "Guaire .i. uasal" ('noble'), "no gairci" (or 'fierceness').

The name of Guare, of which *Guariu* is the dative singular, is still preserved in the family name of O'Guaire, anglicised Gorey. It was borne by two priests who died at Clonmacnois within a short time of one another. In the Annals of the Four Masters we read, "A. D. 944. Guaire, priest of Cluainmic-nois, died." While in the Chronicon Scotorum we read, "A. D. 943. Guaire, son of Maelacan, priest of Cluain-[Muc-Nois] quievit."

The family of O'Shaughnessy, or tribe of Cinél Aeda, is descended from Guare Aidne, called 'the generous,' who was son of Colmán, and governed Connaught in the seventh century, and died A. D. 662.

He was buried at Clonmacnois, as we learn from the poem on the kings and chieftains interred there. However, this Guare could not be the subject of this inscription, which must belong to a much later date than the period of his death.

Drawn by Dr. Petrie, at Clonmacnois, in 1822.

PLATE XLVII.

Fig. 118.

ŌR DU DORAID.

(Pray for Doraid.)

This name has not been identified with any one connected with Clonmacnois. That there was some remarkable man[a] so called may be inferred from the existence of the name Mael Doraid, meaning 'servant of Dorad.'

Drawn by Dr. Petrie, at Clonmacnois, in the year 1822.

Fig. 119.

ŌR DO DONAELDAN.

(Pray for Donaeldan.)

No such name as Donaeldan is known. The inscription should probably be read DOMNALDAN; but it is impossible to test the accuracy of the reading, as the stone has disappeared, and it is very likely that it has been incorrectly read.

Drawn at Clonmacnois by Colonel Burton, and given to Dr. Petrie by Mr. Cooper.

[a] Mael is occasionally prefixed to words which are not men's names. The O Maeldoraidhs (O'Muldorys) were a distinguished family in Ciuel Conaill. (*See* O'Donovan's Battle of Magh Rath, p. 335.)

Fig. 120.

R E C H T A R

This is perhaps a fragment of the name Reachtabhra, which again occurs on a stone found at Roscrea, or should we regard it as for *Rechtare*, and compare the O. Ir. noun *rectire* (gl. præpositus) Z^2, 229, dat. sing. *rectairiu* (gl. villico) Z^2, 780 ? If the former, this is probably the tombstone of the priest whose death is thus given in the Annals, A. D. 948 :—" Reachtabhra, son of Maenach, priest of Cluainmicnois, died."

A small cross marks the beginning of this inscription, and the design of the larger one is interesting, being formed of interlaced bands, surrounded by a circle, and with a smaller circle entwined at the centre.

Drawn by Dr. Petrie, at Clonmacnois, 1822.

PLATE XLVIII.

Fig. 121.

D U N A D A C H .

Dunadach may mean 'having a *dunad*,' which word frequently occurs in the Félire of Oengus, meaning a 'troop.'

The occurrence of the name on a tombstone at Clonmacnois is of great interest, since it is the first of a series of names in this collection which may, with more or less probability, be connected with the family of Conn na mbocht, the members of which were all distinguished men at Clonmacnois, whose descent from Gorman is thus traced :—

Gorman, ob. 753.
Torbach, ob. 807.
Aedhagan, ob. 834.
Eoghan, ob. 845.
Luchairen, ob. 863.
Egertach, ob. 893.
Aenacan, 947; Dunadach, ob. 953.
Dunadhach, ob. 953.
Dunchadh, ob. 1005.
Joseph, ob. 1022.
Conn na mbocht.
Maelfinnen, Maelchiarain.
Cormac.

Dunadach, bishop of that place, was the son of Egertach, the house-steward of the little church of Clonmacnois, in the beginning of the tenth century. He seems to have been educated at Inis Enagh, near Lanesborough, in Lough Ree, his tutor there having been Caenchomrac, who, according to the Four Masters, died on the 23rd of July, A. D. 898. This Dunadach had a brother named Oenacan, at the entry of whose death in 947, we are told by the same authority, that they were of the Mughdhorna-Maighen—a tribe in the county of Monaghan: and the connexion with Conn na mbocht is proved by the following passage in the Chronicon Scotorum:—

"A. D. 948. Oenagan, son of Egertach, Airchinnech of Eglais Beg, germanus atavi of Conn na mbocht, Bishop of Clonmacnois, quievit." Six years later the death of Dunadach occurred, as recorded by the Annalists in the following passages:—"A. D. 953. Dunadhach, son of Egeartach, Bishop of Cluain-mic-nois, died." (Four Masters.) "A. D. 954, Dunadhach, son of Egertach, Bishop of Cluain-muc-Nois, quievit." (Chronicon Scotorum.)

Drawn by Dr. Petrie at Clonmacnois, in the year 1822.

Fig. 122.

OROIT DO CORMACAN.

(Pray for Cormacán.)

This name is a diminutive of Cormac. (*See* observations on the suffix *án*, page 50, *supra.*)

There was a poet of this name, whose death is thus given in the Annals of the Four Masters:—"A. D. 946. Cormacán, son of Maelbrighde, the chief poet, the playmate of Niall Glundubh, died." O'Donovan adds in a note:—"He was the author of the poem describing a circuit of Ireland made by Muircheartach, son of Niall Glundubh, king of Aileach, in the winter of A. D. 942." This poem was edited by O'Donovan for the Irish Archæological Society. *See* Tracts Relating to Ireland, vol. i. (Irish Archæological Society.)

Abbey O'Gormagan, in the county of Galway, derives its name from a person so called; and it appears from the Annals of Loch-Cé that Maelpetair O'Cormacán, "Master of Roscommon," died in 1234.

Found among the ruins of the church on the island of Inisbofin, in Lough Ree.

Drawn by M. S., from a rubbing of the stone taken by the Rev. James Graves in 1869.

PLATE XLIX.

Fig. 123.

O̅R DO FERGAL.

(Pray for Fergal.)

There are two tombstones at Clonmacnois which bear this name. It is probable that one of them belonged to Fergal O'Ruairc, King of Connaught, said to have been the builder of the great belfry at Clonmacnois, which was completed in the twelfth century by Ua Maeleóin. Dr. Petrie describes this tower in his work on Ecclesiastical Architecture, p. 409, and refers to the following passage in the Registry of Clonmacnois:—"And the said Fergal hath for a monument built a small steep castle, or steeple, commonly called in Irish, Cloictheagh, in Cluain, as a memorial of his own parte of that cemeterie." We read in the Annals of the Four Masters of a victory gained by this king, in the year 961, over the men of Munster, on the Shannon; and, in 963, of his defeat by Domhnall Ua Neill, who carried off his hostages. He was killed in the following year, as thus recorded:—"A. D. 964, Fearghal Ua Ruairc, King of Connaught, was slain by Domhnall, son of Conghalach, lord of Breagha and Cnoghbha." (Four Masters.)

Drawn by Dr. Petrie at Clonmacnois, in 1822.

Fig. 124.

$\overline{\text{OR}}$ DO HUAR . . .

(Pray for Uar . . .)

This name may have been Uarach or Uarcridhe. The last-mentioned occurs in the Chronicon Scotorum at the year 684. The *h* is inserted to prevent hiatus.

No name beginning with *Uar* has been found to have belonged to any one connected with Clonmacnois.

PLATE L.

Fig. 125.

FERGAL.

The name Fergal, already commented upon (*see* Note on Fig. 123), is a common one, and it is impossible to identify this particular instance. There was a Fearghal, Lord of Cairbre, whose death is recorded by the Four Masters, at A. D. 974, and to whom this inscription may belong, as we read in the poem on the Tribes interred at Clonmacnois (page 6, *supra*) that "the sons of Cairbre" were buried there.

Drawn by Dr. Petrie at Clonmacnois, in 1822.

Fig. 126.

$\overline{\text{OR}}$ DO EVCHAIG MAG DARMOT.

(Pray for Eochaid Mac Darmot.)

The genitive singular, *Darmot* (which seems to be an ant-stem), has been referred to the i-stem Diarmait (anglicised Dermid); but this is clearly wrong, as the genitive singular of Diarmait is always *Diarmata*. *Euchaig* is the dative singular of the noun *Euchaid*, or *Eochaid*, gen. *Echach*, *Echoch*, Zeuss, G. C., ed. Ebel, pp. 259, 260. *Mag* must be for *Mac*, the dative singular of *Mac*, 'son.' The sinking of the tenuis *c* to *g* on so old a stone is very remarkable.

The only person of this name mentioned in the Annals lived in the sixth century:—"A. D. 597. Eochaidh Mac Diarmata, Bishop and Abbot of Armagh, died." (Four Mast.) We learn from the Registry of Clonmacnois that the family of Mac Dermot possessed a burial-ground at Clonmacnois, which was purchased by Tomaltach Mac Dermot, who became chief of Moylurg, in the year 1169, and died in the year 1206. The Mac Dermots continued to inter the bodies of their chiefs there till the year 1736. Tomaltach rebuilt the great church of Clonmacnois for the cemetery of the Clann Malrunay, the tribe name of the Mac Dermots of Moylurg; and, in the poem on the Tribes interred at Clonmacnois, we find that the O'Mulroneys of the River Boyle were buried there. The ruins of Temple Mac Dermod, or the Cathedral Church, are still standing.

Drawn by Dr. Petrie at Clonmacnois, in 1822.

PLATE LI.

Fig. 127.

ŌR̄ COMGÁN.

(Pray for Comgán.)

This name, which sometimes appears in the corrupt form of Comdhan, has been already discussed. (*See* Note on Fig. 13). It has not been identified with any one connected with Clonmacnois.

In many ways this stone is a remarkable one. The design is an Irish cross, with semicircular terminations filled in with the triquetra, an emblem of the Trinity; while the centre, instead of being circular, is a diamond, filled in with four triquetras, arranged so as to form a cross, and the inscription itself is singular, for the preposition *do*, or *ar*, after *oroit* is omitted, probably by accident.

Drawn by M. S., from a rubbing of the stone taken in 1869.

This slab was drawn by Mr. George V. Du Noyer, in the year 1854, who, however, failed to notice the triquetras at the termination of the shaft and arms. In his notes on this stone he suggests that this may be the tomb of Comghan Foda, who died A. D. 868; but this is not likely, as he was anchorite of the Monastery of Tallaght (Tamhlacht), near Dublin.

Fig. 128.

[ŌR̄ D]O MUIRGUS DEIC[OLAE].

(Pray for Muirgus Deicola.)

The name Muirgus is a common one in Irish history. No explanation has hitherto been given of *deic*. It may, as above suggested, be the beginning of the Latin *deicole*, the dative singular of *deicola*, an quivalent of the Irish *céle dé*, or Culdee. (*See* Dr. Reeves' essay on the Culdees, Trans. of the Royal Irish Academy, vol. xxiv., p. 5.)

It is possible that the name Muirgus in this inscription may be identified as that of a Lord of Hy-Many, whose death is thus given in the Annals of the Four Masters:—"A. D. 985. Muirgeas, son of Domhnall, Lord of Ui Maine, was slain;" and also in the Chronicon Scotorum :—At 984, "Muirghius, son of Domhnall, King of Ui Maine, jugulatus est. Cluain-muc-Nois was burned on the night of Friday before great Easter."

Drawn by Dr. Petrie at Clonmacnois, in 1822.

This inscription was also drawn by Mr. George V. Du Noyer, who has mistaken the O of the word DO for a D. (*See* Antiquarian Sketches, Royal Irish Academy, vol. v. No. 78.)

PLATE LII.

Fig. 129.

R E T A N].

This name may perhaps be read Retara. It is also possible that it may have been Retan, or Redan, a name which occurs in the Annals of the Four Masters at the year 954, and in the parallel passage of the Annals of Ulster, A. D. 955.

This Redan was father to Maelbrighde, Abbot of Clonmacnois and Lann Ela, the latter of which was a church in the O'Molloy's Country, King's County. (*See* Mart. Donegal, Introd., p. xliv.)

The design of the very beautiful ornament upon this stone helps to confirm the opinion suggested by this identification of the name, that it was work of the early part of the tenth century. It was formed of a band so interlaced as to make a large cross of the Maltese pattern, with a smaller cross at the centre; and the angles are filled in with four larger and four smaller triquetra knots, all flowing from the graceful interweaving of a single band.

Drawn by M. S., at Lemanaghan (Liath Mancháin), in the King's County. (*See* p. 8, *supra.*)

PLATE LIII.

Fig. 130.

OR DO MAELFINNIA.

(Pray for Maelfinnia.)

This name is compounded of Mael and Finnia, the servant of Finnia. There are two inscriptions at Clonmacnois commemorating the name of Maelfinnia, both of which may have belonged to persons mentioned by the Annalists as connected with that place, and who bore that name.

This may probably be identified as the tombstone of the Abbot of Clonmacnois, mentioned by the Four Masters at A. D. 991:—"Maelfinnia, the son of Spelan, successor of Ciaran son of the Artificer, died;" and again, in the Chronicon Scotorum, A. D. 992:—"Maelfinnia, son of Spelan, one of the Ui Becon, comarb of Ciaran Mac-an-tsair, quievit." From this latter entry we learn the name of the tribe from whom Maelfinnia sprang. They were descendants of Becon, who was the seventh in descent from Eochaidh Muigh-mheadhoin, Monarch of Ireland in the fourth century. This tribe was seated in Meath, probably at Rath-Becon, in the barony of Ratoath. (Genealogies of the Hy-Fiachrach, Irish Archæological Society, p. 13.)

Drawn by Dr. Petrie at Clonmacnois, in 1822.

Fig. 131.

ŌR DO ODRAN HÁU EOLAIS.

(Pray for Odrán, descendant of Eolas.)

The name Odrán (a diminutive of Odar, 'pale'), is now anglicised Horan. *Háu* is the dative singular of *háue*, the old Irish form of the modern *ua* or *ó* : *haue* (gl. nepos), Zeuss, G. C. ed. Ebel, p. 1021; nominative plural *háui*, *ib.*, p. 48, dative plural *auib*, *ib.* p. 1020, accusative *auu*, Book of Armagh. Goidelica, 2nd ed., p. 86. Eolais is the genitive singular of a noun either cognate or identical with *eolas*, *heulas*, 'peritia,' Zeuss, G. C., ed. Ebel, p. 35.

This is one of the seven inscriptions in this collection where the surname is given, and it can be identified with that of an ecclesiastic of Clonmacnois whose death is thus recorded by the Annalists, A. D. 994 :—"Odhran Ua-h-Eolais, scribe of Clonmacnois, died." (Ann. Four Mast.)

He was, in all probability, the *Ua*, or grandson of Eolas, chieftain of Magh-Rein (in the south of the county of Leitrim), about the year 900, from whom his descendants, the Leitrim families of Reynolds, Mulvey, &c., derived their tribe name of Muinter-Eolais.

Drawn by M. S., from a rubbing made by Mr. O'Neill, who gives a sketch of this stone in the Sculptured Crosses of Ancient Ireland, Plate xxii.

PLATE LIV.

Fig. 132.

ŌR DO FLANNCHAD.

(Pray for Flannchad.)

This was probably the tomb of the Abbot of Clonmacnois, whose death is thus recorded, A. D. 1002 :—"Flannchadh Ua Ruaidhine, successor of Ciaran son of the Artificer, of the tribe of Corca Mogha, died." (Ann. Four Mast). The same event is given in the Annals of Ulster, at the same year, and in the Chron. Scotor. at A. D. 1001.

The tribe to which this person belonged came from the territory of Corca-Mogha, parish of Kilkerrin, in the barony of Killian, in the north-east of the county of Galway. (*See* Tribes and Customs of Hy Many, Irish Archæological Society, p. 84.)

Drawn by Dr. Petrie at Clonmacnois, in 1822.

A sketch of this stone has been published by Mr. O'Neill, in the Sculptured Crosses of Ancient Ireland, p. 26. Dr. Petrie gives an engraving of this monument in his Eccl. Architecture of Ireland, p. 324.

Fig. 133.

ŌR DO BONUIT.

This name has not been met with in any of the Annals or Martyrologies. It is difficult to explain its form. If it were Bonait it might be the diminutive of *buan*, 'good.' (*See* Cormac's Glossary, and for examples of diminutives in *-ait*, Zeuss, G. C., ed. Ebel, p. 274.) But the fourth letter is certainly *u*, and not *a*, on the stone.

Drawn by Dr. Petrie at Clonmacnois, in the year 1822.

This stone was also drawn by Mr. George V. Du Noyer, in 1864, who failed to observe a remarkable distance between the O and the N of Bonuit.

PLATE LV.

Figs. 134 and 135.

L A I T H . . A I T H .

The letters on these two fragments may have formed the first syllables of the name Flaithbertach, and it is remarkable that there are two bishops of Clonmacnois of this name in the 11th century, mentioned in the following passage from the Annals of the Four Masters :—" A. D. 1013. Flaithbhertach, son of Domhnall, that is of the Clann-Colmain, successor of Ciaran and Finnen, died;" and in the Chronicon Scotorum :—" Flaithbhertach, son of Domhnall (he was of the Clan Colmain, comarb of Ciaran and Finnian), quievit in Christo." From his being called Comarb, or successor of Finnian, we learn that he presided over the establishment of Clonard, of which Finnian was the first bishop, as well as over that of Clonmacnois. That the Clann Colmain, from whom he sprung, possessed a burial-ground at Clonmacnois is proved by the passage in the poem on the tribes interred at Clonmacnois, where it is said "many a blue eye and a white limb lie under the earth at Clann Colmain's tomb."

With regard to the second ecclesiastic connected with Clonmacnois who bore that name, we have the following notice in the Annals of Clonmacnois:—" A. D. 1038. Flathbertagh Mac Loyngse, Lector and Bushopp of Clonvicknose, died;" and in the Annals of the Four Masters :—" A. D. 1038, Flaithbeartach, son of Loingseach, Bishop and Lector of Clonmacnois, died;" while in the Chronicon Scotorum his death is recorded as having taken place in the year 1035.

Fig. 136.

[O̅R̅ D Ф B R A N [U C H E] L L A C H Á I N.

(Pray for Bran, descendant of Cellachan.)

The name Bran, which occurs on two other inscriptions in the collection, signifies 'raven;' and Cellacháin (if the conjectured reading be right) is the genitive singular of Cellachán, a diminutive of Cellach, which latter name is found on another Clonmacnois stone. (*See* Fig. 12.)

It has been suggested by Mr. Hennessy that this inscription may be read Bran U hUallacháin, and that it may refer to a descendant of Uallachán, who was the fifteenth in descent from King Cathair Mór, and lived about the year 700. The posterity of Uallachán (the O'Hualaghans, or O'Holahans, were one of the chief branches of the Clann-Colgan, whose territory is now represented by the barony of Philipstown, King's County. (*See* Four Masters, A.D. 1414, note [l].)

This name has not been identified with that of any person on record as connected with Clonmacnois.

Drawn by Dr. Petrie at Clonmacnois, in the year 1822.

PLATE LVI.

Fig. 137.

O̅R̅ D O M A R T E . . .

This figure is copied from a drawing of Dr. Petrie's. The last two letters in the plate can hardly be right. Could the name have been Martenín, a diminutive of Martan?

Drawn by Dr. Petrie at Clonmacnois, in the year 1822.

Fig. 138.

FECHTNACH.

This name has been already discussed. (*See* notice of Fig. 83, p. 46, *supra.*)

Drawn by Dr. Petrie at Clonmacnois, in the year 1822.

PLATE LVII.

Fig. 139.

O̅R̅ DO MUIREDACH.

(Pray for Muiredach.)

Two stones bearing the name of Muiredach are found at Clonmacnois, and the Annalists record the death of three persons so called, who belonged to that place, and one of whom, we also learn, was buried there. The stone now under consideration may have been the tomb of Muiredach, son of Fergus, successor of Patrick, who died A. D. 966. The fact that a Muiredach, son of Fergus, was buried at Clonmacnois is stated in an ancient poem on the interments at that place, found among the MSS. in the Burgundian Library at Brussels, a copy of which is now preserved in the Catholic University, Dublin, where the poet says:—"Muireadach, son of Fergus, was one of those who lay under the tombstones at Cluain."

Drawn by Dr. Petrie at Clonmacnois, in the year 1822.

Fig. 140.

[O̅R̅] DO MAELPHATRAIC.

(Pray for Maelphátraic.)

This name occurs once before in this collection (*see* Plate xxv., Fig 61), where it is spelt Maelpatric. Here the infection of the initial of Pátraic is clearly expressed by the insertion of the letter H after P, and the introduction of the letter *a* before *c* is due to progressive vocalic assimilation.

This inscription is noticed by O'Donovan, in his Irish Grammar, page 43.

The Annalists record the deaths of two persons called Maelpatrick, who were ecclesiastics at Clonmacnois. (*See* notice of Fig. 61.) The second of them is thus mentioned by the Four Masters:—"A. D. 1028. Maelpadraig Ua Baeghalain [anglicised O'Boylan], priest of Cluain-mic-Nois, died."

Drawn by Dr. Petrie at Clonmacnois, in the year 1822.

PLATE LVIII.

Fig. 141.

O̅R̅ DO .... BRIGTE.

(Pray for .... Brigte.)

The name upon this stone was probably Maelbrigte, the part of the slab which contained the first syllable having been broken away. If this be so, it is the third instance we have met with of the occurrence of this name on the tombstones at Clonmacnois. (*See* notices of Figs. 81 and 84.) At the date 954 the Four Masters record the death of Maelbrigte, son of Redan, who was Abbot of Clonmacnois and Lynally (Lann Ela), in the King's County. The name Redan occurs upon a tombstone found in the churchyard of Lemanaghan. (*See* notices of Fig. 129.)

Drawn by M. S., from a rubbing made by the Rev. James Graves, at Clonmacnois, in 1869.

Fig. 142.

[C] OSCRACH.

Coscrach occurs as an adjective in the 150th verse of the Duan Éirennach. (Irish Nennius, p. 242, Irish Archæological Society.)

The name *Coscrach*, signifying 'victorious,' from *coscur*, 'victory,' is still a common family name in Ireland, anglicised Cosgrave. It frequently occurs in the Annals, as borne by chieftains, but not by ecclesiastics. This name has not been identified with that of any one immediately connected with Clonmacnois. It may possibly be the stone of Cosgrach, a Bishop of Clonfert, whose death, in the eleventh century, is thus recorded in the Annals of the Four Masters :—"A.D. 1040. Cosgrach, son of Aingeadh, successor of Flannan and Brenainn, died, after a well-spent life."

Drawn by Dr. Petrie at Clonmacnois, in the year 1822.

PLATE LIX.

Fig. 143.

[OR D . . . . IN GOR . . .

(Pray for . . . . . Gor . . .)

This inscription may have been *Or do anmain Gormain*, 'Pray for the soul of Gorman.' Were the stone restored, so as to make the cross complete, there would be room for the missing letters. If this suggestion be correct, we have here the second instance in which the name of Gorman appears on the tombstones of Clonmacnois. (*See* Fig. 100, Plate xxxix.)

Drawn by Dr. Petrie at Clonmacnois, in the year 1822.

Fig. 144.

OR DO TH . . GAN.

This may be a fragment of the name Tadgán, which has been already discussed in the notice of Fig. 132.

Drawn by Dr. Petrie at Clonmacnois, in the year 1822.

PLATE LX.

Fig. 145.

DAIGREI.

(Of Daigre.)

Daigre is a name that occurs thrice in the Martyrology of Donegal, and once in the Annals of the Four Masters, as borne by an anamchara of Clonmacnois, who died at Glendalough in the year 1056. The terminatiou *ei* (not *i*) on an inscription seems that of the gen. sing. of a latinised form, *Daigreus*.

The name seems to correspond with Daigh remarkable as borne by the great artist of Ireland in the sixth century. *See* Martyrology of Donegal, page 223; and Note, page 219, where the sons of Daigre are called the sons of the artist.

Drawn by Dr. Petrie at Clonmacnois, in the year 1822.

Fig. 146.

FOGARTA . .

This is evidently a fragment of the name Fogartach, gen. *fogartaig;* whence the familiar name Fogarty. The old Irish form of the name would be Focartach, with the tenuis *c* for *g*.

It is probable that this inscription belongs to Fogartach the Fair, of Ulster, whose death is thus recorded:—"A. D. 1065. Fogartagh Fyn, an anchorite and sadge, died at Clonvicknose." (Annals of Clonmacnois.) "A. D. 1066. Fogartach Finn, one of the Ulidians, a wise man and an anchorite, died at Cluain-mic-Nois." (Four Masters.)

Drawn by Dr. Petrie at Clonmacnois, in the year 1822.

PLATE LXI.

Fig. 147.

ŌR DO CHUNN.

(Pray for Conn.)

Cunn is the dative singular of *Conn*, gen. *Cuinn*, whence the Anglo-Irish Quin. A distinguished man belonging to Clonmacnois was named Conn na mBocht, or Conn of the Poor, from his devotion to the poor, and their relief and care. He was a lay brother of Clonmacnois, and father of a great family of scholars, lay and ecclesiastical. He appears to have been the founder and superior of a community of poor lay monks, of the Céli Dé (or Culdee Order), in connexion with that great establishment. (*See* Dr. Reeves on the Culdees, page 19.) In the Annals of the Four Masters, A. D. 1032, we read :—"Conn na mBocht, head of the Culdees, and anchorite of Cluain-mic-Nois, the first that invited a party of the poor of Cluain at Iseal Chiarain, and who presented twenty cows of his own to it." of this was said :—

> "O Conn of Cluain! thou wert heard from Ireland in Alba;
> O head of dignity! it will not be easy to plunder thy church."

And again :—"A. D. 1059. Conn na mBocht, the glory and dignity of Cluain-mic-Nois, died at an advanced age."

This Conn was descended from Gorman, who died in the year 610, while on his pilgrimage at Clonmacnois, and a long line of ancestors, all of whom held some office at Clonmacnois.

In the present collection we have already met with the name of another member of this family (*see* Plate xlviii., Fig. 21)—Dunadach, Bishop of Clonmacnois, who died sixty years before the founding of this hospital. His connexion with Conn is proved by the following passage in the Annals of the Four Masters:—"A. D. 1005. Dunchadh, son of Dunadach, lector of Cluain-mic-Nois, and its anchorite, afterwards head of its rule and history, died. He was the senior of the race of Conn na mBocht."

The descent of Egartach, the father of Dunadach, from Gorman, is also given by the Four Masters, A. D. 863.

Joseph, the father of Conn, was Anmchara, or 'soul-friend,' in the monastery. He died in the year 1022. His son Conn survived him for thirty-seven years, and his death is recorded in the Annals of Ulster, in the following passage:—"A. D. 1060. Daniel Desech, chief soule friend of Ireland, and Conn na mBoght, .i. of the poore, in Cluain-mic-Nois, ad Christum vocati sunt."

Again, in the Annals of the Four Masters:—"A. D. 1059. Conn na mBocht, the glory and dignity of Cluain-mic-Nois, died at an advanced age." His death is recorded in the Chronicon Scotorum as occurring three years earlier than in the Annals of Ulster:—"A. D. 1057. Conn na mBocht, of Cluain-mic-Nois, quievit."

It is only in the Chronicon Scotorum that we learn what rank he held in the Church. He is called "Bishop" in the same work, at the year 948. He left behind him several sons, many of whom, with their sons also, became distinguished men in this monastery. Names identical with those of three of his sons and two of his grandsons are inscribed upon the next five tombstones, all of which are adorned with a cross of exactly the same style, and the same ornamental design in the central circle.

Drawn by Dr. Petrie at Clonmacnois, in 1822.

Fig. 148.

ŌR DO MAELFINNIA.

(Pray for Maelfinnia.)

This name has occurred on another tombstone in this collection (*see* Pl. xli., fig. 128), and it is remarkable that while it is only found twice in the ancient Annals, as borne by ecclesiastics connected with Clonmacnois, it should be also seen on only two of the sepulchral slabs in this ancient cemetery.

This second Maelfinnia of Clonmacnois may then have been he of whom we read in the Annals of the Four Masters:—"A.D. 1056. Maelfinnen Mac Cuinn-na-mBocht, the father of Cormac, successor of Ciaran, died, i.e. Maelfinnen, son of Conn, son of Joseph, son of Donnchadh, son of Dunadach, son of Egertach, son of Luachan, son of Eoghan, son of Aedhagan, son of Torbach, son of Gorman, of the Ui Ceallaigh-Breagh."

Drawn by Dr. Petrie at Clonmacnois, in 1822.

PLATE LXII.

Fig. 149.

[ŌR DO MA]ELCHIARÁN.

This is probably a fragment of the name Maelciarán, or the servant of Ciarán. If the stone were restored to its original form, there would be space for the usual prayer, and the inscription would read Ōr do Maelchiarán.

The death of Maelciarán Mac Cuinn-na-mBocht is recorded in the following passages :—"A. D. 1079. Maelciarán Mac Cuinn-na-mBocht, successor of Ciaran, died. He was the glory and veneration of Cluain-mic-Nois in his time." (Annals of the Four Masters.) "A. D. 1079. Macquin, heade of the poore of Clon-mic-Nois [and others] *Mortui sunt.*" (Annals of Ulster.) From this last entry we learn that he succeeded his father in the government of the hospital at Clonmacnois. He was killed at the attack made upon his hospital by Murchadh O'Melaghlin, which is thus described in the Annals of Clonmacnois:—"A. D. 1069. Murrogh Mac Connor O'Melaghlyn, prince of Meath, did so oversette the family of Moyle-Kyeran Mac Conn Ne Moght, in Isill-Kyeran, and the poor of that house, that the steward of that family was slain by them, for which cause Moyvoura was granted to the poor."

The Four Masters also record that, in the year 1070, "The causeway from the Cross of Bishop Etchen to Irdom-Chiaran was made at Cluain-mic-Nois by Maelciarán Mac Cuinn-na-mBocht, and the causeways from Cross-Chomgaill to Uluidh na-dtri-gcross ['monument of the three crosses'], and thence westwards to the entrance of the street."

The monument of the three crosses, here referred to, is still pointed out at Clonmacnois.

The death of this person is recorded at the year 1076, in the Chronicon Scotorum.

Drawn by M. S., from a rubbing of the stone taken by the Rev. James Graves in 1869.

Fig. 150.

OR̄ DO GILLACHRIST.

(Pray for Gillachrist.)

This name is formed by the prefix Gilla, servant, to the name of Christ. (*See* notice of the name Gillaciaran, p. 51, *supra.*)

This name may probably be identified with that of another son of Conn. His death is thus recorded by the Four Masters :—"A. D. 1085. Gillacrist Mac Cuinn-na-mBocht, the best ecclesiastical student that was in Ireland in his time, the glory and ornament of Cluain-mic-Nois, died."

Another Gillacrist died at Clonmacnois thirty-eight years later, as recorded by the Chronicon Scotorum:—"A. D. 1123. Gillacrist Ua Maeleoin, Abbot of Cluain-muc-Nois, fountain of knowledge and charity, head of the prosperity and affluence of Erin, quievit." And we learn also, from the same authority, that:—"A. D. 1120, the great belfry of Cluain-muc-Nois was finished by Gillacrist Ua Maeléoin and by Toirdhealbhach Ua Conchobhair." This event is also recorded by the Four Masters :—"A. D. 1124. The finishing of the Cloictheach of Cluain-mic-Nois, by Ua Maeleoin, successor of Ciarán," who thus give his death:—"1127. Gillacrist Ua Maeleoin, Abbot, successor of Ciaran of Cluain-mic-Nois, fountain of the wisdom, the ornament and magnificence of Leath Chuinn, and head of the prosperity and affluence of Ireland, died."

Drawn by Dr. Petrie at Clonmacnois, in 1822.

PLATE LXIII.

Fig. 151.

OR̄ DO MAELCHIARAN.

(Pray for Maelciaran.)

This is the second instance of the occurrence of the name Maelciaran, or servant of Ciaran, found on the tombstones of Clonmacnois, and it may be identified with that of the learned man whose death is thus recorded by the Four Masters:—"A. D. 1101. Maelchiaran Ua Donnghusa, learned senior of Clonmacnois, died."

Drawn by Dr. Petrie at Clonmacnois, in the year 1822.

Fig. 152.

OR DO MAILMAIRE.

(Pray for Mailmaire.)

This name, which signifies the servant of Mary, was borne by a celebrated man in Clonmacnois, in the early part of the twelfth century, whose death is thus recorded by the Four Masters :—"A. D. 1106. Maelmuire, son of Mac Cuinn-na-mBocht, was killed in the middle of the Daimhliag of Clonmacnois, by plunderers." O'Donovan adds in a note :—"He was the transcriber of Leabhar-na-hUidhre, a considerable fragment of which is still preserved, in his own handwriting, in the Library of the Royal Irish Academy." We learn that this Maelmuire was the son of Cellechar, the son of Conn na mBocht, from an entry in the book itself. At the top of p. 55 occurs a note, partly illegible, intimating that it was a "probatio of the pen of Maelmuri, son of the son of [Conn na mBocht];" and on p. 37, col. 2, a scribe named O'Cuirnin entreats a prayer for "Maelmuri, son of Celechar, grandson of Conn na mBocht, who wrote and selected this book from various books." (*See* O'Curry's Lectures, pp. 182, 570.)

Drawn by M. S., from a rubbing taken by the Rev. Dr. Todd, in 1848.

PLATE LXIV.

Fig. 153.

OROIT AR THURCAIN LASAN

DERNAD IN [C]HROSSA.

(Pray for Turcain, by whom this Cross was made.)

The name Turcain has not been identified.

This inscription is found on the Carn of the Three Crosses, from which the causeway which connects the Nunnery Church, or Relig-na-Cailleach, with the Cemetery of Clonmacnois, derives its name. This monument must have been in existence in the time of Maelchiaran, son of Conn of the Poor, as in the passage already quoted (page 67), we find that the causeway made by him extended from Uluidh-na-dtri-gcross, or 'the station monument of the three crosses,' to Cross Chomgaill; and, even before this, in 1026, when the paved way from Garrda a Banabbaid ('the garden of the abbess') to this monument was made by Breasal Conailleach. (*See* Annals of the Four Masters, page 812, note; and A. D. 918.)

Drawn by M. S., from a rubbing of the stone found in the collection of Dr. Petrie.

The Rev. James Graves has described this stone in the Journal of the Kilkenny and South-East of Ireland Archæological Society, vol. iii., second series, page 302 :—"The slab lies at the mound situated between the burying-ground and the Nunnery, where tradition says that St. Kieran's maid servant was buried in punishment after the saint's cow was lost."

Fig. 154.

ŌR DO MAEL[EO]AIN.

(Pray for Mael[eo]ain.)

The name Mael Eoain (anglicised Malone) means 'tonsured servant of Eoan' (Johannes). It was adopted by a branch of the royal house of O'Conor, in the eleventh century. That the O'Conor family possessed a burial-ground at Clonmacnois is stated in the Registry of that place. (*See* Journal of the Kilkenny and South-East of Ireland Archæological Society, second series, vol. iii., page 451.)

This name may, perhaps, be identified with the Ua Maeleoin whose death is thus recorded in the Chronicon Scotorum:—"A.D. 1153. Aedh Ua Maeleoin, successor of Ciaran of Cluain-mic-Nois, fountain of the prosperity and affluence of Leath Cluinn, a man of charity and mercy, completed his life."

An older form of this name, Mael-Iohain, is found at Fig. 162.

Drawn by Dr. Petrie at Clonmacnois, in the year 1822.

PLATE LXV.

Fig. 155.

[HU]ARIADEN (?)

The name upon this stone cannot be read with certainty. The conjectured *hua* ('nepos') occurs on Figs. 165 and 169. The *riaden* (leg. *rladén*) may be a form of the name Rédán, which occurs in the gen. sing. *Rédáin*. (Four Masters, A.D. 954.)

This cross belongs to the same class, and is probably of the same date of those of Maelquiaran, and Ronan and others of the ninth century;—an Irish cross, quadratc in the centre, and with loops at the terminal points.

Drawn by M. S., from a rubbing of the stone made at Clonmacnois by the Rev. James Graves, in the year 1870.

Fig. 156.

TIRUCIST.

The name inscribed on this stone has not been identified, nor can this reading of the inscription now be verified, as the stone has disappeared.

The design upon this stone is quite peculiar, as it does not occur again in any other stone as yet discovered in Ireland; but it is found on the bases of the shrines of St. Moedog and St. Molaise, on the side of the box of the Stowe Missal, and on the back of the shrine of St. Patrick's bell; all of which date from the tenth to the twelfth century. We may then presume that the stone belongs to the same period.

Drawn by Dr. Petrie at Clonmacnois, in the year 1822.

PLATE LXVI.

Fig. 157.

[OR̄] DO CHÁINIG.

(Pray for Cáinech.)

This name has not been identified. It has been suggested that it may be related to the name Cainnech, which occurs in the Annals of the Four Masters, at A. D. 928, as borne by a daughter of Canannan, who was wife of the King of Ireland. However, as the *ái* is probably a diphthong, the name can hardly be the same.

Drawn by Dr. Petrie at Clonmacnois, in the year 1822.

Fig. 158.

OR̄ DO MAELMHICHIL.

(Pray for Maelmíchíl.)

This name, meaning 'the servant of Michael,' occurs three times on the tombstones of Clonmacnois.

In this instance the vocalic infection (or, as Irish grammarians term it, 'aspiration') of the letter M of Míchel (rare on so early a monument) is due to the lost vowel with which the governing noun *Mael* originally ended in the dative singular. (*See* Zeuss. Gram. Celtica, ed. Ebel, pp. 180, 181.)

A similarly formed name, Cara Míchel, 'friend of St. Michael' (now Carmichael), is found in Scotland. O'Donovan, Ir. Topog. Poems, Introd., pp. 55, 56.

Drawn by Dr. Petrie at Clonmacnois, in 1822.

PLATE LXVII.

Fig. 159.

MAELMICHÉIL.

(Maelmichael.)

This is another form of the name just noticed (Fig. 159.) It will be observed that as *mael* is in the nominative singular, the M of Micheil is not aspirated here, although the C is, owing to its coming between two vowels.

This is the only instance we have met with of a slab ornamented with two small Latin crosses at the top.

Drawn by Dr. Petrie at Clonmacnois, in 1822.

Fig. 160.

MAELIOHAIN EP̄S̄.

(Maeliohain Episcopus.)

This name signifies 'the servant of Johannes.' The abbreviation EP̄S̄, if it represent an Irish word, should be read *epscop*; if it represent a Latin word, *episcopus*. The occurrence of the name of the person buried, with his title added, is uncommon in Ireland, only five other instances having been found, four of which are at Clonmacnois (*see* Figs. 26, 72, and 128); but such often occur in Gaulish Latin inscriptions, as well as Roman, from the fifth to the seventh centuries. (*See* Inscriptions Chrétiennes de la Gaule; Le Blant, tome i., p. 127).

Dr. O'Donovan (*see* Annals of the Four Masters, vol. iii., p. 4, note) has suggested that this name may be identified with that of the Bishop of Clonmacnois whose death is thus recorded:—"A. D. 1172. Tiernagh O'Malone, successor of Ciaran of Clonmacnois, died."

Drawn by Dr. Petrie at Clonmacnois, in 1822.

PLATE LXVIII.

Figs. 161, 162.

L E T . . . .

M A L E C .

The letters on these two stones are so mutilated, that it is impossible to say what names they may have stood for. It is doubtful whether Fig. 162 was a tombstone, or only formed part of the ornament of some building. It seems too small to have been a tombstone.

Dr. Petrie drew these stones at Clonmacnois in 1822. Fig. 162 now forms part of the Petrie collection deposited in the Royal Irish Academy.

Fig. 163.

T H O M A S .

This name may be identified with another descendant of Conn na mBocht, so many of whose family have been already mentioned.

In the year 1253, after the death of Cellach O'Gillapatric, Bishop of Clonmacnois, Thomas O'Quin, a friar minor, was consecrated at Rome as his successor. He was a Franciscan friar, and was confirmed by King Henry III., on the 20th of February, 1252, English style (*see* Harris' Edition of Ware's Bishops, p. 171.) He held the see for fifteen years, and his death is thus recorded:—"A. D. 1278. Thomas O'Quin, Bishop of Clonmacnois, died."

Drawn by Dr. Petrie at Clonmacnois, in 1822.

Fig. 164.

This slab was probably a tombstone, though Dr. Petrie failed to find any traces of letters remaining on the fragment when he found it. The ornamented circle occurs in other instances upon these slabs (*see* Figs. 95 and 109), but never before without some form of cross in the centre.

Drawn by Dr. Petrie at Clonmacnois, in the year 1822.

PLATE LXIX.

Fig. 165.

ŌR DO . . . . . CILLIN ICANERNAD IN LECS .

(A prayer for . . . . . . illin, by whom this stone was made.)

The first word in this inscription may be Cillin; and so this may be the tombstone of Cormac O'Killin to whom reference has been already made. (*See* notice of Fig. 49.)

His death is recorded in the Annals of the Four Masters:—"A. D. 964. Cormac Ua Cillene, successor of Ciaran, a bishop, and a wise man of great age, died." Further particulars are related of him in the Chronicon Scotorum, under the same date, where it is recorded that "Cormac Ua Cillin, of the Ui Fiachrach Aidhni, Comarb of Ciaran and Coman, and Comarb of Tuaim-greine, by whom the great church of Tuaim-greine and its cloigtech were constructed, Sapiens et Senex, et Episcopus, quievit in Christo." "This," adds Mr. Hennessy, in a note (p. 216), "is the earliest record extant of the erection of a round tower." He was also the builder of Temple Killen, a church at Clonmacnois, the ruins of which may still be seen.

As to the rest of the inscription—for *icanernad* we should probably read *lasanernad*, i.e. *lasan-dernad*, the eclipsed *d* being here, as is sometimes the case, omitted. (See the analysis of the inscription on the shrine of the Bell of St. Patrick. Reeves' Antiquities of Down and Connor, p. 370.)

Drawn by Dr. Petrie at Clonmacnois, in 1822.

Fig. 166.

ŌR DO CH:::::

DO MUGROIN HU BORGAN.

(Pray for Ch . . . . . . for Mugron, descendant of Borgan.)

This title has not been identified. In the Annals of the Four Masters, at the date 1025, the name Mugroin occurs as borne by the ancestor of Muireadach, a lector of Clonmacnois. (*See* notice of Fig. 173.)

Drawn by Dr. Petrie at Clonmacnois, in 1822.

PLATE LXX.

Fig. 167.

DÍCHOE[M].

If this reading be right, the name is probably a woman's, from the intensive prefix *di*, and the adjective *coém*, now *caomh*, and meaning very 'loveable.'

Drawn by M. S., from a rubbing of the stone taken by the Rev. James Graves, in 1869.

FIGS. 168, 169.

MAEL.....

$\overline{\text{OR}}$ DO CHONODEN.

(Mael . . . . .)

(Pray for Conoden.)

In the first of these two inscriptions the letters have been so much mutilated that it is impossible to know the name of which they formed a part.

The name Conoden, in the second, has not been identified. The death of a "Conodar," Abbot of Fore, in Westmeath, is recorded in the Irish Annals (Ulster, Four Masters, and Chron. Scotorum) under the year 706.

Drawn by Dr. Petrie at Clonmacnois, in the year 1822.

It has been published before by Mr. O'Neill, in his Sculptured Crosses of Ireland, and a drawing of it is given by Mr. George Du V. Noyer, in the sixth volume of his sketches, now in the Royal Irish Academy.

The readings given by these gentlemen do not quite agree with Dr. Petrie's. Mr. O'Neill has it Clonden.

PLATE LXXI.

FIG. 170.

$\overline{\text{OR}}$ DO AED $\overline{\text{MC}}$. . . $\overline{\text{MC}}$ TAIDG HUI.

CELLAICH DO RIG HUMANE.

(Pray for Aedh, son of Taidg O'Kelly, for [the] King of Hy-Many.)

The second name in this inscription is unfortunately so obliterated that it is uncertain what it may have been. It looks very like Brian. It is evident from the remaining words that the Aed for whom this tombstone was raised was a son or grandson of Tadhg O'Kelly, King of Hy-Many. There are twenty-one of this name mentioned by the Four Masters; but one chieftain so called fought at the battle of Clontarf, A. D. 1013, who had a grandson named Aed, child of his son Diarmaid. He is called Tadhg Mor O'Kelly, son of Murchadh; from him all the septs of the O'Kellys of Hy-Many are descended. (Annals of the Four Masters, vol. ii., page 774; Tribes and Customs of Hy-Many, Note, page 99.)

The death of Aedh, son of Tadhg O'Kelly, is thus recorded by the Four Masters:—"A. D. 1014. Aedh, son of Tadhg, son of Murchadh Ui Ceallaigh, lord of Ua Maine, was slain at Clonmacnois." It appears that the Danes, after their defeat at the battle of Clontarf, in the year following attacked and burned Clonmacnois; so that it was probably on this occasion, and in defence of the place, that Aedh met his death.

Drawn by Dr. Petrie at Clonmacnois, in the year 1822.

PLATE LXXII.

Fig. 171.

$\overline{\text{OR}}$ DO RIACAN . . . . .

(Pray for Riacan, Bishop.)

This name has not been identified, and it is not possible to read the letters in the drawing; the stone is unfortunately missing. It is not impossible that the person referred to was Flanagan O'Riagau, O'Riagan, Bishop of Kildare, ob. 920 (Four Masters), or Riagan, Bishop of Dromore, ob. 1101 (Ware).

Drawn by Dr. Petrie at Clonmacnois, in the year 1822.

Figs. 172 and 173.

. . . . . LAIꞆ OROIT.

The occurrence of the word *oroit*, on the second of these stones, written in full, gives this stone a peculiar interest. This form occurs only nine times in the sepulchral slabs as yet found in Ireland.

Drawn by Miss Boxwell, from stones found at Clonmacnois by the Rev. James Graves, in the year 1869.

Fig. 174.

+ $\overline{\text{OR}}$ DO.

(Pray for.)

There is no trace on this stone of any name having been carved upon it. It would seem that the sculptor was interrupted in his work, when he had only been able to accomplish the first three letters of the inscription.

As the design of the cross upon this stone is in all respects similar to that of Suibine Mac Maele Humai, and others carved at the end of the ninth century, we may presume that the stone is of somewhat the same date.

Drawn by Miss Boxwell, from a rubbing made by the Rev. James Graves, in the year 1869.

PLATE LXXIII.

Fig. 175.

. . . . . DIAM.

This stone is so much mutilated that it is impossible to say what the name may have been. If we read Diamain, or Diamuin, we may explain it by the adjective *diamain*, 'pure.' (Cormac's Glossary, p. 62; *diamuin*, Ebel's Zeuss, 18, 250.) The stone is lying in a low, grassy mound in Sir Edmund Armstrong's demesne, near the village of Ferbane, in the King's County, which is probably the site of the original foundation of Gallen Priory, described in page 11, *supra*, of this work.

Drawn by M. S., from rubbings taken by the Rev. James Graves and Mr. Hennessy.

Fig. 176.

ŌR DO [MAEL]MICHEIL.

(Pray for Mael-Michcil.)

This is the third instance of the occurrence of this name at Clonmacnois. (*See* notices of Figs. 158, 159.)

The design of the cross and form of ornament found on this stone resembles that belonging to the crosses of the tenth and eleventh centuries.

Drawn by M. S., from a rubbing.

PLATE LXXIV.

Fig. 177.

ARMEDA.

This name has not been identified. If rightly read, it would be the genitive singular of an i-stem *Armid* or *Airmid.* We have the name Airmedhach.

Drawn by M. S., at Iniscloran, in Lough Ree, in the year 1869.

Fig. 178.

+ DO CENNEDIG.

(+ For Cennedig.)

The formula of this inscription is a singular one, being a small Maltese cross before the preposition do, instead of the usual form *Oroit.* The name Cennedig, anglicised Kennedy, may perhaps be identified with that of the descendant of Congal, steward of the "Fort of the guests" at Clonmacnois, whose death is thus recorded :—"A. D. 1128. Cennedig Ua Conghail, Airchinnech of Lis Aeigheadh, at Cluain-mic-Nois, died." (Four Masters.)

The name of Congal, King of Teffia, has already appeared in this work. We find the tombstone of his son, Conaing, who died in the year 821, in this collection. Clonmacnois was the cemetery of the chiefs of the southern Hy-Niall race, to whom the lords of Teffia belonged, and their interment at this place is also proved by the following passage in the poem of Enoch O'Gillain. (*See* page 5.) The men of Teffia, the tribes of Breagh, were buried under the clay of Cluain."

Drawn by Dr. Petrie at Clonmacnois, in the year 1822.

Fig. 179.

ŌR DO MURETHACH.

(Pray for Murethach.)

This is the second instance o the occurrence of this name on a tombstone at Clonmacnois. (*See* Plate lviii., Fig. 139.) Here *th* is written for the aspirated *d,* as often in Old Irish MSS. (*See* Ebel's Zeuss, p. 63.)

There were two ecclesiastics of this name connected with Clonmacnois, whose deaths are thus recorded:—

"A.D. 1011. Moriegh Ultach, anchorite of Clonvicknose, died" (Annals of Clonmacnois); and "A.D. 1017. Muireadach Ultach, anmchara of Cluain-mic-Nois, died." (Annals of the Four Masters.) Twelve years later the death of a bishop of Clonmacnois who bore that name is thus recorded:—

"A.D. 1025. Muireadhach, son of Mugron, successor of Ciaran and Comman, died. He was of the family of Imleach Fordeorach" (probably Emlagh, in the parish of Kilkeevin, barony of Castlerea, and county of Roscommon). His death is also recorded in the Chronicon Scotorum, at A.D. 1028. His father's name, Mugron, is found on another tombstone at Clonmacnois. (*See* Plate lxix., Fig. 166.)

Drawn by M. S., from a rubbing taken in the year 1869 by the Rev. James Graves.

The Editor has to offer her best thanks to Mr. O'Looney for the following poem, and for the translation which he has kindly added to it. It was copied by Professor O'Curry from a manuscript in the Burgundian Library at Brussels, and his copy is now preserved in the Catholic University of Dublin:—

ON THE KINGS AND CHIEFTAINS BURIED AT CLONMACNOIS.

h-i ccaċraiġ in toirrnide	In the city of Ciaran,
Ciaran crabad co n-ġrinde	The prayerful, the pious, and wise,
batar amra flaiċemain	There were illustrious chieftains,
Fil mor do rioġoib inde.	There are many kings therein.
Fionaċta Muad Muireadaċ	Finnachta,[a] Muad,[b] Muiredach,[c]
Conċobair boinne báine	Concobar of the white Boyne;
Aed Allain mac Ferġoile	Aed Allen, son of Fergal;[d]
Diarmaitt mac Aeda Slane.	Diarmait, son of Aed Slane.
Ġúaire Aidne adamra	Guaire Aidne[e] the admirable;
Follaṁain fertair flanoail[1]	Follamhain,[f] . . . . . .
Caṫal mar mac Muirġiora	Cathal[g] the beautiful, son of Muirgus;
Maelduin mac Aeda Allάin.	Maelduin,[h] son of Aed Allen.

[a] *Finnachta.—See* Fig. 45, Pl. xvii., and notice of Fig. 45 at p. 27.

[b] Here the word Muad may be read as an epithet of Finnachta, "the noble;" but it may also be a proper name. There was a prince so called, eldest son of Donchadh, son of Aedh, son of Fathmuine, of the race of Fiachach, son of Niall of the Nine Hostages. (*See* the Irish Life of St. Colman Ela.)

[c] *Muiredach.—See* Fig. 139, Pl. lviii., and notice of Fig. 139 at p. 63.

[d] *Aed Allen, son of Fergal.—See* Fig. 74, Pl. xxix., and notice of Fig. 74 at p. 37.

[e] *Guaire Aidne.—See* Fig. 117, Pl. xlvi., and notice of Fig. 117 at p. 55.

[f] *Follamhan.*—A. D. 828. Follamhain, son of Donnchadh, was slain by the Munstermen: and A. D. 866. Follamhain, of Sil-Mureadaigh, ancestor of the O'Fallons. (Four Mast.)

[g] *Cathal.—See* Fig. 116, Pl. xlvi., and notice of Fig. 116 at p. 54.

[h] *Maelduin.—See* Fig. 1, Pl. i., and notice of Fig. 1 at p. 15.

Muirġios Diarmuid Tomultaċ
  Ailill Indreaċtaċ Eallaċ
  A ṫri mic im Ragallaċ
  Domnall cain Caṫal Ceallaċ.

Conaing Teṫba tonnglaine
  Ailill Brig Leiṫ leir lonnmur
  Aoḋ mac Brenuin borrḟadaċ
  Diarmaid breac Conla Conġal.

Conall oirgeaċ aiġṫide
  Fiann mac Colla cloṫ néṁiḋ
  Fergus mor mac ailġile·
  Diarmaid mac Conaing ceiliḋ.

Uaṫta Aed mac Fiṫċeallaċ
  Aird rig airḋerc ḟer ḟíorglan
  Conċuḃair mac Innreaċtaiġ
  Flaiṫnía ua Ċinn Faelaḋ.

Duḃ da ṫuaṫ mac Daṁine
  Ro damair rinne ruaḋa
  Ard ruire na n-airgíalla
  Aed mac Colcain cúlbuad.

Fíanġalaċ fíal ḟlaiṫeaṁail
  Findġal ba ḟlaiṫ condulġe
  Breasal, Cernaċ comroṁac
  Conġul Oengus Aeḋ Suiḃne.

Aoḋ balb mac Tipraite
  Uata Eocrán díorma dreaċdac
  Innreaċtaċ ua Fiṫcallaḋ
  Domṅall mac Caṫail creaċtaċ

Muirgios,[a] Diarmait, Tomaltach,[b]
  Ailill, Indrechtach, Eallach,
  Ragallach, with his three sons;
  Donnell the mild, Cathal, and Cellach.[c]

Conaing,[d] from Teffia of the bright wave;
  Ailil of Brigleith, righteous and valiant;
  Aed,[e] son of Brennan the turbulent;
  Diarmaid Breacc, Conla, and Congal.[f]

Congal the brave, the slayer;
  Flann, son of Colla the famous;
  Fergus[g] the great son of Ailgil;
  Diarmait, son of Colla the wise.

Uatha,[h] Aed son of Fith-Cellach,
  A high conspicuous kiug of truly pure men;
  Concobar, son of Innrechtach,
  King champion of Ui CennFaeladh.

Dubh da thuath, son of Damhin,
  Who endured red spear points,
  The great chief of the Airgiallans;
  Aed,[i] son of Colcan, triumphant in battle.

Fiangalach,[j] generous and princely;
  Fingal, a chief without reproach;
  Breasal, Cearnach the warlike,
  Congal, Oengus,[k] Aed, and Suibhne.[l]

Aedh Balb, son of Tiprait;
  Uatha Eochran, of beautiful hosts;
  Imrechtach ua Fithcellach,[m]
  Donnell,[n] son of Cathal of the wounds.

[a] *Muirgios.—See* Fig. 128, Pl. li., and notice of Fig. 128 at p. 59.

[b] *Tomaltach.*—He was father of Muirgios and Diarmait. (*See* Ann. Four Mast. at A. D. 810–832.)

[c] *Cellach.—See* Fig. 12, Pl. iv., and notice of Fig. 12, p. 18.

[d] *Conaing.—See* Fig. 18, Pl. xxxviii., and notice of Fig. 98, p. 48.

[e] *Aed, son of Brenainn,* chief of Teffia, died A. D. 556. (Ann. Four Mast.)

[f] *Congal.*—King of Teffia, father of Conaing. (*See* Four Mast. at A. D. 823.)

[g] *Fergus.—See* Fig. 67, Pl. xxvii., and notice of Fig. 67 at p. 35.

[h] *Uatha.—See* Fig. 39, Pl. xv., and notice of Fig. 39, p. 26.

[i] *Aed.*—A. D. 606. Aed, son of Colgan, chief of the Oirgialla, and of all the Airtheara, died on his pilgrimage at Cluain-mic-Nois. (Ann. Four Mast.)

[j] *Fiangalach.*—One of the chieftains of Leinster, who fought for Aed Allen, and died A. D. 733, was so named (Four Mast.)

[k] *Oengus.—See* Fig. 79, Pl. xxx., and notice of Fig. 79 at p. 39.

[l] *Suibhne. See* Fig. 82, Pl. xxxi., and notice of Fig. 82 at p. 39.

[m] *Fithcellach.*—A chief of Hy Many, who died A. D. 688. (Four Mast.)

[n] *Donnell, son of Cathal.*—The Four Masters record that he died by his brother's hand in the year 923.

Muiredaċ mac Feargusa
Mic Róeḋa cetaib sciaṫraċ
Caṫal mór mac Aililla
Caṫal mac Finneaċ Fiaċraċ.

Donnċaḋ barrcas bregmaige
balc ri albada Etair
Cernaċ mac cain Congalaiċ
Aongus mac Colmain Cetaig.

Claine Ruruig ruamrai
Rointir dar caṫa cruu
Sirreaċtaċ naċ taiṫbeu
Rí rod rainic aniuu.

Ni fairsing an flaiṫemnus
Inda fil feiḃ ro ċuala
Ni mor for seaċt bfertroigeḋ
Ferann gaċ cori fir uadhaḋ.

Amra fer fil etara
Cesa tráig ro bo tuile
Máel saer seaċnaill, setduide.

Sluag rí ḃ-fer n-Eren
Acas uile carṫa an doṁansa
Edir rí acas rúaṁa
Mindreaċ ua Donnċada
Fil fo lecaiḃ lis Ċlúana.

Cét Ciarán naoṁ náird niṁe
Pettor Pól fir foirgliḋe
In toige ard airgide
h-í caṫraig an toirnide.
h-i c-catraig.

Muiredach,[a] the son of Fergus,
The son of Roedh, with hundreds of shield-bearers.
Cathal[b] the great, the son of Ailill;
Cathal,[c] the son of Finnach Fiachra.

Donnchadh of the curly hair, from Breagh Moy,
The powerful and noble king of Etar;
Cernach the comely, son of Congallach;
Angus,[d] son of Colman Cetach.

The race of Ruruigh, very admirable,
Who were wont to shed blood in battle;
Alas! that he cannot live again,
The king who came to thee to-day.

Far from wide is the domain
Where they lie—so I have heard—
About seven feet to each man
Is all now is given to these warrior chiefs.

One great man there is among them,
Whose approach is like the flood upon the strand,
The noble and swift Maelsechnaill.[e]

The kings' hosts of the men of Erin,
And all lovers of this world,
Both kings and royal champions,
And the mild-faced[f] Ua Donnchada,
Lie beneath the tombstones of Cluain.

There are a hundred Ciarans, saints of high heaven
Peter and Paul, witnesses of truth;
The silver statue of the tall Virgin,[g]
In the city of the prayerful one.

[a] *Muiredach, son of Fergus,* successor of Patrick, died A. D. 966. (Ann. Four Mast.)

[b] *Cathal, son of Ailill.*—Died A. D. 812. He was lord of Ui Fiachraich. (Ann. Four Mast.)

[c] *Cathal, son of Fiachra.*—Died A. D. 805. He was lord of Rath Airthir.

[d] *Angus, son of Colman.*—The death of Angus, son Colman Mor, in the year 616, is recorded by the Four Masters. He was lord of the Ui Neill, and is mentioned by Adamnan in his Vita Columb., lib. i., c. 13. In the Annals of Ulster his death is entered under the year 620, and in the Annals of Clonmacnois under 619.

[e] *Maelsechnaill.*—*See* Fig. 86, Pl. xxxiii., and notice of Fig. 86 at p. 42. Maelsechnaill, or Malachy, was father to King Flann, to whose memory the Abbot Colman erected the great cross at Clonmacnois. The death of Malachy is given by the Four Masters at the year 860, who add, "Of his death was sung—

'Mournfully is spread her veil of grief over Ireland,
Since the chieftain of our race has perished Maelsechlain of the flowing Sinainn.'"

[f] The mild face alluded to in the poem was the face of Maelsechlainn, who was the grandson (Ua) of Donnchadh, King of Ireland, ob. 792.

[g] In Ciaran's "Prayer of Protection," mention is made of the altar, statue and shrine of the Blessed Virgin at Clonmacnois, and the special devotions to the "smooth hair of Mary."

Mr. Hennessy has been good enough to favour the Editor with the following Irish poem, found by him in the Library of Trinity College, Dublin, in a MS. classed H. 1. 17, during the passage of these sheets through the press. Written, as it professes to be, by Conaing Buidhe O'Mulconry, one of the hereditary historians of the O'Conor family, it is entitled to a higher degree of credence than the Brussels' poem. Conaing Boy O'Mulconry must have composed it before the year 1224, when Cathal Crobhderg died, whose name occurs in the last stanza of the poem.

Conaing buiḋe O Maoilconaire cc.

A reileag laoċ leiṫ(e) cuinn,
Cia doḋ ṁaithiḃ nach moluim,
A ġreis gan locht ar alar
A ṗort inar ċes Ciaran.

A ṫempuill ṁóir ṁoluid các
Fád ċadar is fad ċónach,
Díar ṁeirḟeang roba minġlór
Dha riġ Eirenn fat altóir.

Toirrḋealḃaċ don leaḋ abor di,
Ruaiḋri dan leṫ ard eili,
Diar garg ṁin gan taiḋe attenn
Dha airdriġ aille Eirionn.

On ċranncaingil siar iarroin
Leabaiḋ ṁic Ruaiḋri raṫṁoir
Slat oigḟer do ḃi ag broghad
Ri ar an ccoigeḋ Conċoḃar.

Diarmuid Mac Maġnura ṁóir,
Dar Ordaiġe Iosa onóir,
Craoḃ ro ċin on Aoḋ Engach,
Taoḃ fri taoḃ is Toirrḋealḃach.

CONAING BUIDHE O'MULCONRY, CECINIT.

Cemetery of the heroes of Leth-Chuinn,[a]
Whom of thy nobles do I not praise?
O structure without fault in its midst!
O spot in which Ciaran suffered!

Great Temple[b] which all men praise,
For thy respect, and for thy prosperity;
Two slender-fingered whose glory was bright—
Two kings of Ireland—are under thy altar;

Toirdhelbhach[c] on the hither side of it;
Ruaidhri[d] on the other side;
A fierce-mild pair of unlimited power,
Two noble arch-kings of Ireland.

Westwards from the Chancel, after that,
Is the bed of the son of Ruaidhri the lucky;
A youthful scion who was flourishing—
Conchobhar[e]—who was king over the province.

Diarmaid[f], son of Magnus the Great,
For whom Jesus ordained great honour,
A branch that descended from Aedh the Valiant,
Is side by side with Toirdhelbhach.

[a] *Leth-Chuinn.*—"Conn's half," or the northern half of Ireland. The principal families of Connacht and Leinster derive their descent from Iberemon, son of Milesius (to whom the northern portion of Ireland is alleged to have been assigned), through Conn of the Hundred Battles, from whom the northern division was called Leth-Chuinn.

[b] *Great Temple.*—The church here referred to is apparently Temple-Conor, alias Temple-Ciarain; for an account of which, *see* Petrie's Eccl. Archit., pp. 272-3.

[c] *Toirdhelbhach.*—Turlough (the Great) O'Conor, monarch of Ireland; ob. 1156. In the Annals of the Four Masters, Turlough is said to have been buried "beside the altar of Temple-Ciarain."

[d] *Ruaidhri.*—Roderic O'Conor, son of Turlough the Great, and the last monarch of Ireland. He died in 1198, and is stated (Four Masters) to have been buried at the "north side of the altar of the great church."

[e] *Conchobhar,*—Conor Maenmaighe, or Conor of Moenmoy, son of Roderic; slain 1189

[f] *Diarmaid.*—This was apparently Dermot, son of Maghnus, son of Turlough Mór O'Conor, who was slain in 1248.

A leacsa leabṫa Ġuaire
  Raġallach fatt uir úaine
  Muireḋach, Tadg na ttri ros (sic)
  Innreachtach fud is Ferġos.

Murġaile, Tomultaċ trén,
  Muirġios a ṁac mor an sgel,
  Dar dia caḋuis do Cluain
  Mo riġ naille re' hen uair.

A leac na riġ nuallach nard,
  Fud atait cuirp na ttrí Ttaḋg,
  Fud ata fór ar fior daṁ
  Tri Conċoḃair dhá Ċaṫal.

IS fud ata ant aoḋ Engaċh,
  Creaċ oile ṫeallaiġ ṫeaṁrach;
  Ata fud, follas a raṫ,
  Diarmuid, Caṫal, is Ceadach.

Ata fan leic na luiġe,
  O heiḋin flaiṫ fionn ṁuiġe,
  Doṁnall is Taḋg a hEaċhtaigh,
  Aoḋ balḃ Aoḋ ṁac Inreachtaiġ.

O stone and O bed of Guaire's[a],
  Under thy green sod are Raghallach,[b]
  Muiredhach,[c] and Tadhg of the three Rosses;[d]
  Innrechtach[e] is under thee, and Fergus.[f]

Murghaile[g], Tomultach the Valiant,
  And Muirghius[h] his son, great the tidings;
  Who earned more respect for Cluain,
  Than all other kings together.

O flag of the proud exalted kings!
  Under thee are the bodies of the three Tadhgs;
  Under thee also, true for me,
  Are three Conchobars,[i] and two Cathals.[i]

Under thee is the Aedh Engach,[j]
  Another sorrow of the hearth of Tara;
  Under thee are, manifest the grace,
  Diarmaid,[k] Cathal, and Cedach.

Under the flag are lying
  O'Heyne,[l] chief of a fair plain,
  Domhnall[m] and Tadhg[m] from Echtghe,[n]
  Aedh Balbh,[o] Aedh[p] son of Innrechtach;

[a] *Guaire's bed.*—The grave of Guaire Aidhne, King of Connacht, renowned for his generosity, who died in 662.

[b] *Raghallach.*—Son of Uada, King of Connacht, and ancestor of the sept of O'Fallon, slain 645.

[c] *Muiredhach.*—Muiredhach Muillethain, King of Connacht; ob. circa 762.

[d] *Tadhg of the Three Rosses.*—This should probably be "Tadhg of the Three Towers," King of Connacht, who died in 954, and from whom Turlough Mór O'Conor was the sixth in lineal descent.

[e] *Innrechtach.*—The son of Muiredhach Muillethain, referred to in note [c], and also a King of Connacht.

[f] *Fergus.*—The father of King Muiredhach Muillethain.

[g] *Murghaile.*—The son of Innrechtach, referred to in note [e], and the father of the "Tomultach the Mighty," whose name follows.

[h] *Muirghios.*—The son of Tomultach. His death is entered in the Chron. Scotorum under the year 815.

[i] *Tadhgs, Conchobhars, Cathals.*—These names were borne by so many of the ancestors of the Connacht families whose place of sepulture was at Clonmacnois, that it would be vain to endeavour to identify the persons here referred to, without some more definite description. But it is certain that they were personages who flourished between the years 800-1100.

[j] *Aedh Engach, or Aedh the Valiant.*—Aedh O'Conor, King of Connacht, who died in 1274, is called "Aedh Engach" in the Annals of Loch-Cé. But another person so called, who lived three centuries earlier, seems to be alluded to.

[k] *Diarmaid, Cathal, Cedach.*—The same observation applies to these names as to the names referred to in note [i].

[l] *O'Heyne.*—The O'Heynes were chiefs of Ui-Fiachrach-Aidhne, a territory co-extensive with the present diocese of Kilmacduagh.

[m] *Domhnall and Tadhg.*—These would appear to have been members of the O'Scanlan sept, who ruled, until subdued by the O'Heynes and O'Shaughnessys, the territory of Ui-Fiachrach-Aidhne, including the mountainous district of Echtghe, or Slieve Aughty, on the confines of Galway and Clare. Domhnall O'Scanlan, chief of his name, died about the year 1000. And the name of Tadhg also occurs in the pedigree of the family.

[n] *Echtghe.*—See last note.

[o] *Aedh Balbh.*—"Aedh the Stammerer." Perhaps the father of Uada, King of Connacht; slain 597, (Four Masters.) But he may have been the same as the Aedh referred to immediately after.

[p] *Aedh.*—Also called Aedh Balbh. His death is recorded by the Four Masters under 737.

IS deiċ ríoġ ḟiċead oile
Do luchṫ reime ríoġruiḋe,
Do ríoġaiḃ Cruaċan ro ċreid,
Fo leic na ríoġ ad roilig.

Ruaiḋri san teampull ṫeas,
Diarmuid ṁac Taḋg cnes re cnes
Conċobar, Aoḋ, ceann a gceann,
Ḋa mac Ruaiḋri ríoġ Eirionn.

Brían Breifneaċ, Maṫġaṁuin mín,
Muirġios fan leic ċeḋn [a], adċim,
Muinnter nar er neaċ ḟa ní,
Luchṫ tempuill do ríogh Ruaiḋri.

A leac ṁorra Uí Maoilruanaiġ
Treuċáin is fá núaḋh ġoile.
Fiċe ríoġ fa ccinn fad crois
Ata san núaiṁ do ḋuanais

A leac Uí Ṫaiḋg an teġlaiġe
Fa sáor do luchṫ re leanṁuin,
Flaiṫ ar ḟiċeaḋ fúd ata
Do cloinn Tomulta, mo ġraḋ
Ṫair fine Breifne do ḟíorġnaṫ.

Ata fat úir [a]ċaiḋ ċeall,
Dollaṁnaib uaisle Eirionn,
Mac Coise air naċ gcualla smachṫ
Ag cú ċúaine Chonnachṫ.

Go ccoiṁeadaiġe Críosd na cceard
Mac mo ríġ Caṫal Croiḃḋerg.
Go saoraḋ dia os ḋo do ṫiġ

Ose is riar da gaċ roileg.

A Realeiag.

And thirty other kings—
Of such as had regal rank—
Of the kings of Cruachu who received the Faith—
Are under the flag of the kings in thy cemetery.

Ruaidhri[a] is in the southern church,
Skin by skin with Diarmaid[b] son of Tadhg;
Conchobhar and Aedh are head to head—
Two sons of Ruaidhri, king of Ireland.

Brian Breifnech,[c] Mathghamhain[d] the mild,
And Muirghius[e], under the same flag I see;
Persons who refused none for aught,
Church companions for king Ruaidhri.

O, thou great flag of O'Maelruanaidh![f]
To see thee is cause of fresh tears;
Twenty kings, and their heads under thy cross,
Are in the grave which thou hast closed.

O, flag-stone of Ui-Taidhg an-teghlaigh,[g]
Noble it were to follow thy company;
Under thee are one and twenty princes
Of the descendants of Tomultach, beloved by me
Always beyond the tribes of Breifne.

Under the clay, O holy cemetery,
Is one of the noble poets of Ireland—
Mac Coise[h]—whom I heard not reproved
By the pack-hound of Connacht.

May Christ, (head) of all arts, protect
The son of my king, Cathal Crobhderg;
May God preserve, since from Him all things
come;
For he is the lord of all cemeteries.

CEMETERY.

[a] *Ruadhri.*—See note [d], p. 79.

[b] *Diarmaid.*—This person has not been identified, unless he was the son of Tadhg, son of Turlough Mór.

[c] *Brian Briefnech.*—Son of Turlough Mór, King of Connacht; ob. 1184.

[d] *Mathghamhain.*—Probably Mahon O'Conor, son of Conor Moinmoy, and grandson of Roderick; slain in 1196.

[e] *Muirghius.*—This was probably the Muirgheas, son of Conchobbar, "heir of Connaught," slain in A. D. 986, as recorded in the Chronicon Scotorum.

[f] *Flag of O'Maeluanaidh.*—Here the poet addresses the sepulchre of the Mac Dermot family, without enumerating the names of the persons buried there.

[g] *Ui Taidhg an teghlaigh.*—The descendants of "Tadhg (O'Conor) of the Household," now represented by the Tighes of Connacht.

[h] *Mac Coise.*—Erard Mac Coise, "chief chronicler of Ireland, died at Clonmacnois 1023." (Four Masters).

THE FOLLOWING NAMES OF FAMILIES WHO POSSESSED BURIAL GROUNDS AT CLONMACNOIS ARE TAKEN FROM THE REGISTRY OF CLONMACNOIS.

Vide Journal of Kilkenny and South-East of Ireland Archæological Society, second series, Vol. i., p. 448 :—

Cairbre (Carbury)—Chiefs of Hy Mainy. *See* notice of Fig. 96, p. 47.
Carthy (Mac), Kings of Desmond or South Munster. *See* notice of Fig. 58, p. 33.
Cynnydhe (O'), (O'Kennedy).
Cobhtach (O'Coffey), Hy Maini. *See* Irish MS. Series, p. 99, Derry. *See* notice of Fig. 32, p. 24.
Kyllen (O'). *See* notice of Fig. 49, p. 29; Fig. 164, p. 72.
Colmain (Mac) O'Melaghlins, Kings of Meath, branch of Clanna Neill. *See* notice of Fig. 88, p. 43.
Connor (O'), Kings of Connaught. *See* notice of Fig. 50, p. 30.
Cormacan (O').
Cuaghan (O').
Dersgoil (Ui) O'Driscoll.
Granaill (Mac) M'Ranall.
O'Kelly's (Ui Cellagh) Kings of Hymany. *See* notice of Fig. 61, p. 34.
Mac Dermoda (M[c]Dermots), of Moylurg. *See* notice of Fig. 126, p. 58.
Maelmuaid (Mulmoy).
Neills (O').
Ruairc (O'). *See* notice of Fig. 123, p. 57.
Torpain (O').
Trepy (O').

THE FOLLOWING SURNAMES ARE FOUND ON STONES AT CLONMACNOIS :—

Aed Mac . . . . . Mac Taidg Ui Cellaich.
Bran Ua Caillen (O'Cillen).
Bran Ua Chellacháin.
Cairbre Crom.
Cellach.
Colman Mac Gormain.
Cormacan.
Conaing Mac Conghail.
Dubcen Mac Thadggan.
Eochaid Mac Dermot.
Fland Mac Maelsechlainn (Melaghlin)
Fogartach Mac Broenain.
Mugroin hu Borgan.
Odran Ua Eolais.
Suibine M[c]Maelehumai.[c]

NAMES OF TRIBES INTERRED AT CLONMACNOIS, WHICH OCCUR IN THE POEM OF ENOCH O'GILLAN, p. 4, *supra*.

Aeda (Cenel). *See* notice of Fig. 113, p. 53, and Fig. 117, p. 55.
Briain, Ui (OBrien).
Cairbre (sons of).
Cahill (Clann) O'Flannagans.
Ceallach (Clann) O'Kellys. *See* Tribes of Hy Many, p. 43, for names corresponding to stones.
Colman Clann (O'Melachlainns).

Conaill (Cinel).
Conaille (Cinel).
Connor (Clann) O'Conor.
Creide (Sil) (O'Conors of Connacht)
Donnchada (Ua).
Fallon (O').
Hy Fiachraich, p. 33.
Finnachtaigh (O'). *See* notice of Fig. 45, p, 27.
Flaherty (O').
Flannagan (O').
Floinn (O').
Gailenga (Men of), in the territory of O'Gara.
Mac Coise.
Mac Dermot.
Mac Lonain.
Mulrenin.
Mulroney.
Taidhg an teghlaigh.

NAMES WHICH OCCUR OF KINGS AND CHIEFTAINS BURIED AT CLONMACNOIS IN POEM, p. 76, *supra*.

Aed.
Aed, son of Brennan.
Aed Allan, son of Ferghoil. *See* notice of Fig. 74, p. 37.
Aed of Brigh Leith.
Aed Balb, son of Tiprait.
Aed Slaine.
Aed, son of Colcan.
Aed, son of Fithcellach.
Ailgilla.
Ailill.
Aengus.
Breasal.
Brennan.
Cearnach.
Cathal, son of Muirgus. *See* notice of Fig. 116, p. 54.
Cathal, son of Ailill.
Cellach, son of Raghallach. *See* notice of Fig. 12, p. 18.
Colla (sons of).
Colman.
Conchobair. *See* notice of Fig. 36, p. 42.
Conchobair.
Conaing of Teffia. *See* notice of Fig. 98, p. 48.
Congal.
Diarmaid, son of Aed Slaine.
Diarmaid Brace.
Diarmaid.
Diarmaid, son of Colla (Colman).
Donnell, son of Cathal.
Donchad.
Donnell, son of Raghallach.
Dubhda Tuath, son of Damhin.
Eallach.
Fergus, son of Aigilla. *See* notice of Fig. 67, p. 36.
Fiangalach.
Flann, son of Colla.
Finnachta. *See* notice of Fig. 45, p. 27.
Follamhan.
Guaire Aidne. *See* notice of Fig. 117, p. 55.
Maelduin, son of Aedh Allen. *See* notice of Fig. 1, p. 15.
Maelsechnall. *See* notice of Fig. 86, p. 42.
Muiredach, son of Fergus. *See* notice of Fig. 139, p. 63.
Muirgios. *See* notice of Fig. 128, p. 59.
Muretach. *See* notice of Fig. 173, p. 74.
Murechtach Ua Fithcellagh.
Oengus. *See* notice of Fig. 79, p. 39.
Raghallach.
Suibne. *See* notice of Fig. 82, p. 39.
Tomultach.
Tiprait.
Uatha Eochran. *See* notice of Fig. 39, p. 26.

NAMES OF HEROES BURIED AT CLONMACNOIS, MENTIONED IN POEM OF CONAING BUIDHE O'MULCONRY, p. 79, *supra*.

Aed.
Aed Balbh, i. e. the Stammerer; ob. A. D. 597.
Brian Breifnech; ob. A. D. 1184.
Cathal Crobderg; ob. A. D. 1224.
Cathal.
Cathal.
Cetach.
Conchobar of Moinmoy; ob. A. D. 1189.
Conchobar.
Diarmaid.
Diramait.
Domnall.
Fergus.
Guaire; ob. A. D. 662.
Innrechtach, King of Connaught; ob. circa 762.
Mac Coise; ob. A. D. 1023.
Mahon O'Conor.
Muirgios, son of Tomultach; ob. A. D. 815.
Muirgios, son of Roderic; ob. A. D. 1224.
Muiredach, King of Connaught; ob. A. D. 762.
O'Heyne.
Raghallach; ob. A. D. 645.
Roderic O'Conor; ob. A. D. 1198.
Turlough O'Conor; ob. A. D. 1156.
Tadhg an Teghlaigh.
Tadhg of the Three Rosses, King of Connaught; ob. A. D. 954.
Tomultach.

INDEX TO NAMES ON TOMBSTONES AT CLONMACNOIS,

AND ITS NEIGHBOURHOOD.

☞ The Names which appear to have been identified are marked with an asterisk.

END OF VOL. I.

1

MAILDUIN.

2

GOM[GAN.

3

Scale 1/8.

ŌR DO CHOLUMBON.

Clonmacnois

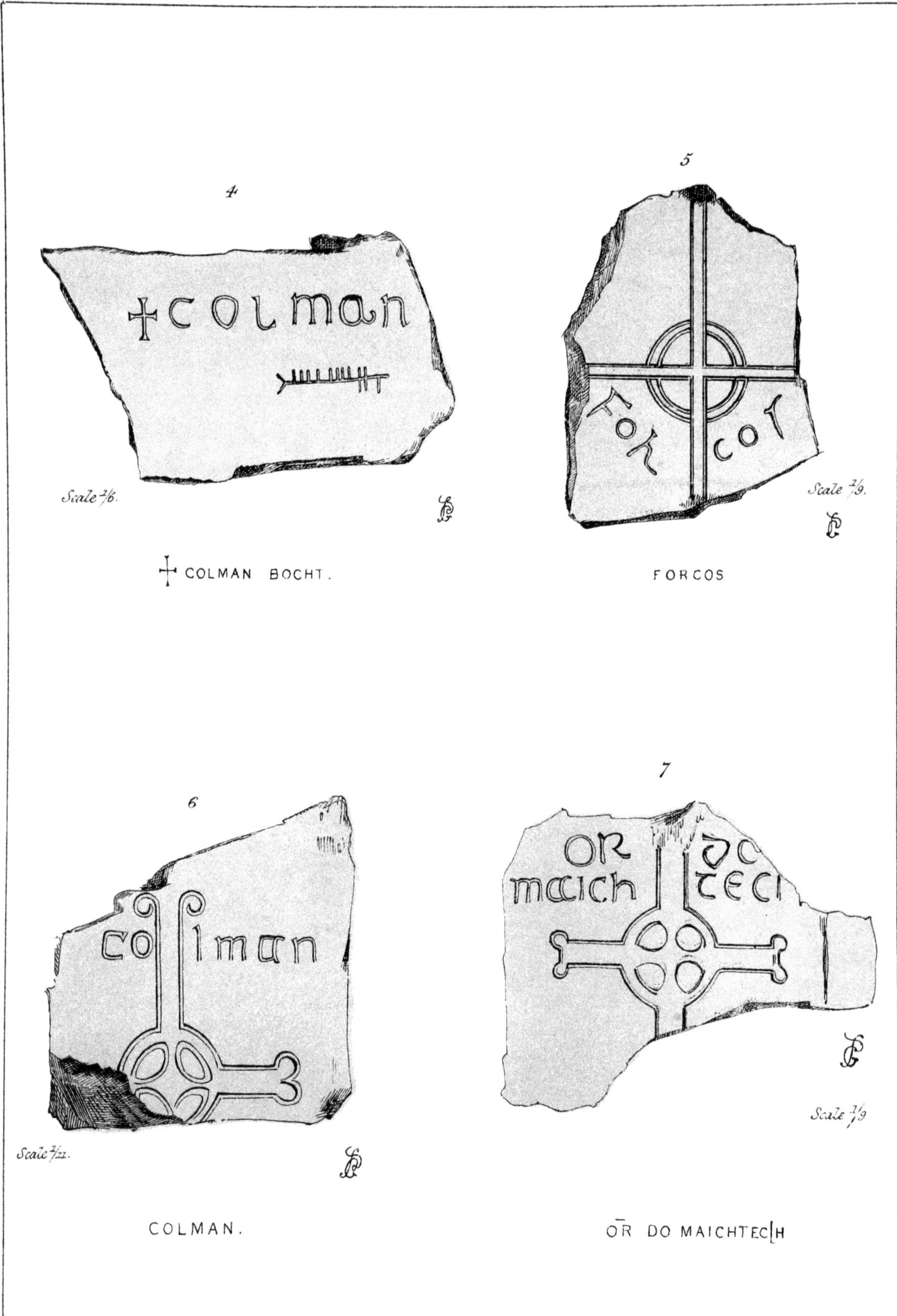

✝ COLMAN BOCHT.

FORCOS

COLMAN.

OR DO MAICHTEC[H

Clonmacnois

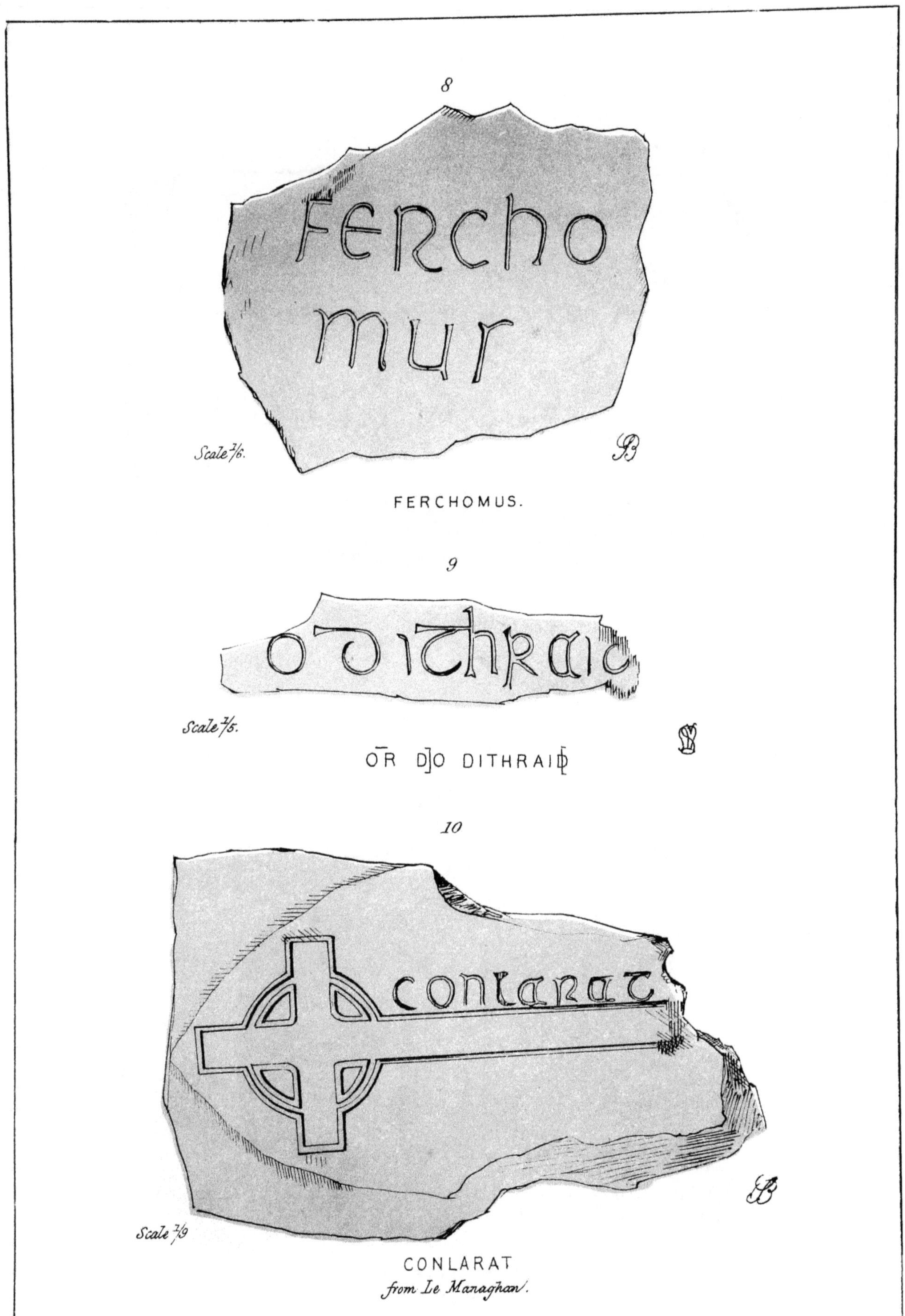

FERCHOMUS.

OR DO DITHRAID

CONLARAT
from Le Managhan.

Clonmacnois

11

Scale 1/4.

OR AR CHUINDLESS.

12

Scale.

[OR] DO CELLACH.

13

Scale 1/8.

ŌR DO COMGAN.

14

Scale 1/12.

ŌR DO LOAN.

15

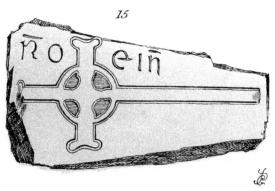

R]OEIÑ

Clonmacnois

16

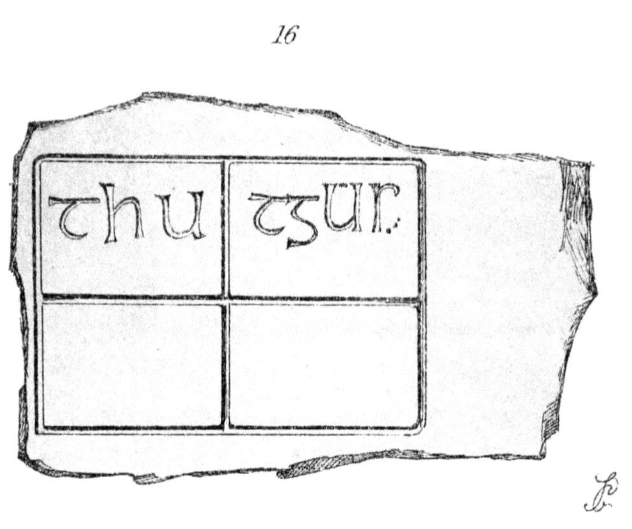

TNUTCAL. [?]

17

Scale 1/10.

OR·I· AC·II

Clonmacnois

18

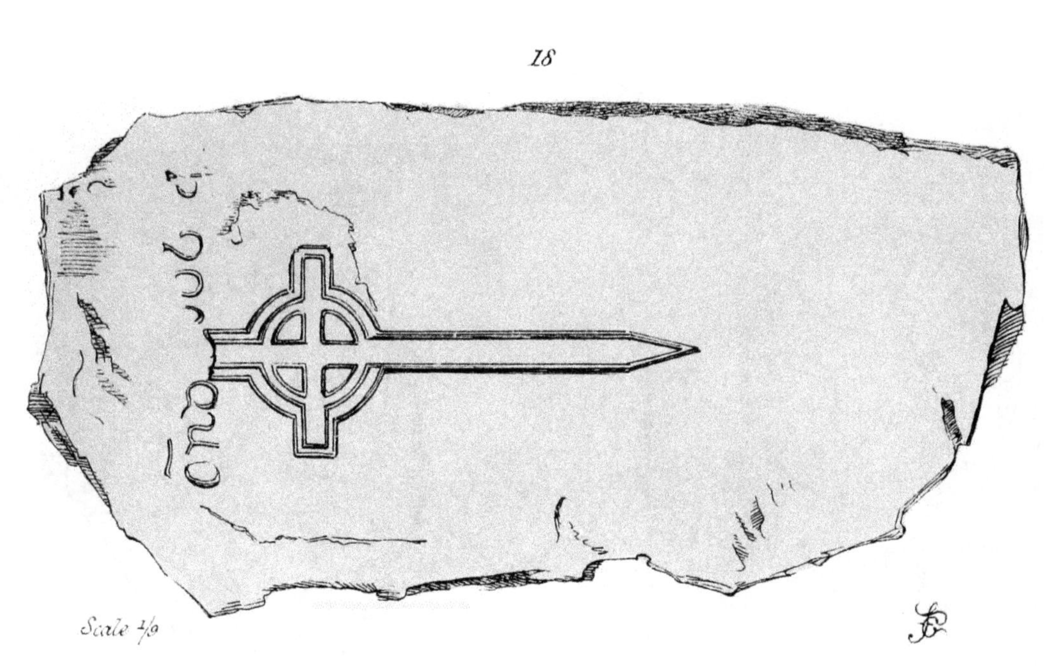

Scale 1/10

ŌR DOU⁝⁝B⁝D.

19

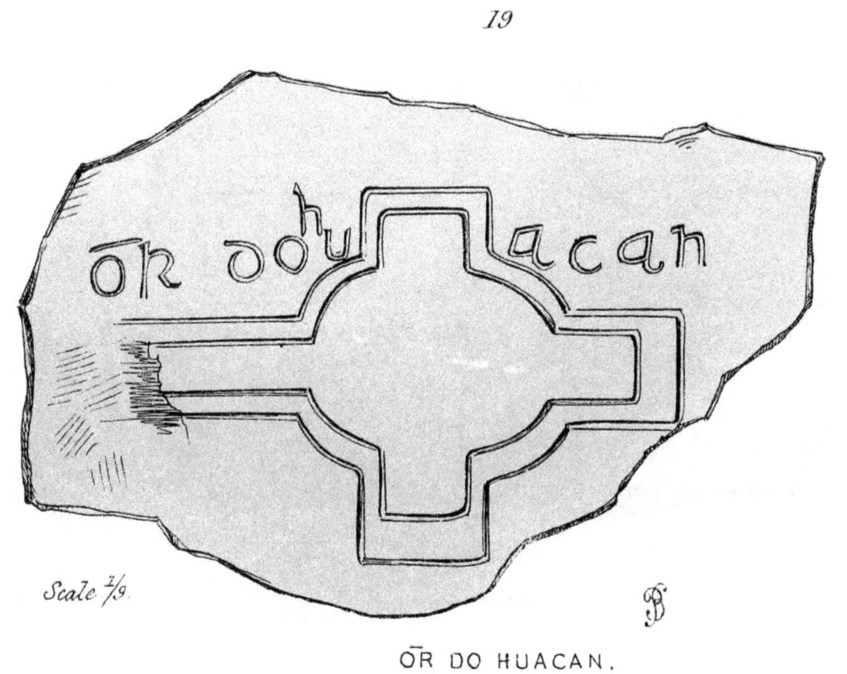

Scale 1/9

ŌR DO HUACAN.

Clonmacnois

20

RUADRI.

21

OROIT AR REMI[D]

22

CONASSACI.

Clonmacnois

23

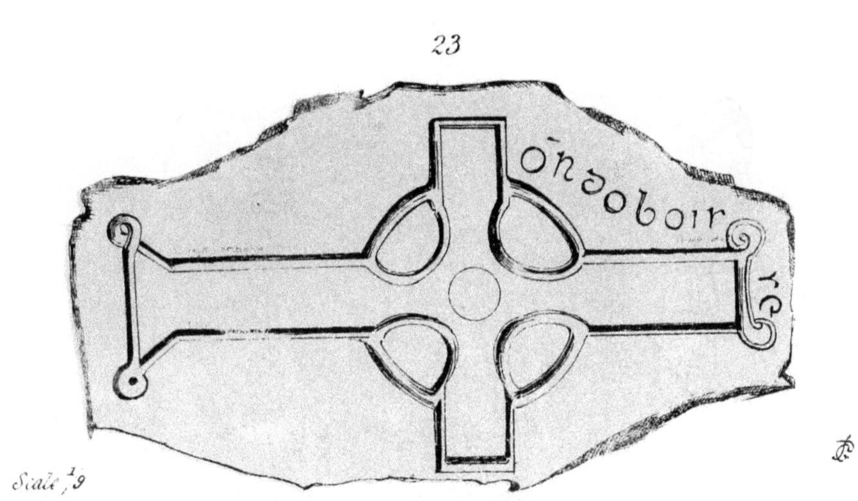

Scale 1/9

ŌR DO BOISSE.

24

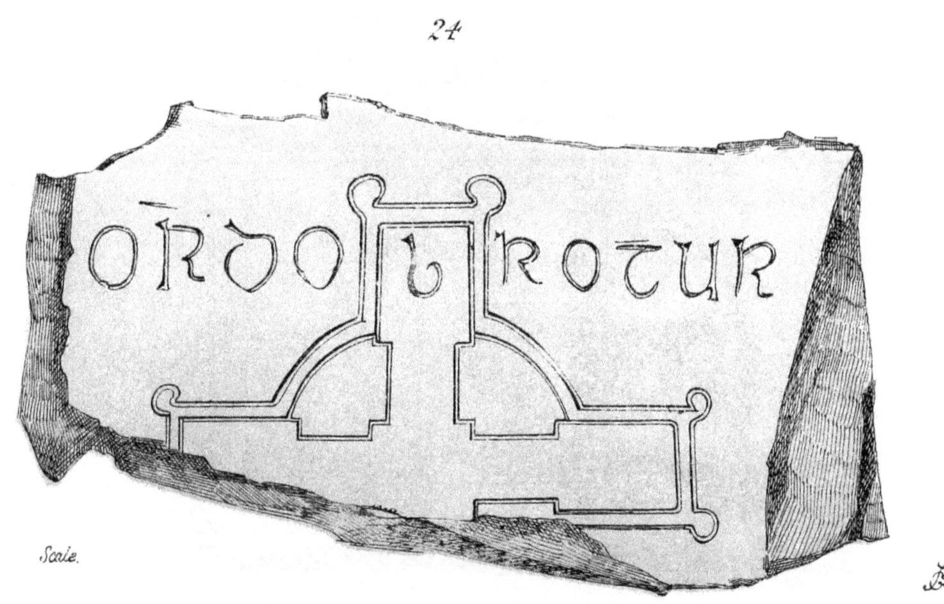

Scale.

ŌR DO BROTUR.

Clonmacnios

25

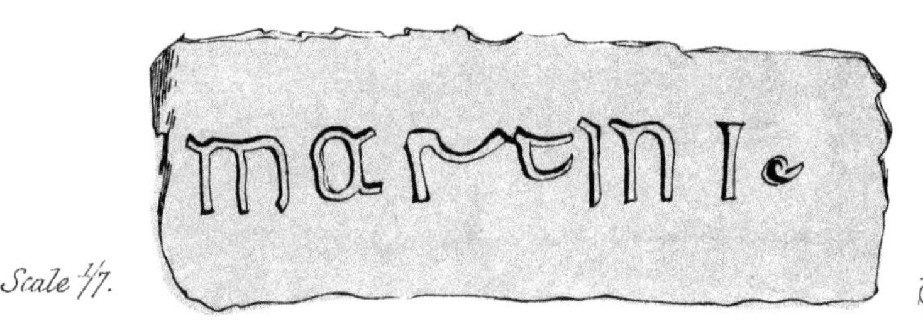

Scale 1/7.

MARTINI

26

Scale 1/8.

EPSCOP DATHAL.

Clonmacnois

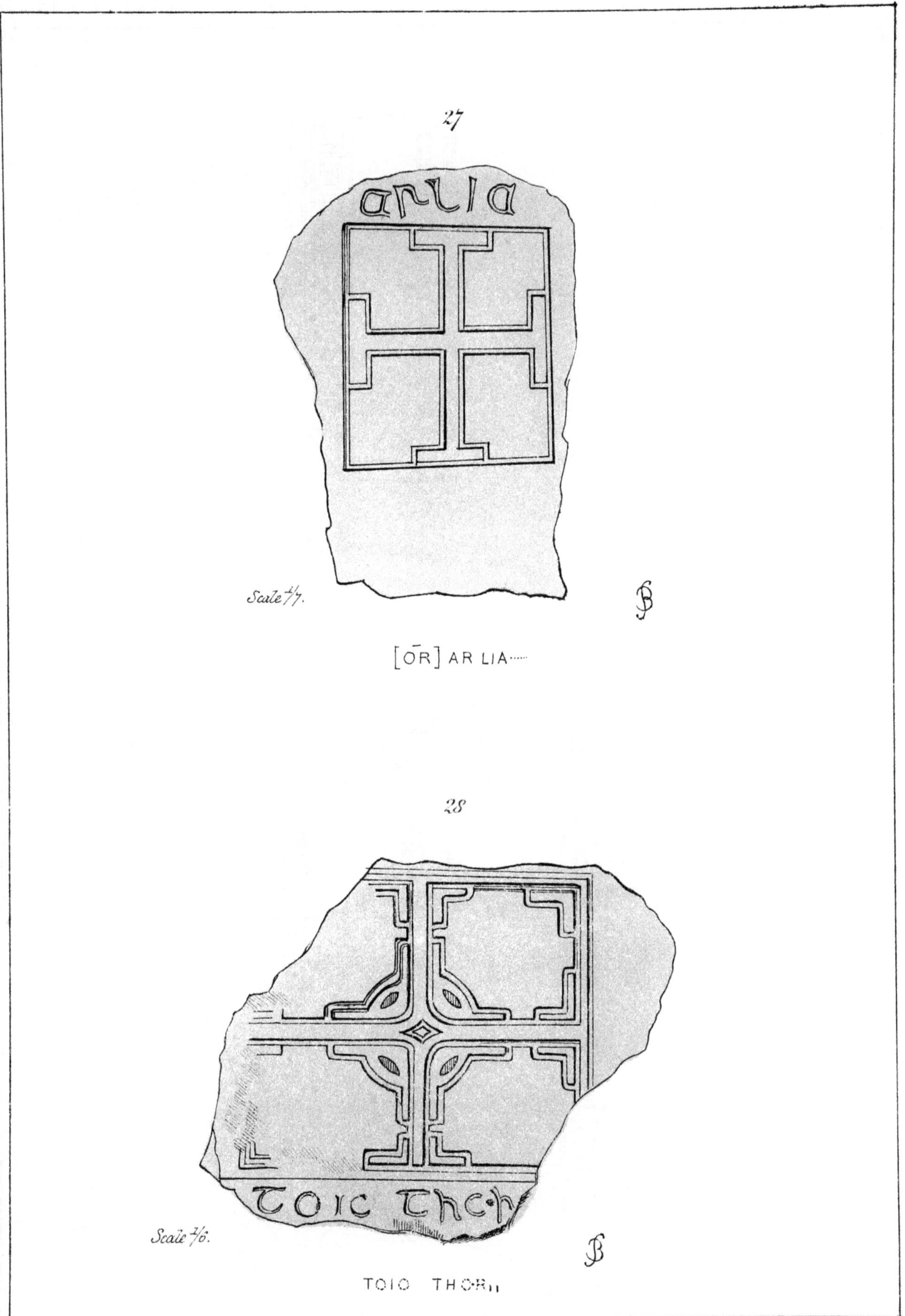

Clonmacnois

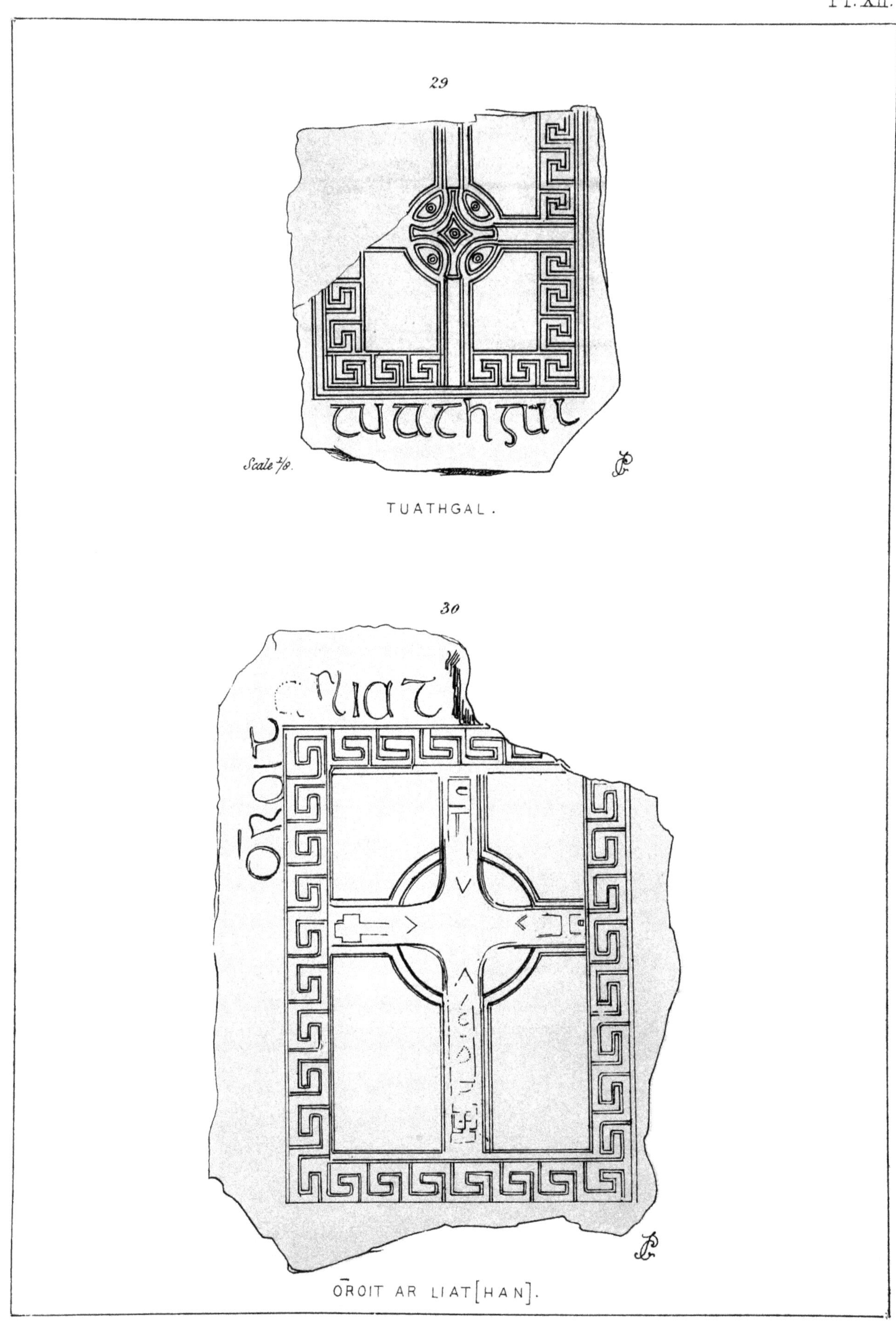

TUATHGAL.

ŌROIT AR LIAT[HAN].

Clonmacnois

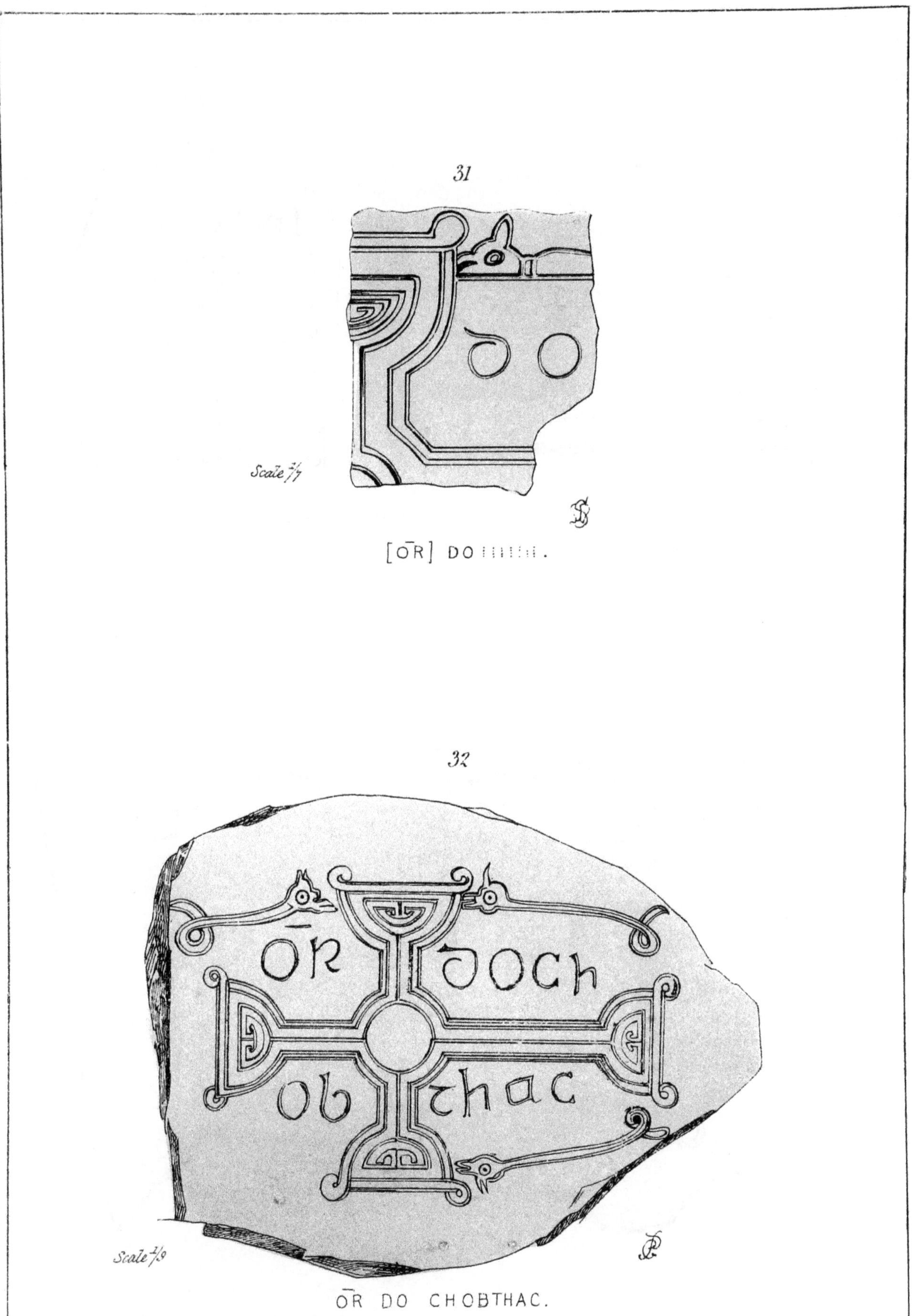

Clonmacnois.

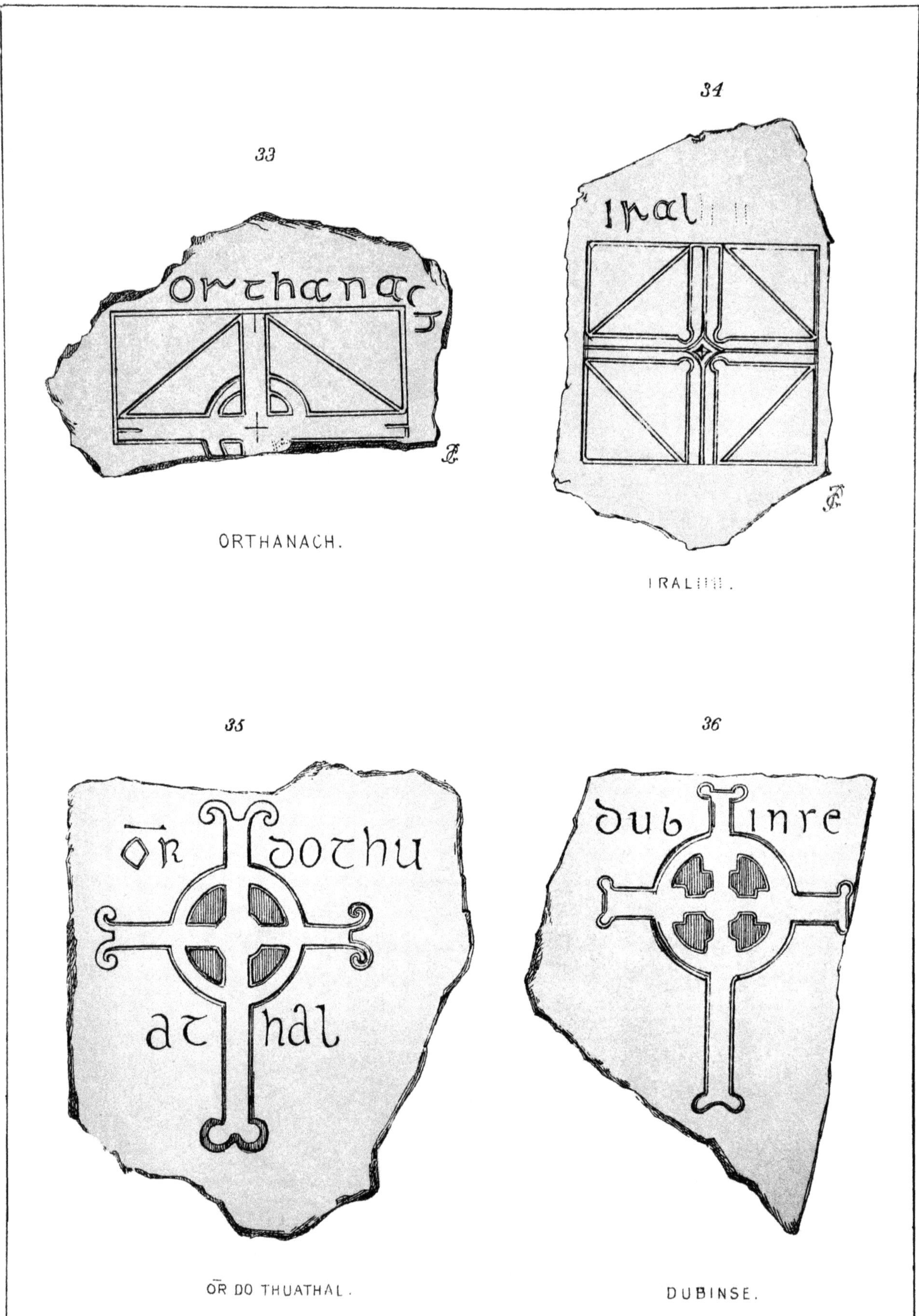

ORTHANACH.

IRAL!!!!.

ŌR DO THUATHAL.

DUBINSE.

Clonmacnois

Pl. XV.

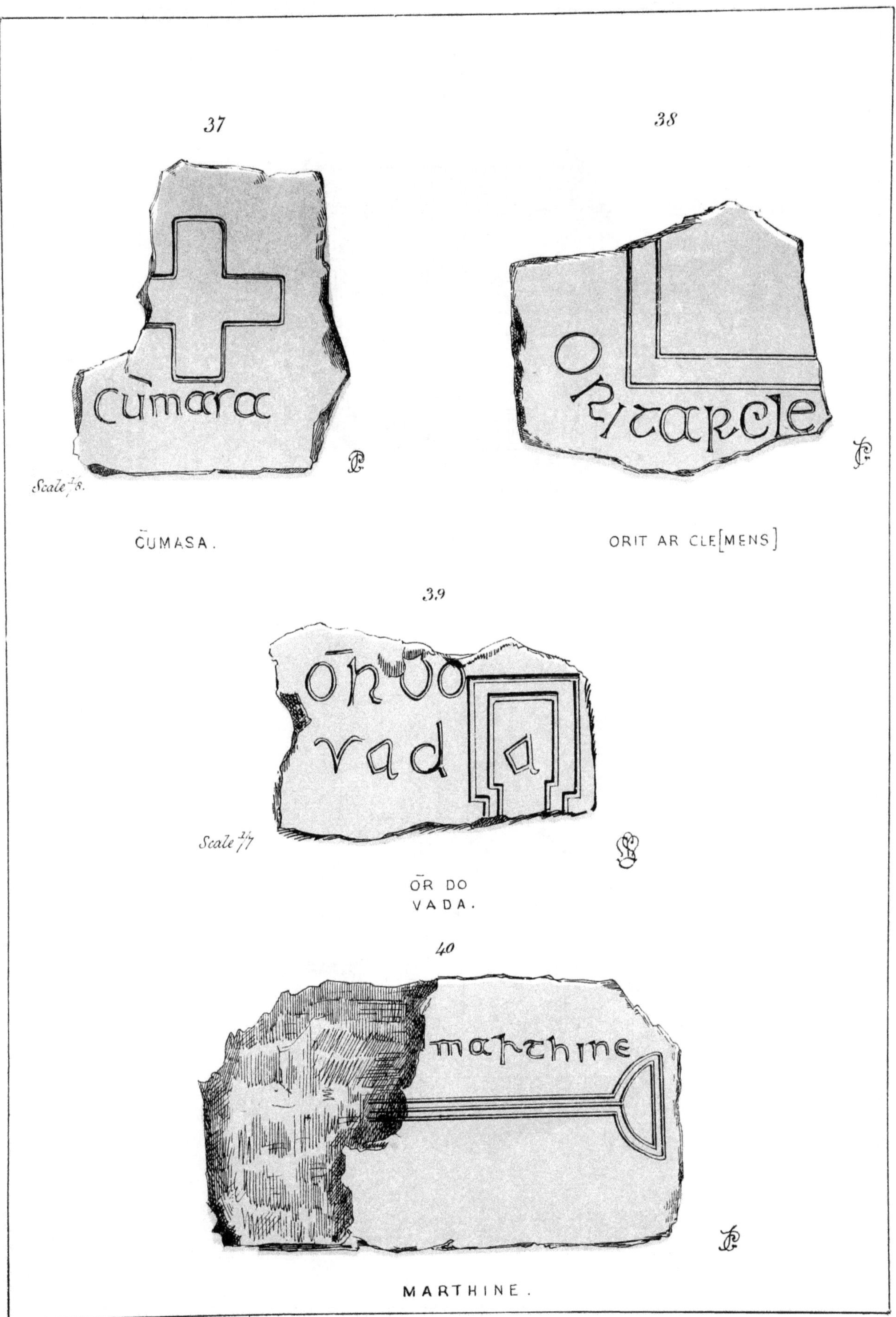

Clonmacnois

41

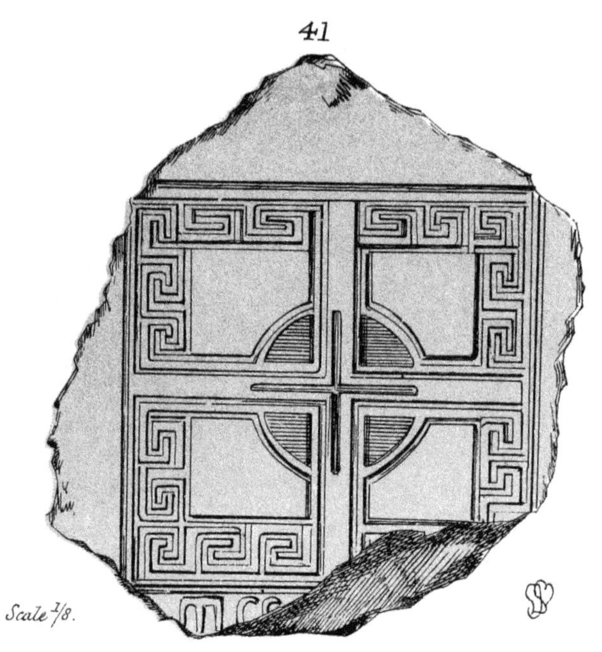

Scale 1/8.

42

Scale 1/7.

ŌR AR FINDAN

Clonmacnois

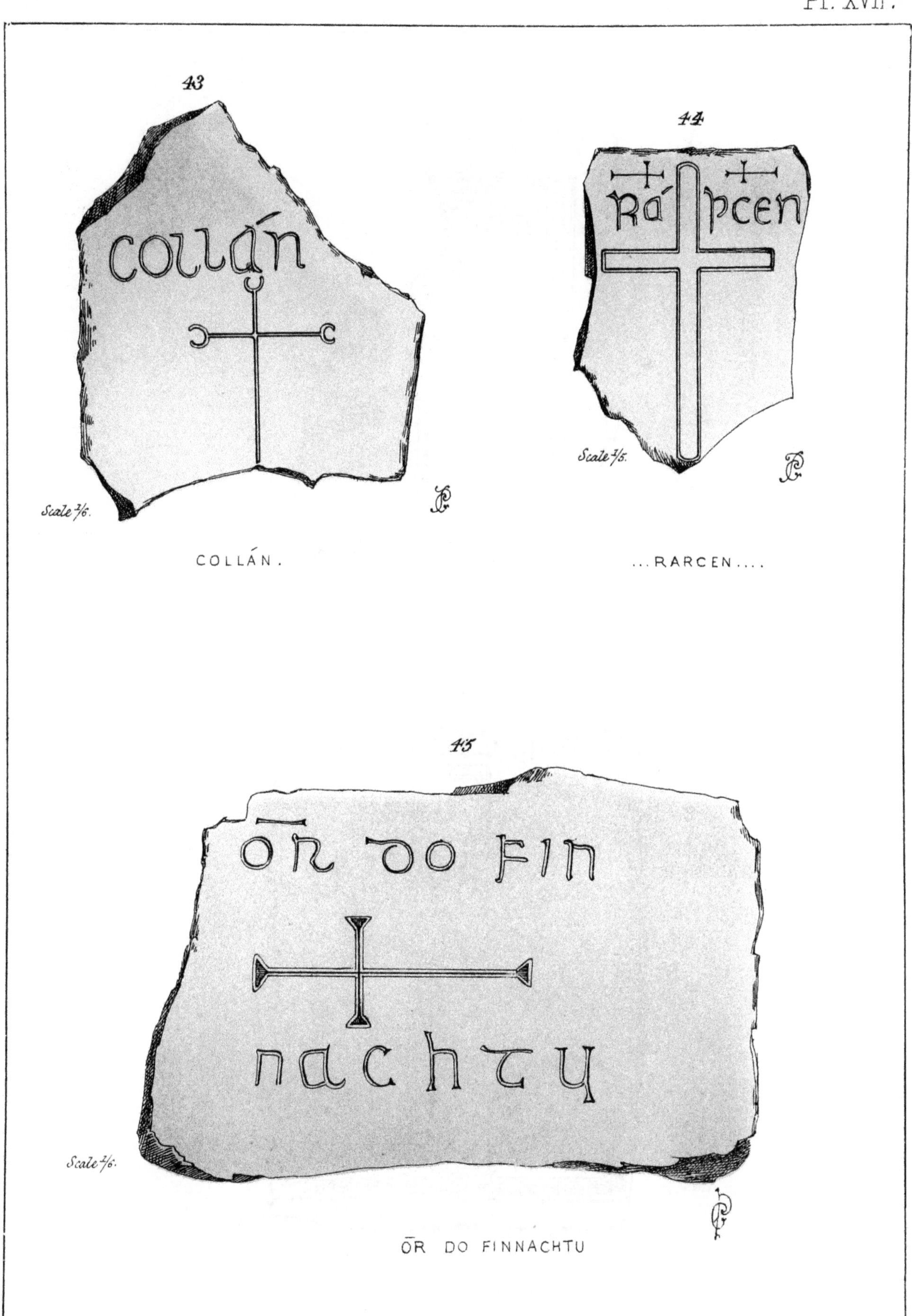

COLLÁN.

...RARCEN....

ŌR DO FINNACHTU

Clonmacnois

46

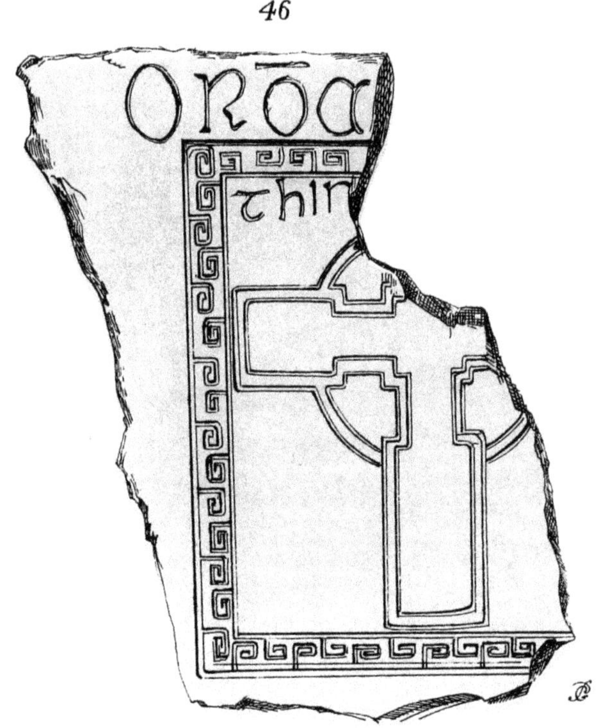

ŌROA[R] THIS ⁞⁞⁞⁞

47

Scale 2/7.

OROIT AR MAELA⁞⁞.

Clonmacnois

48

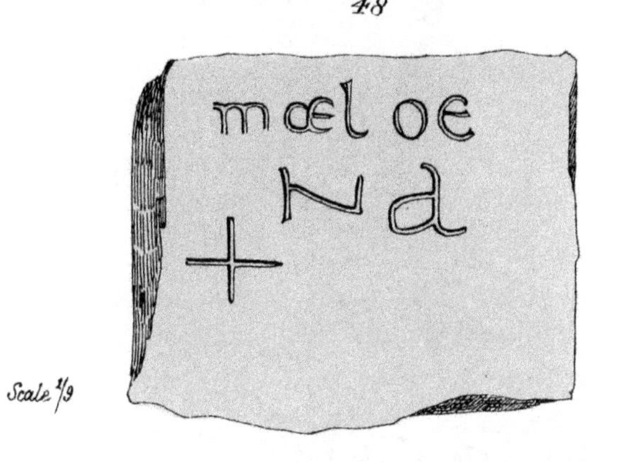

Scale 1/9

MOELOENA

49

Scale 1/7

ŌR DO BRAN U CAILLÉN

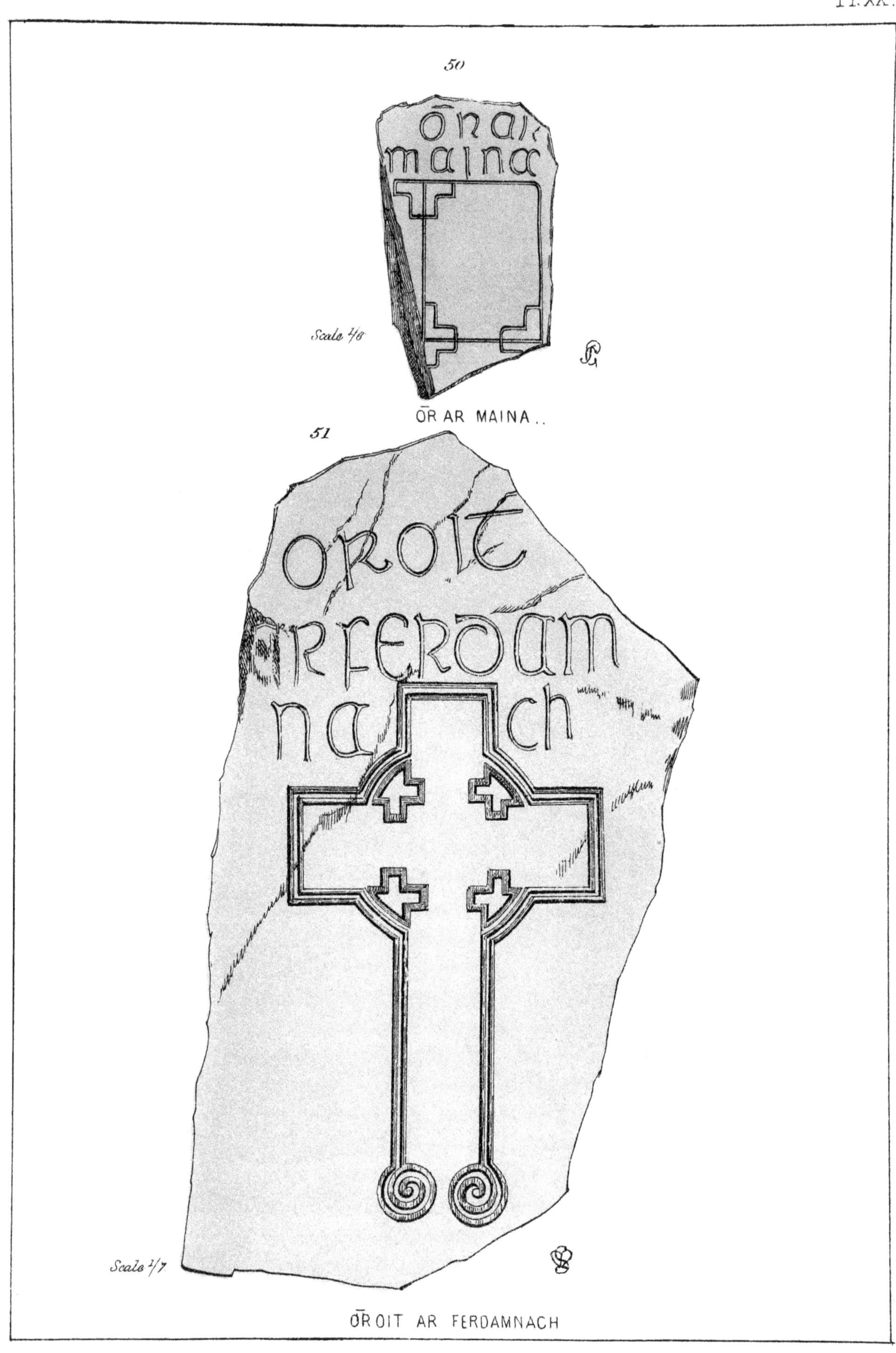

ŌR AR MAINA..

ŌROIT AR FERDAMNACH

Clonmacnois

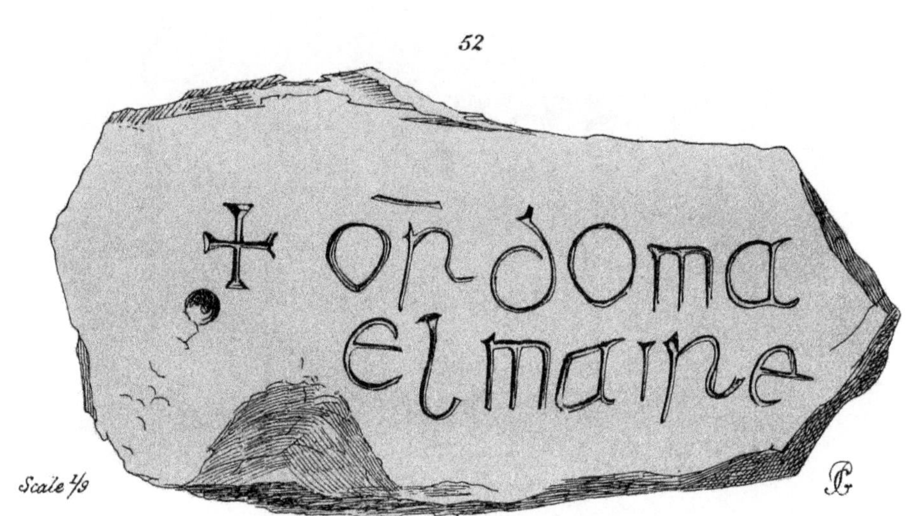

ŌR DO MAILMAIRE.

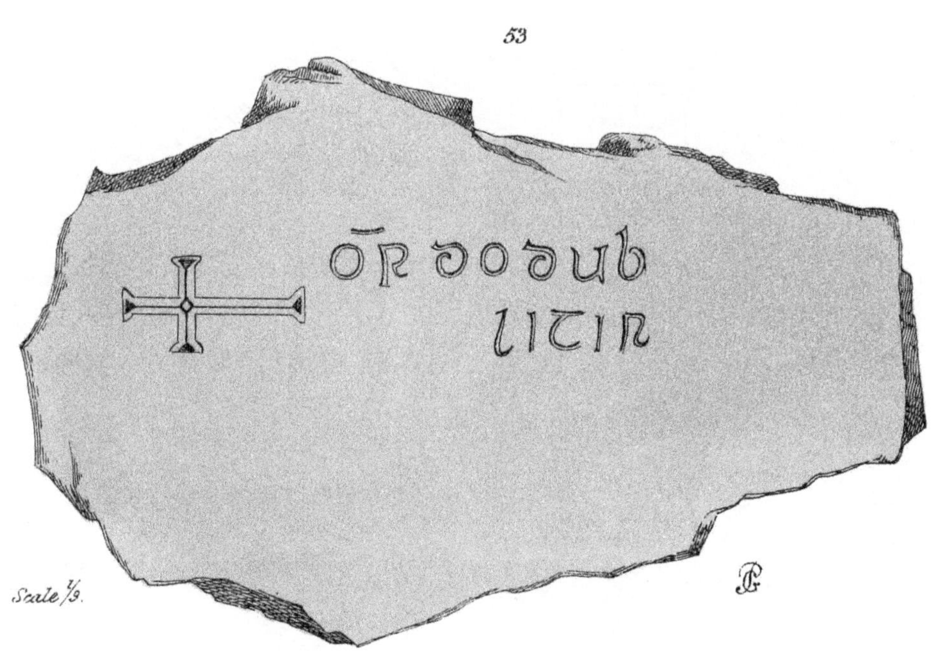

ŌR DO DUBLITIR

54

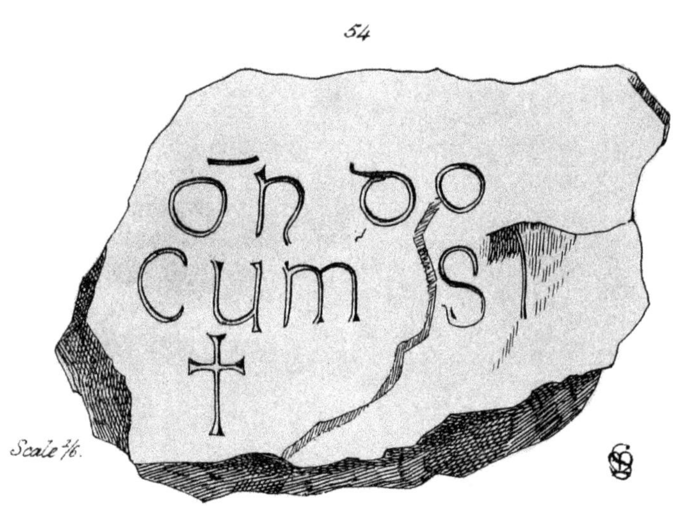

ŌR DO CUM SI...

55

ŌR DO THORPAITH.

Clonmacnois and Athlone.

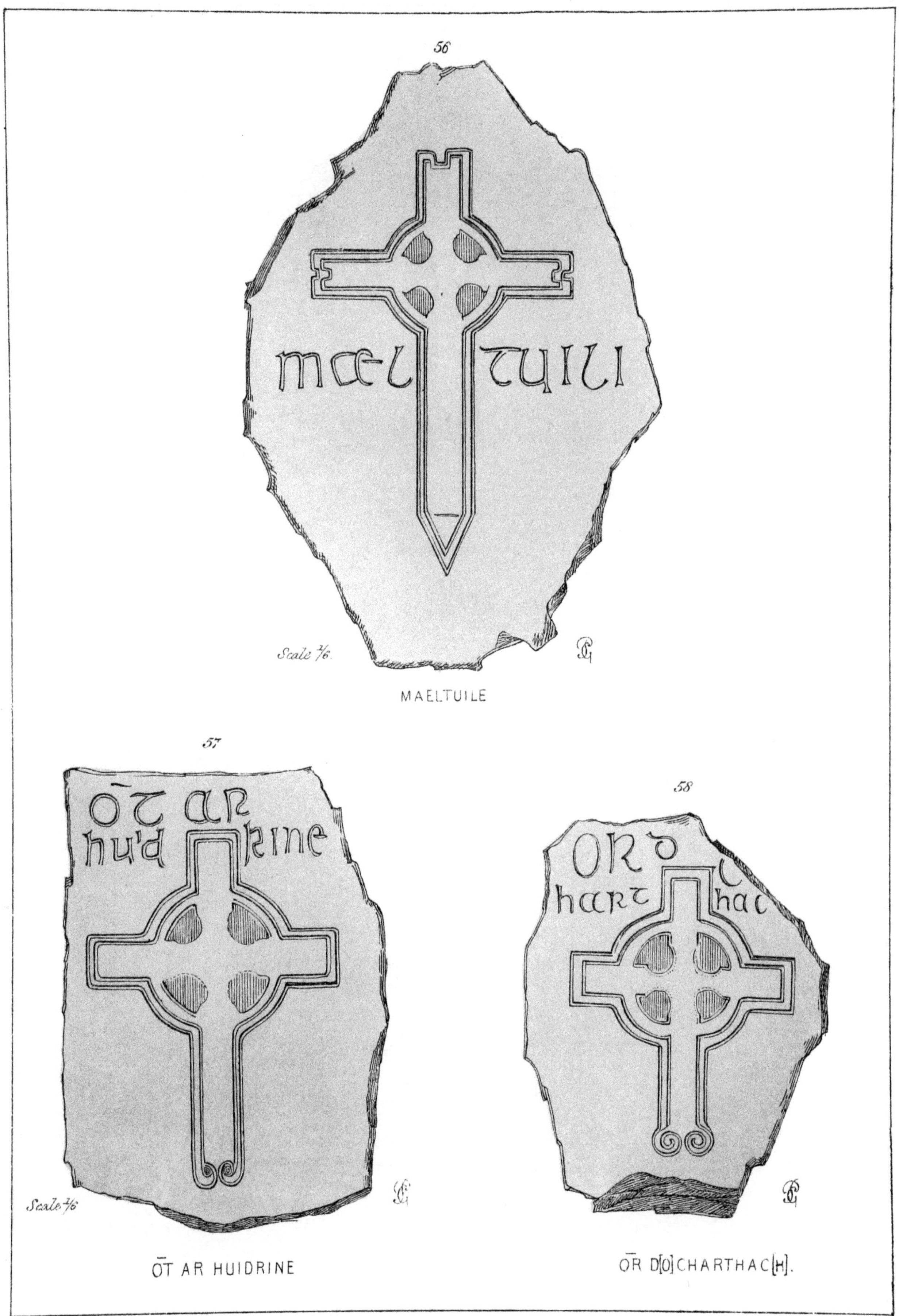

MAELTUILE

ŌT AR HUIDRINE

ŌR D[O]CHARTHAC[H].

Clonmacnois.

59

Scale 1/6

TETC ..

60

Scale 1/8.

ŌR DO FERAGAN

Clonmacnois

61

Scale 1/8.

ŌR DO MAELPATRIC

Clonmacnois

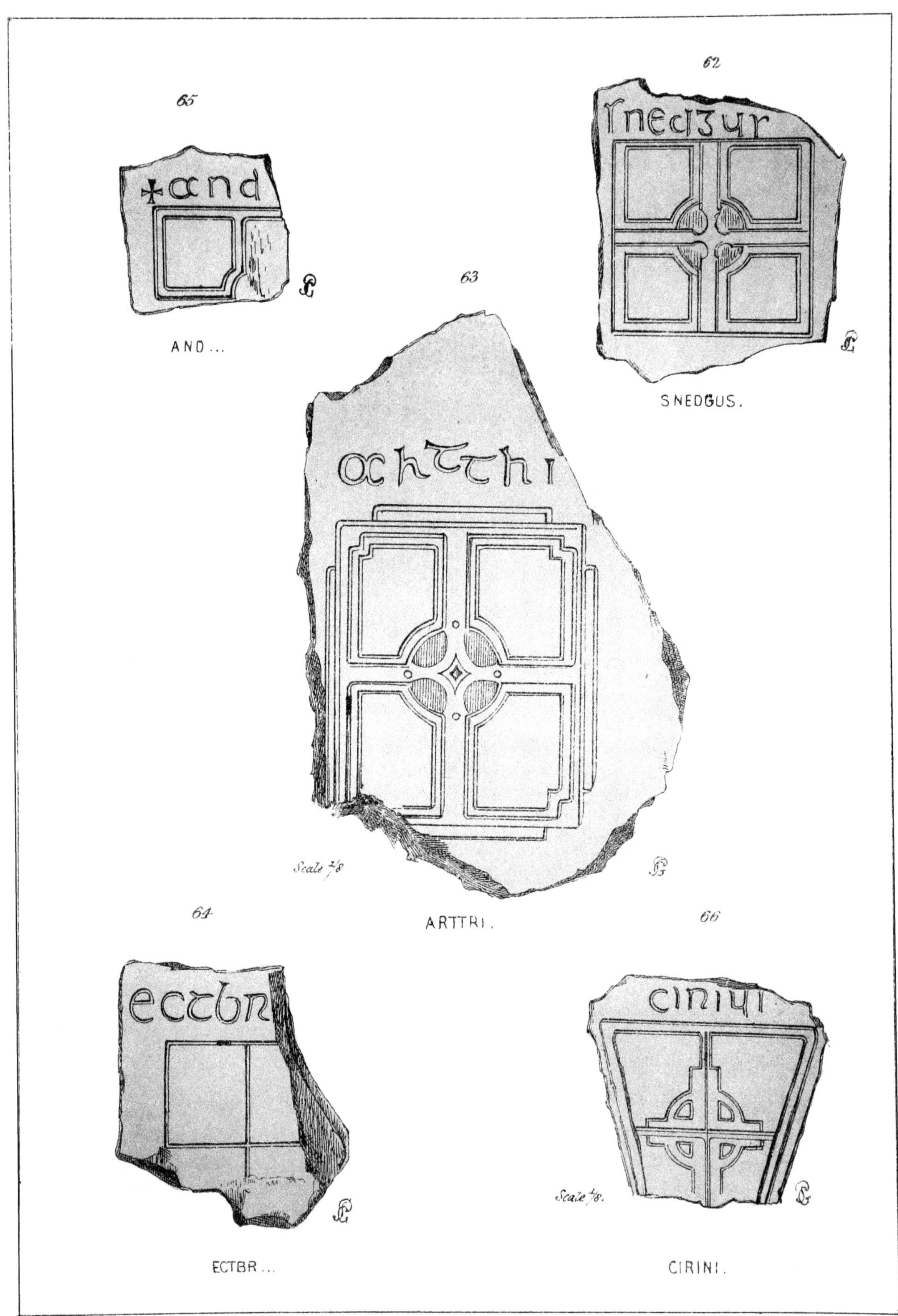

Clonmacnois.

67

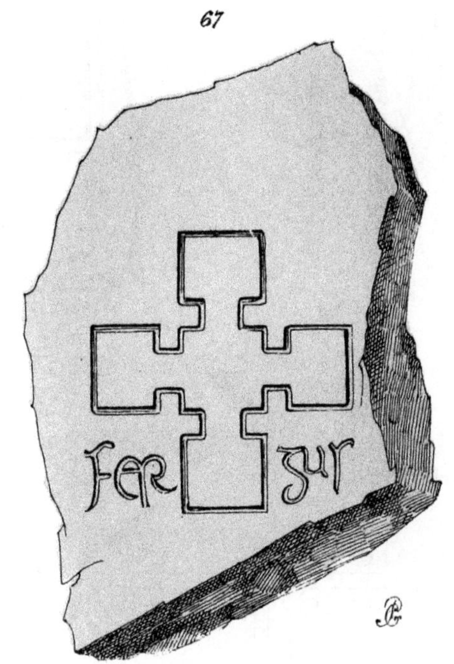

FERGUS

68

Scale 1/10.

LATICEN

Clonmacnois.

Pl. XXVIII.

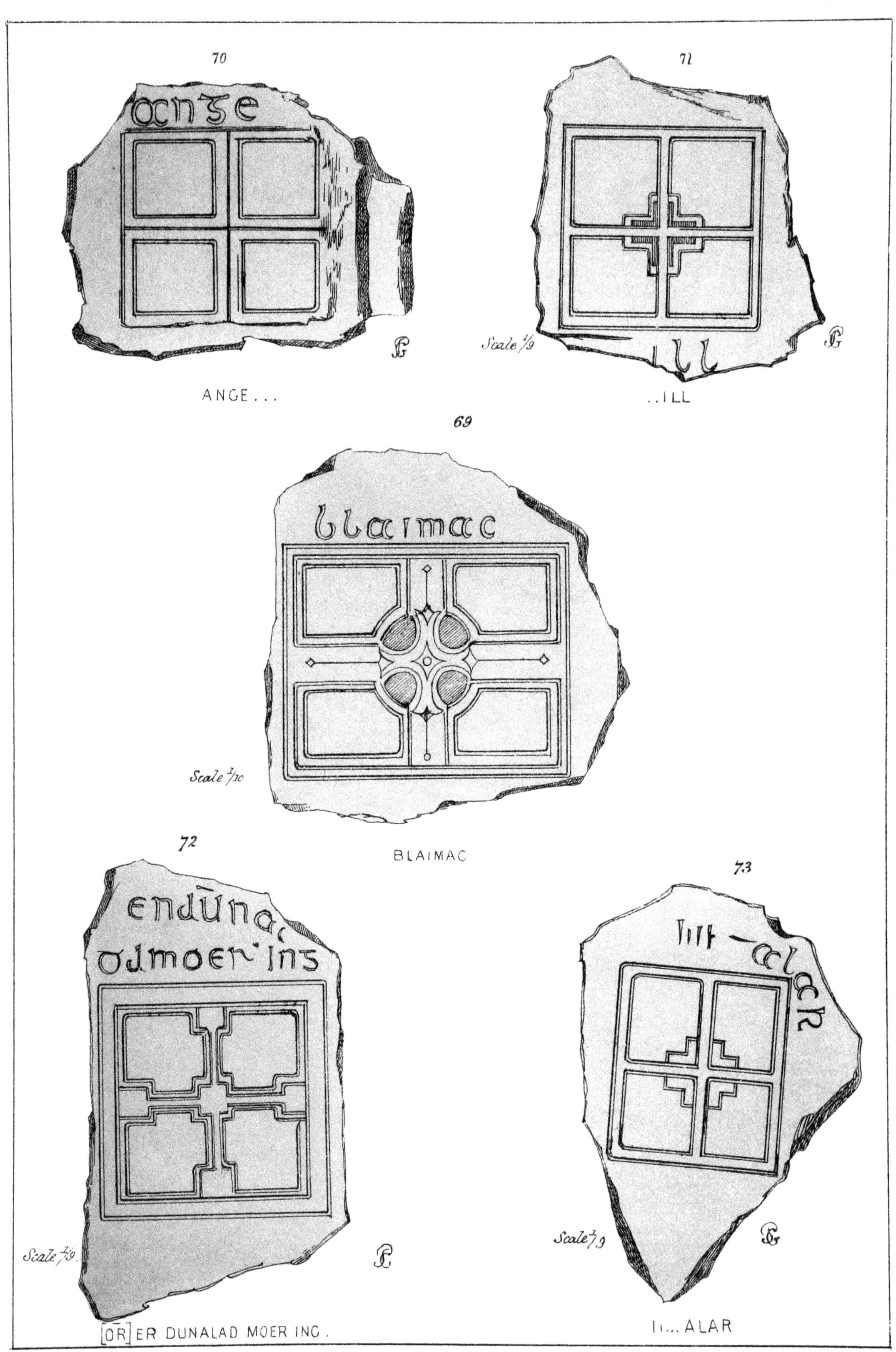

Clonmacnois

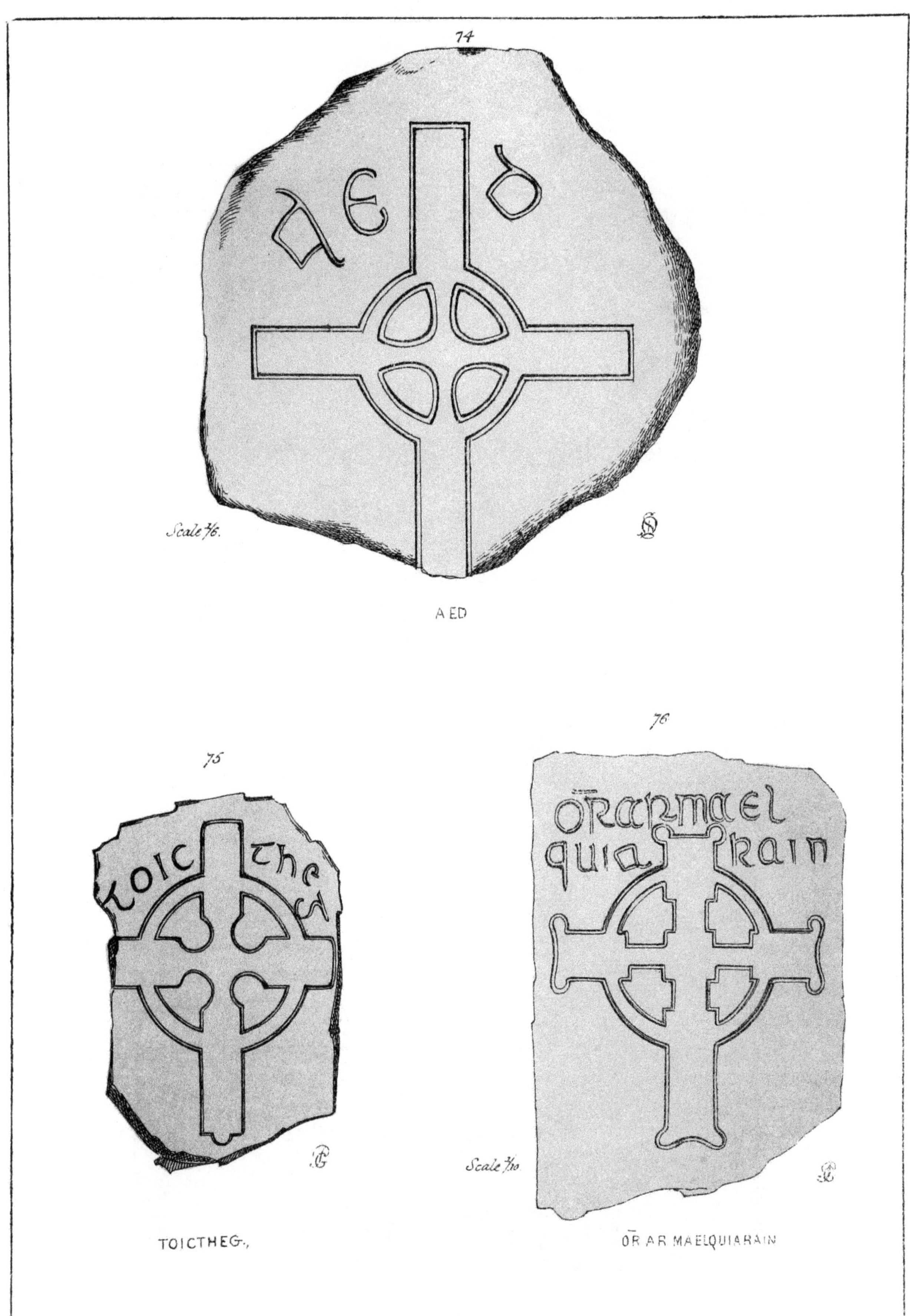

Clonmacnois.

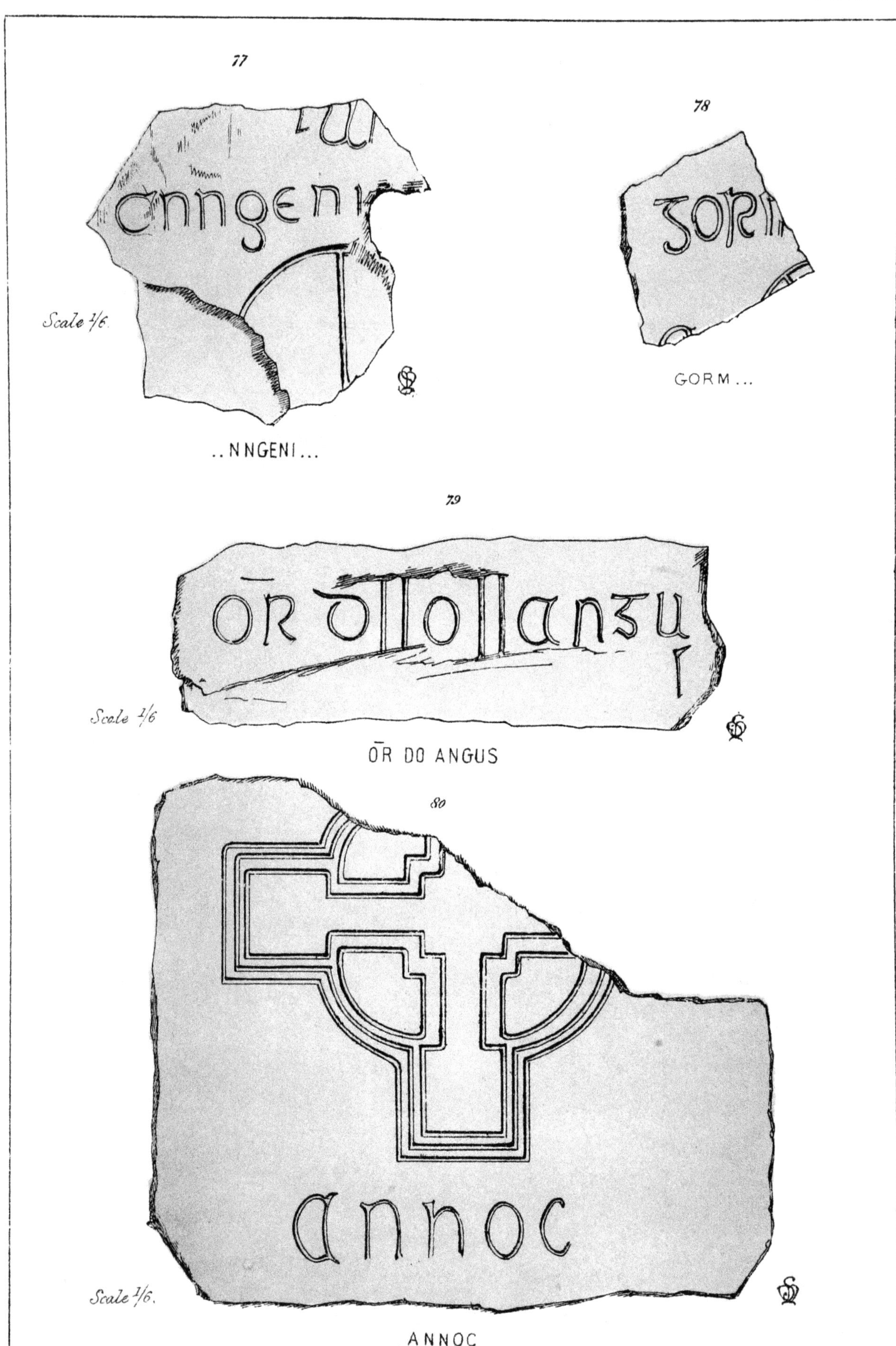

Clonmacnois.

81

ŌR DO MÁELBRIGTE.

82

SVIBINE M̄C MAILÆHVMAI

Clonmacnois.

83

ŌR DO FECHTNACH

85

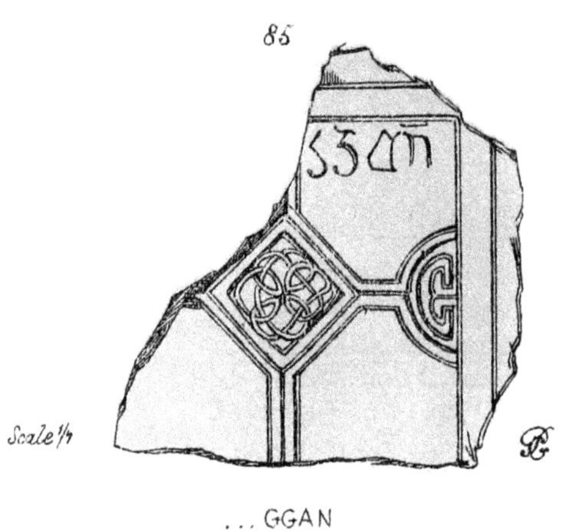

. . . GGAN

84

OROIT AR MAELBRITE

PLATE XXXIII

Vincent Brooks, Day & Son, Lith.

86
Clonmacnois

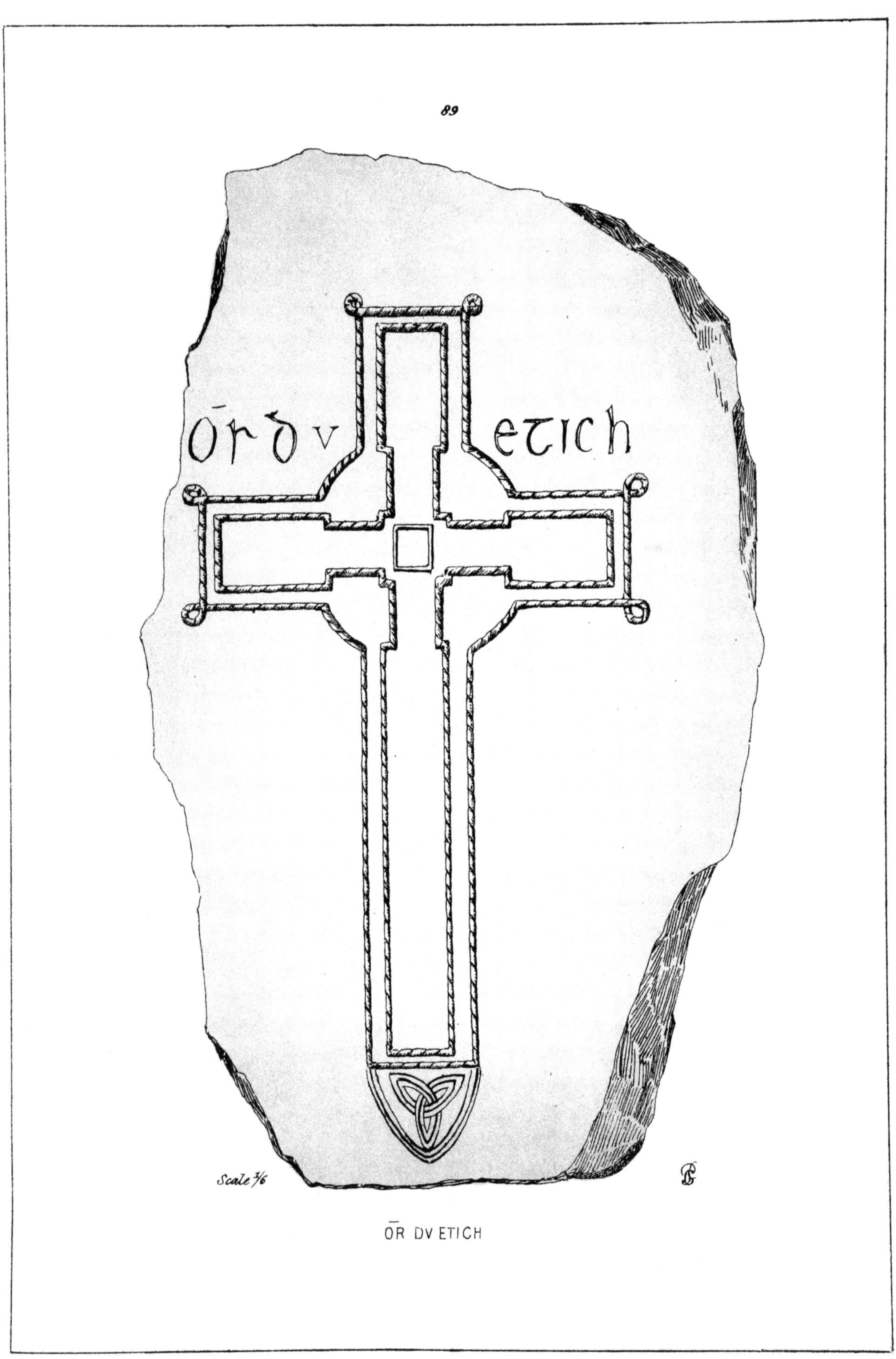

ŌR DV ETICH

Clonmacnois.

90

ŌR DO DAINÉIL

91

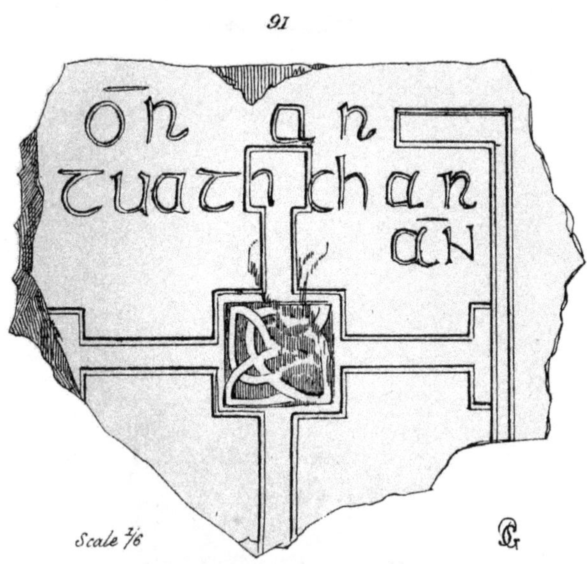

ŌR AR TUATHCHARAN.

Clonmacnois

92

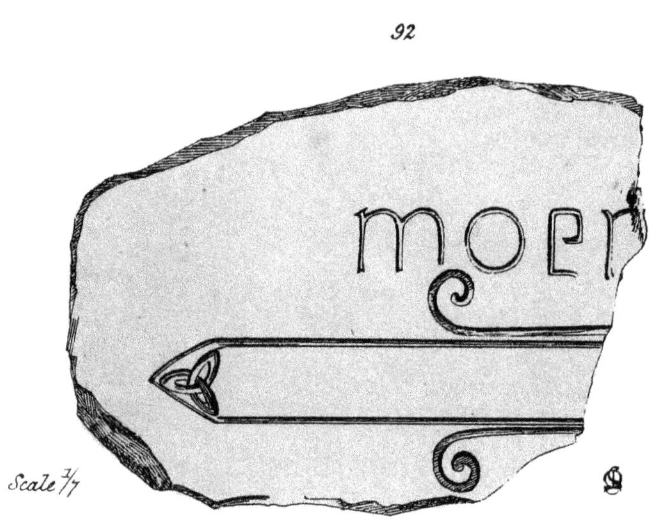

MOEN...

93

..R DO MAIL..RIGG

94

ECHT....

Clonmacnois.

95

Scale 1/12.

ŌR AR FIACHRAICH

97

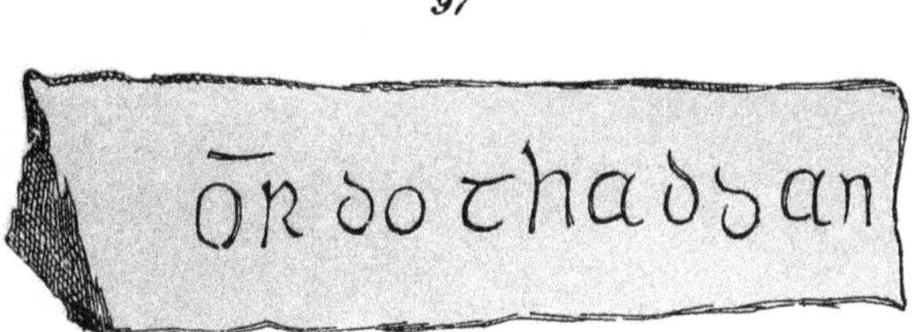

ŌR DO THADGAN

96

ŌR DO CHORBRIV CHRVMM.

Clonmacnois.

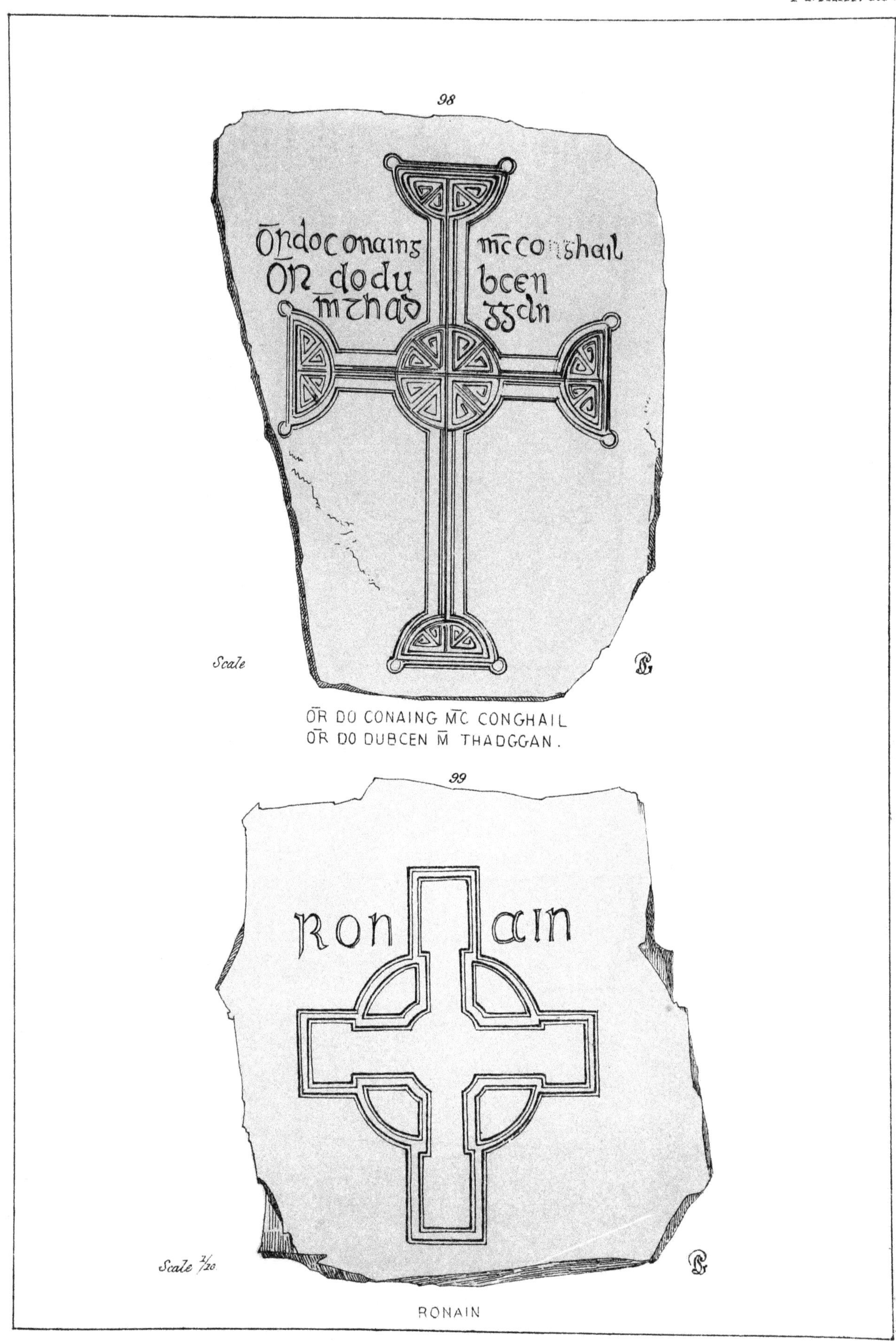

ŌR DO CONAING M̄C CONGHAIL
ŌR DO DUBCEN M̄ THADGGAN.

RONAIN

Clonmacnois.

100

Scale 1/20

OR DO CHO ... IN GORMAI ..

101

Scale 1/7

.... TUI ∴.

Clonmacnois.

102

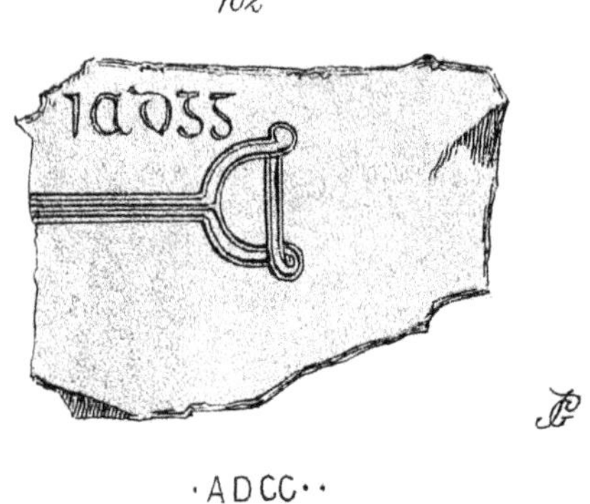

·ADCC··

103

ORÓIT MAR MAELCIARAIN.

103 a

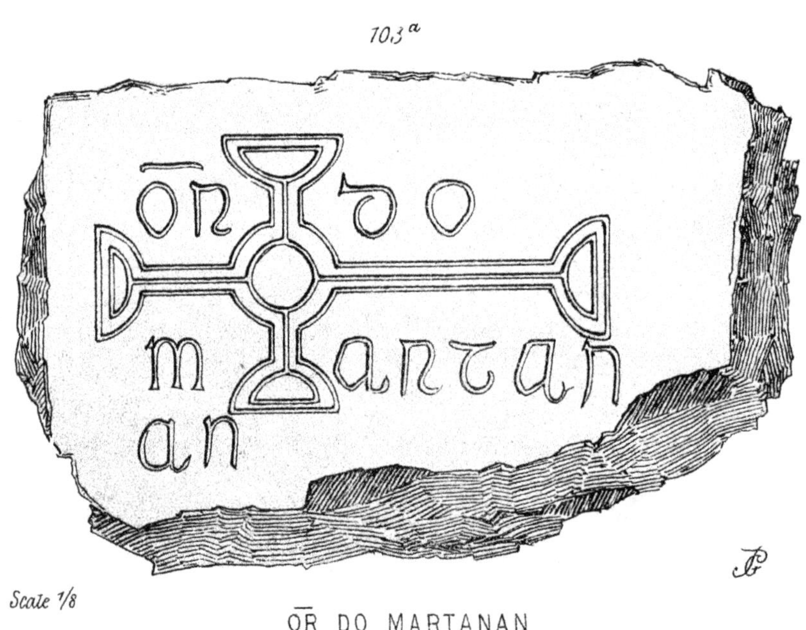

ŌR DO MARTANAN

Clonmacnois

104

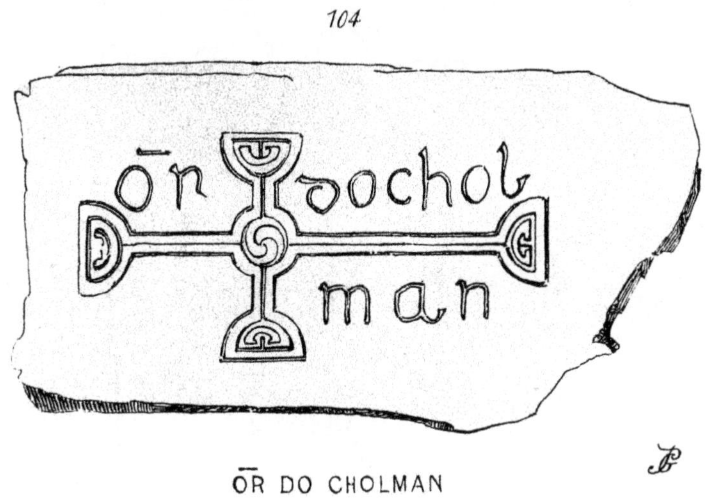

ŌR DO CHOLMAN

105

Scale 1/7

ŌR AR GILLAGIARAIN

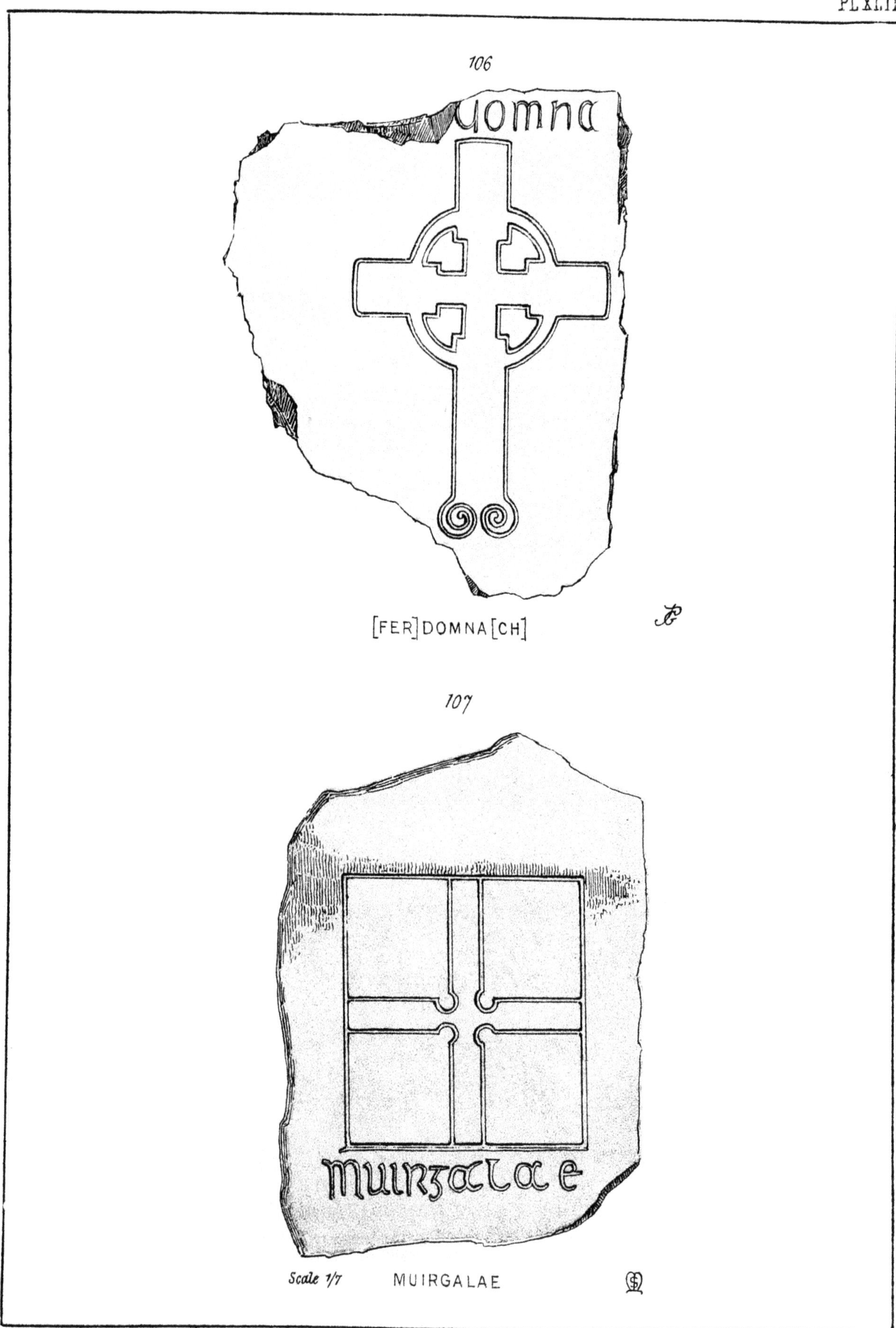

106 [FER]DOMNA[CH]

107 Scale 1/7 MUIRGALAE

Clonmacnois

108

ŌR DO MAEL[MOICH]EIRC[E]

Scale 1/6

109

Scale 1/7

110

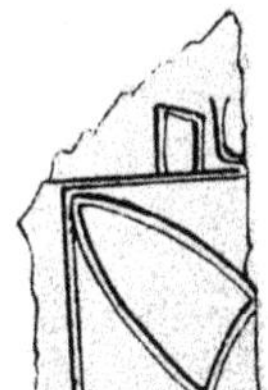

Scale 1/9

111

Scale 1/8

Clonmacnois

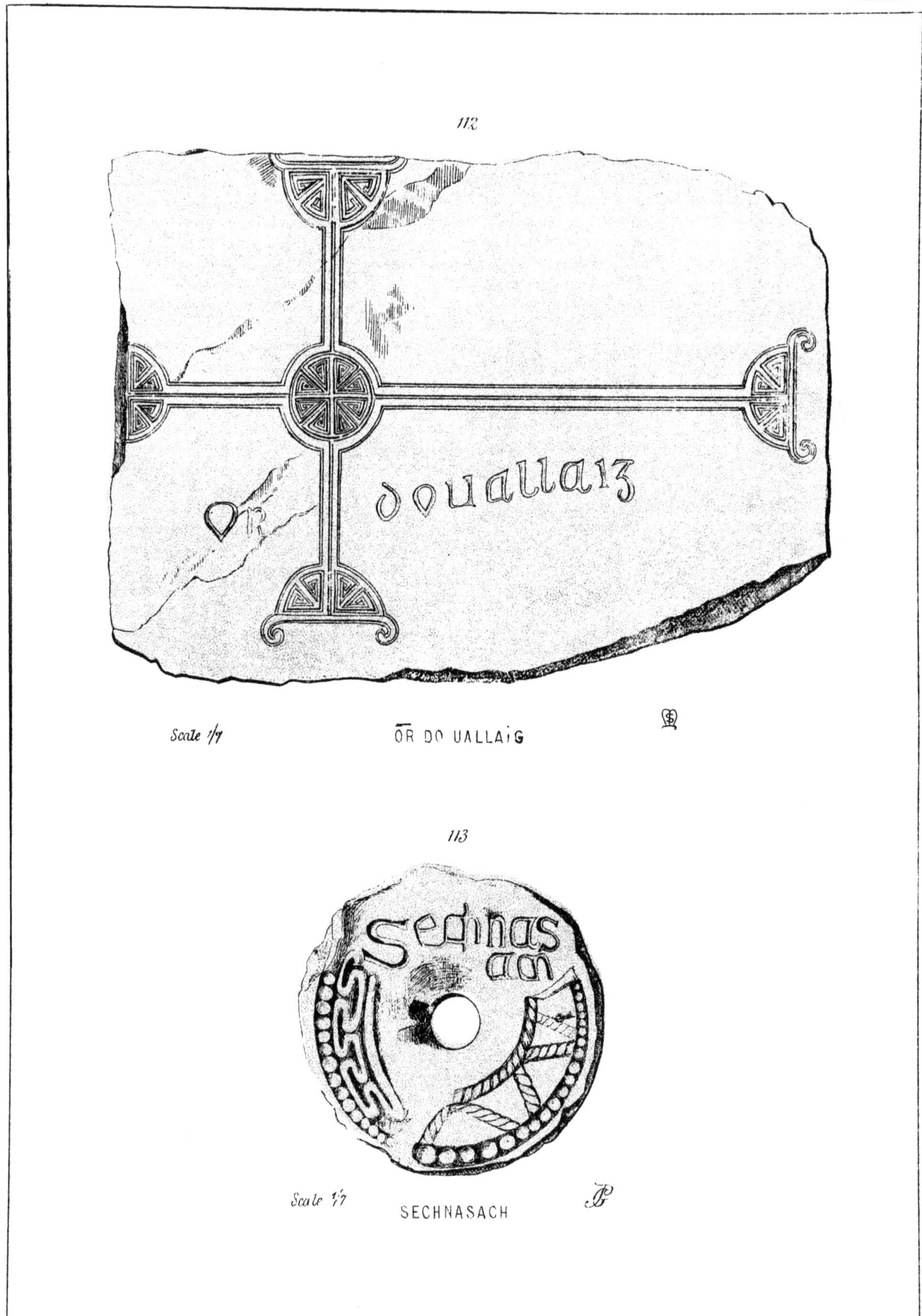

Clonmacnois

114

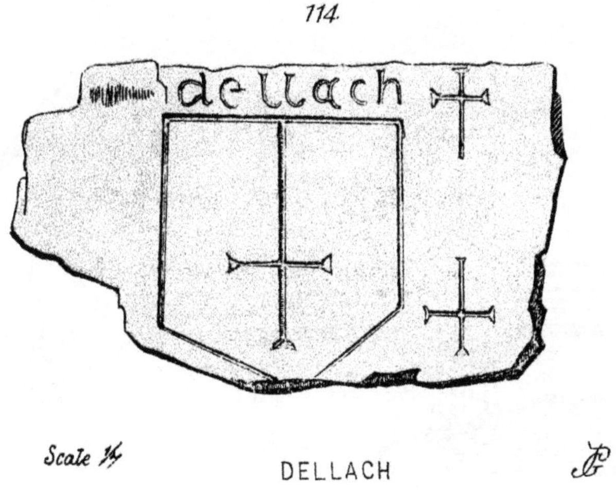

Scale ¼

DELLACH

115

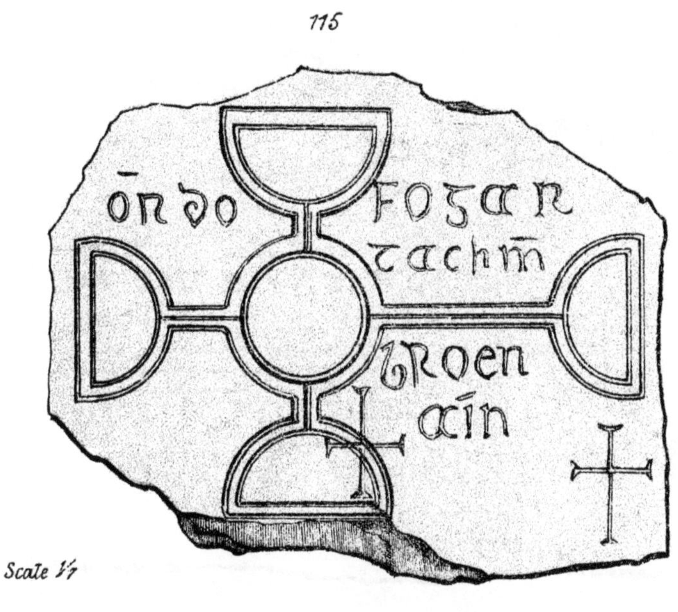

Scale ⅐

ŌR DO FOGARTACH MAC BROENAIN

Clonmacnois

116

Scale 1/7

ŌR DO CHATHUL UIIIUG
ŌR DO BENEDICHT

117

Scale 1/7

ŌR DO GUARIU

Clonmacnois

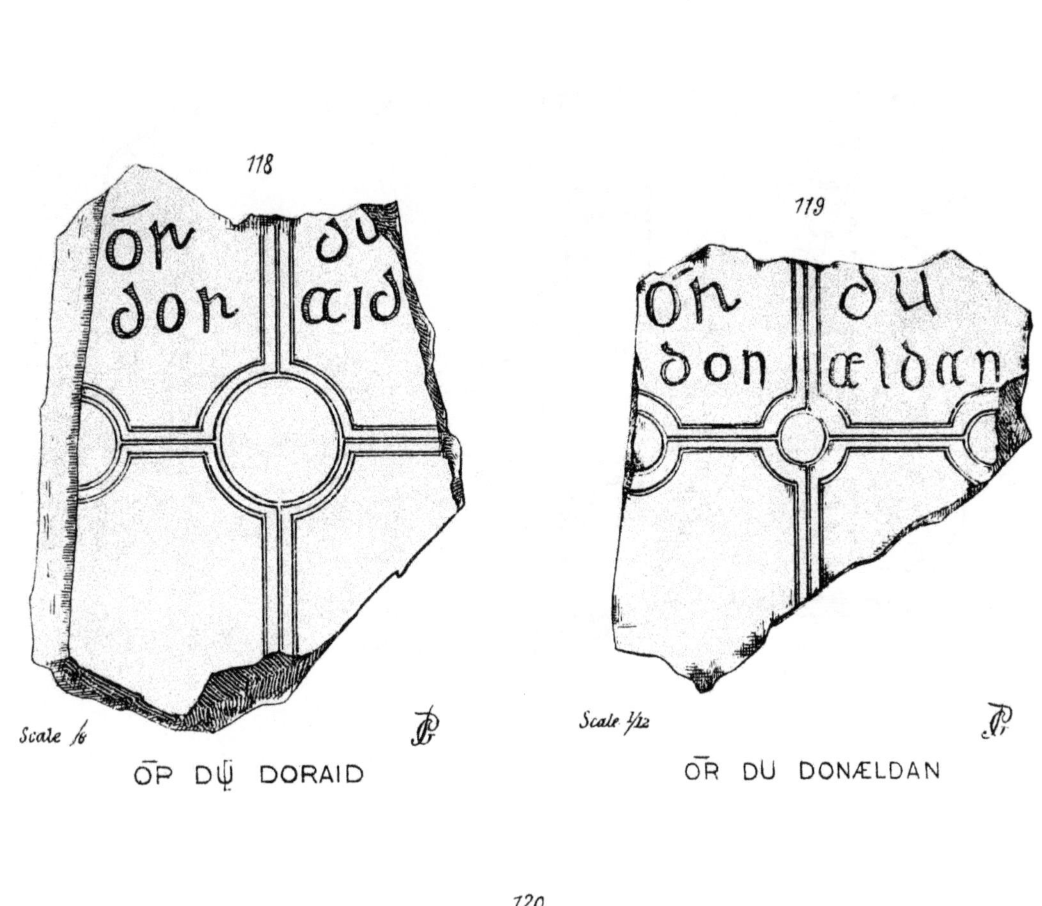

ŌP DΨ DORAID

ŌR DU DONÆLDAN

+ RECHTAR[E

Clonmacnois

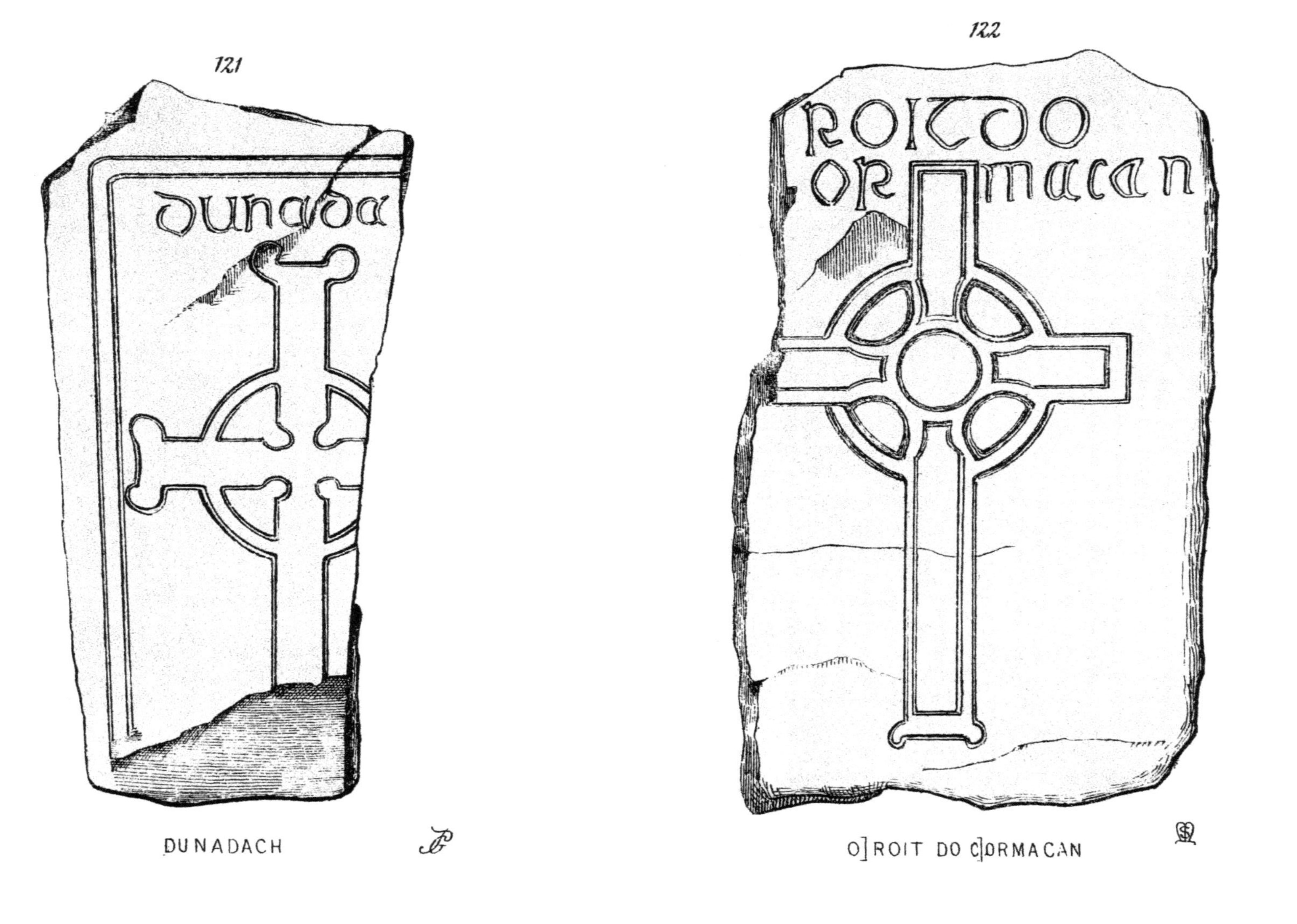

121 DUNADACH

122 O]ROIT DO C]ORMACAN

Clonmacnois.

123

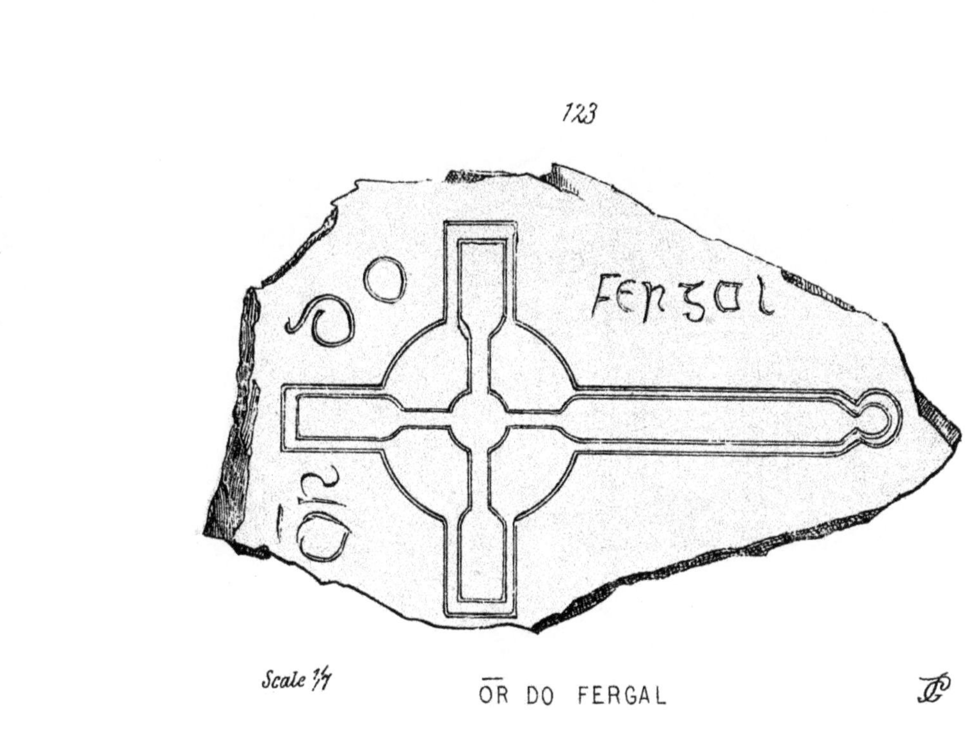

Scale 1/7 ŌR DO FERGAL

124

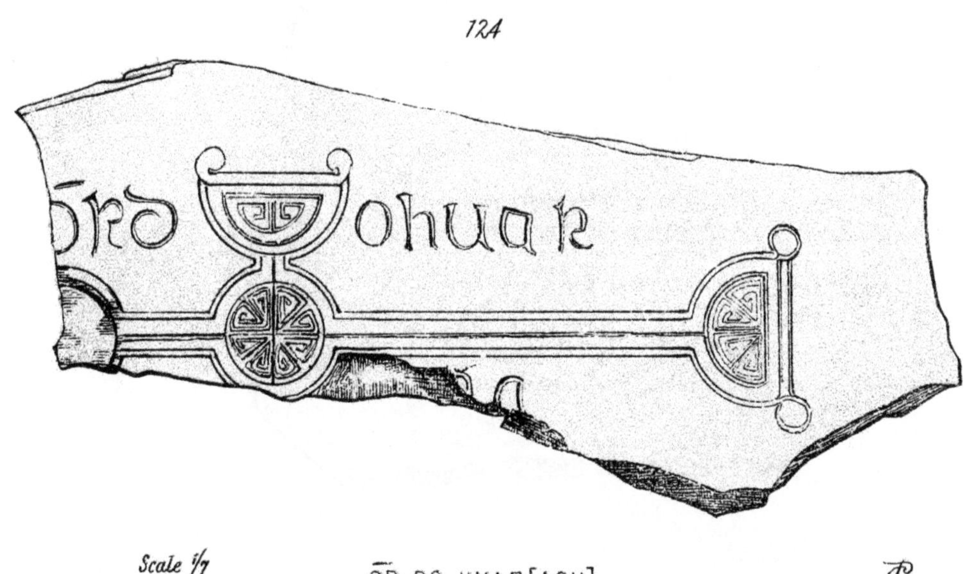

Scale 1/7 ŌR DO HUAR[ACH]

Clonmacnois

125

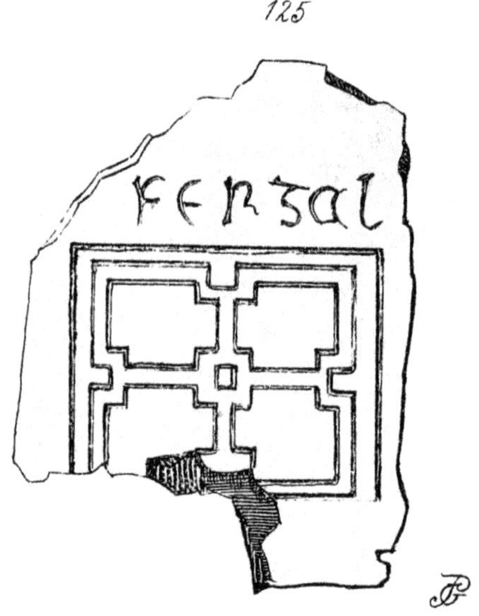

FERCAL

126

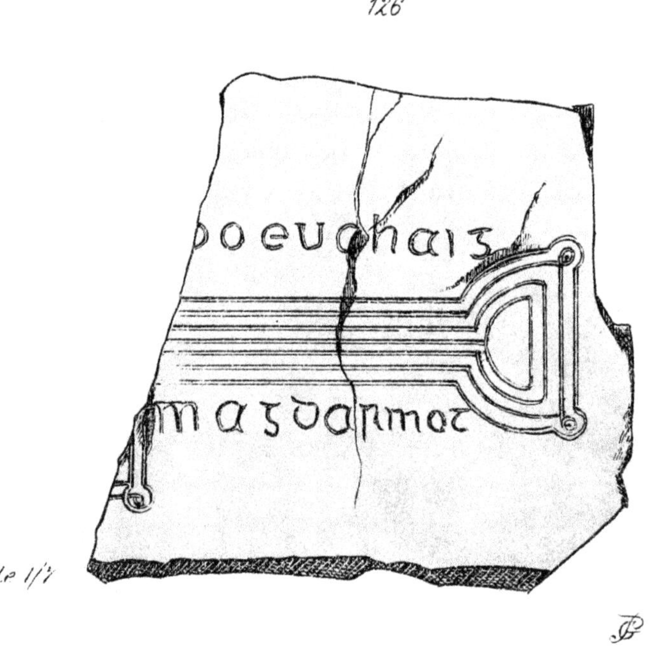

Scale 1/7

ŌR DO EUCHAIG MAG DARMOT

Clonmacnois

104

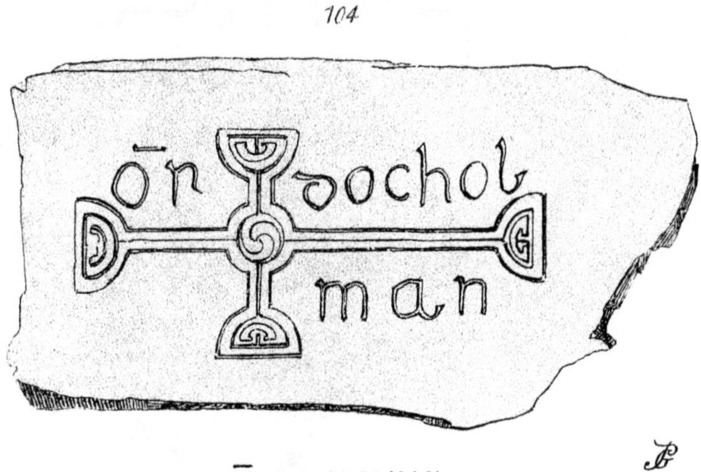

ŌR DO CHOLMAN

105

Scale 1/7

ŌR AR GILLAGIARAIN

Clonmacnois

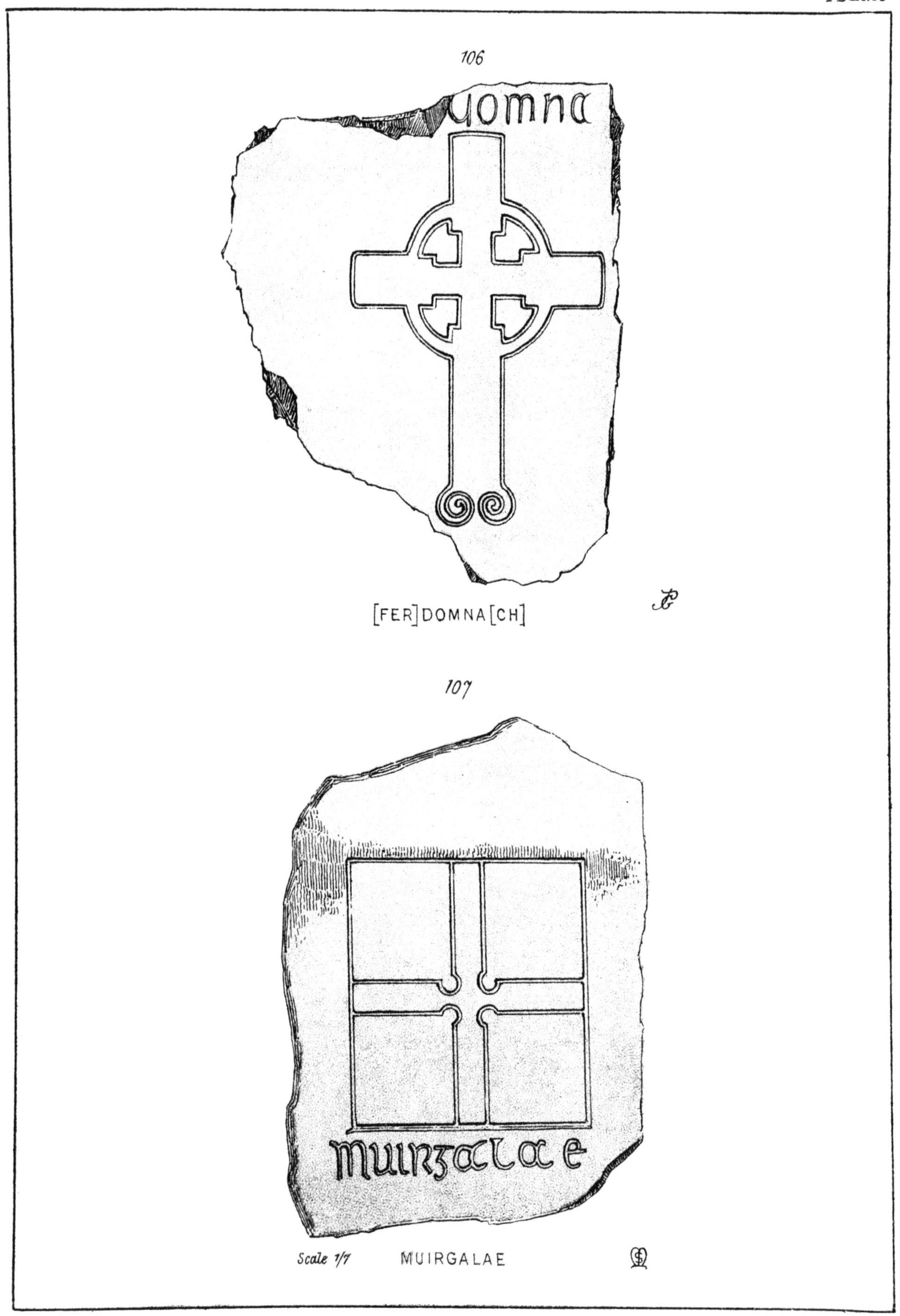

Clonmacnois

130

OR̄ DO MAELFINNIA

131

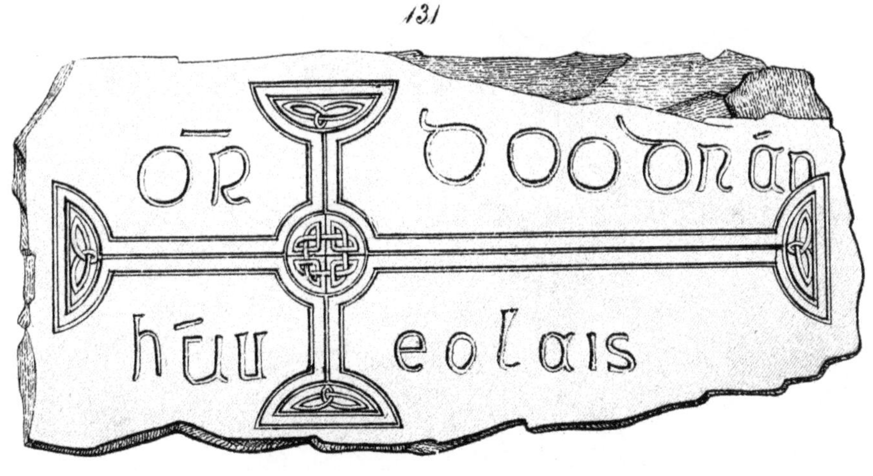

OR̄ DO ODRAN HAU EOLAIS

Clonmacnois

132

ŌR DO FLANNCHAD

133

ŌR DO BONUIT

Clonmacnois.

134

Scale 1/6

··LAITH····

135

Scale 1/6

··AITH····

136

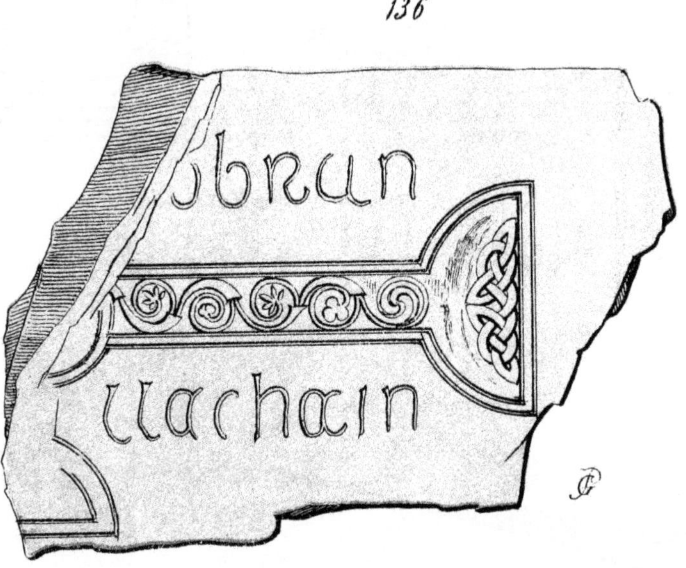

[··]BRAN[···] LLACHAIN

Clonmacnois.

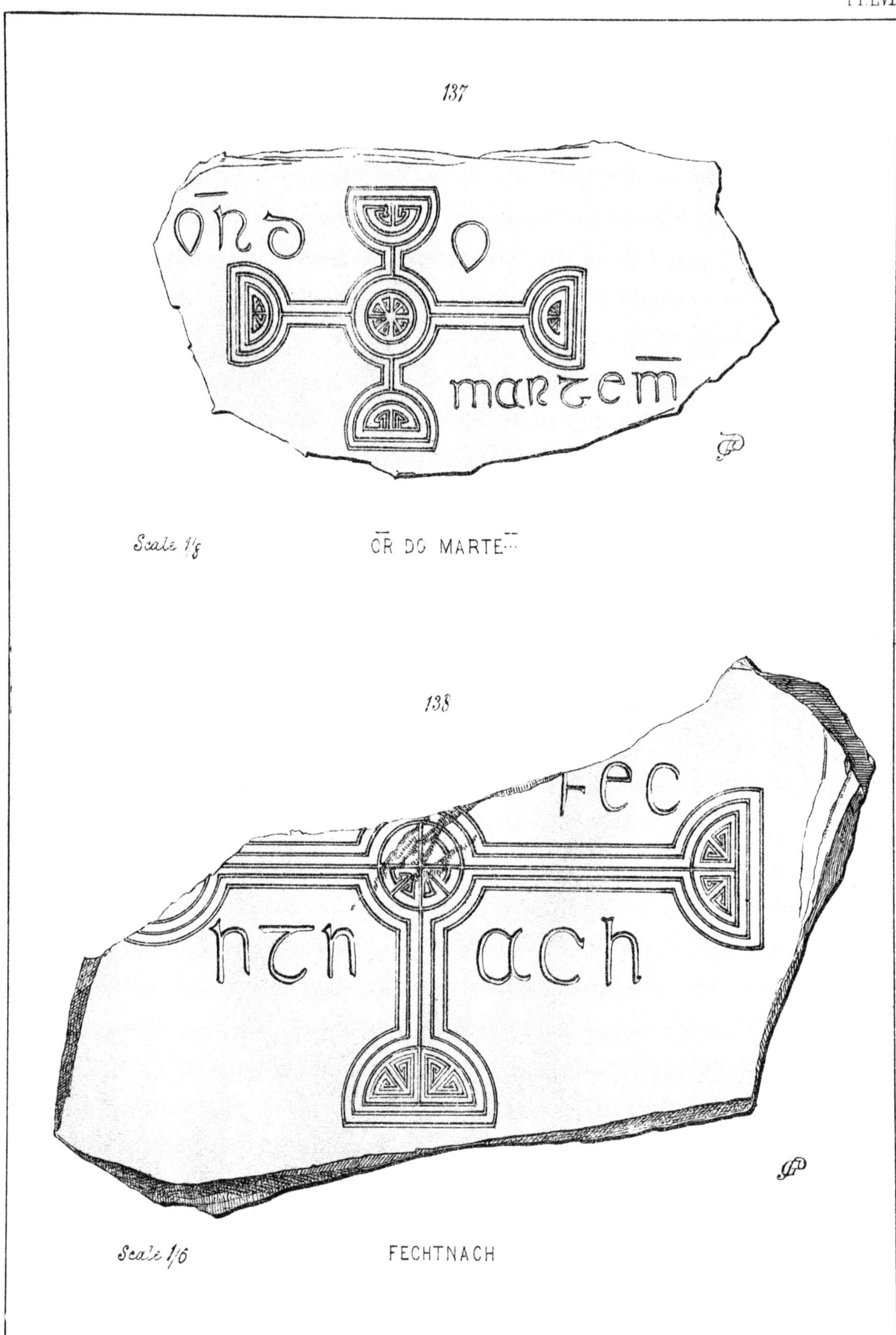

Clonmacnois.

139

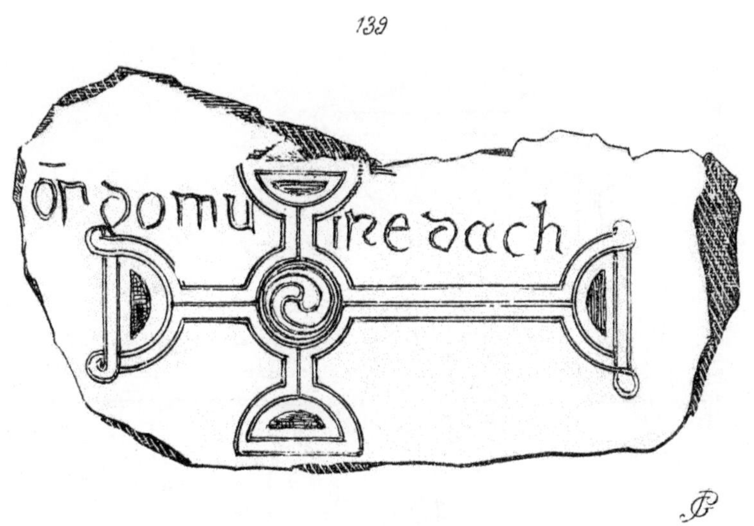

ŌR DO MUIREDACH

140

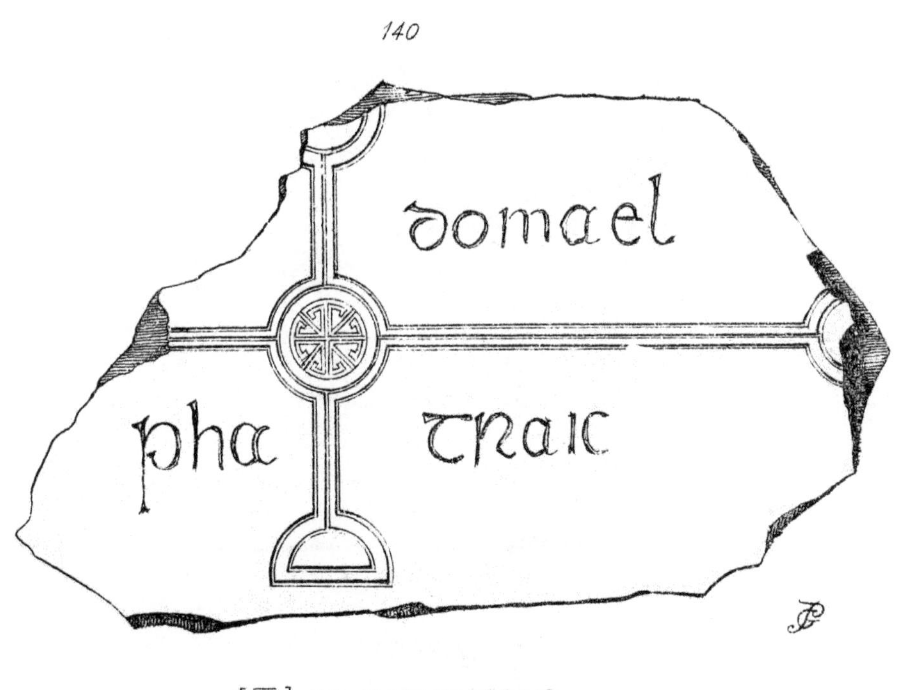

[ŌR] DO MAELPHATRAIC

141

Scale 1/5

OR DO .... BRIGT

142

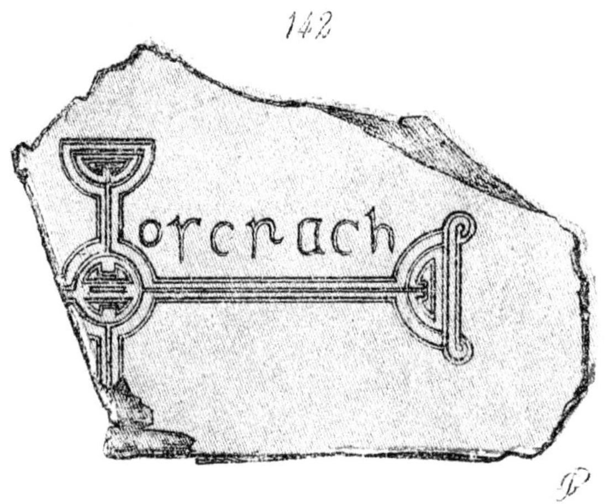

[C]OSCRACH

Clonmacnois

143

Scale 1/6

OR DO ····· IN GOR

144

Scale 1/7

OR DO TH ·· G·UN

Clonmacnois.

145

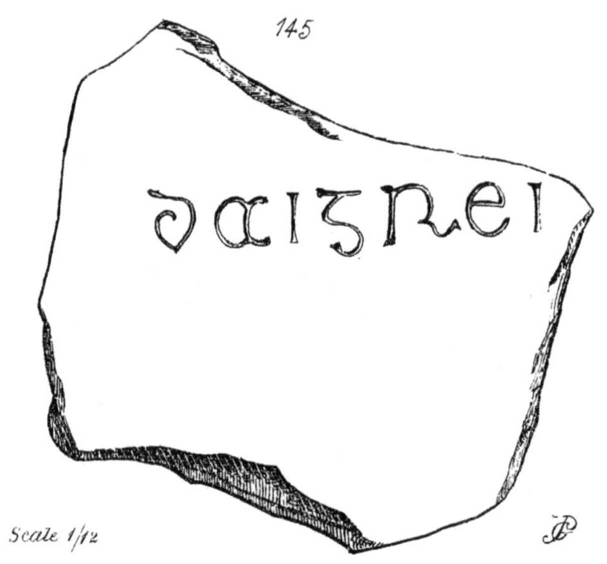

Scale 1/12

DAIGREI

146

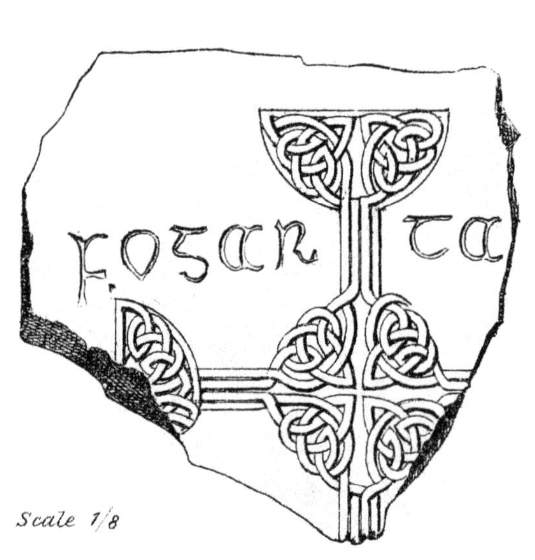

Scale 1/8

FOGARTA[..]

Clonmacnois

147

Scale 1/8 ŌR DO CHUNN

148

Scale 1/9 ŌR DO MAELFINNIA

Clonmacnois.

149

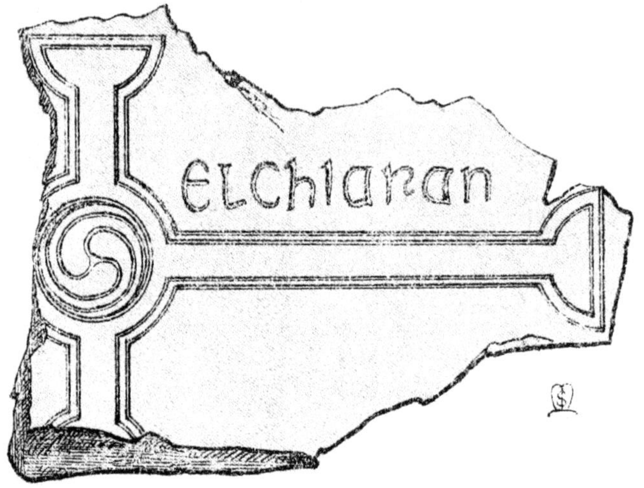

Scale 1/8

[MA]ELCHIARAN

150

Scale 1/5

ŌR DO GILLACHRIST

Clonmacnois.

151

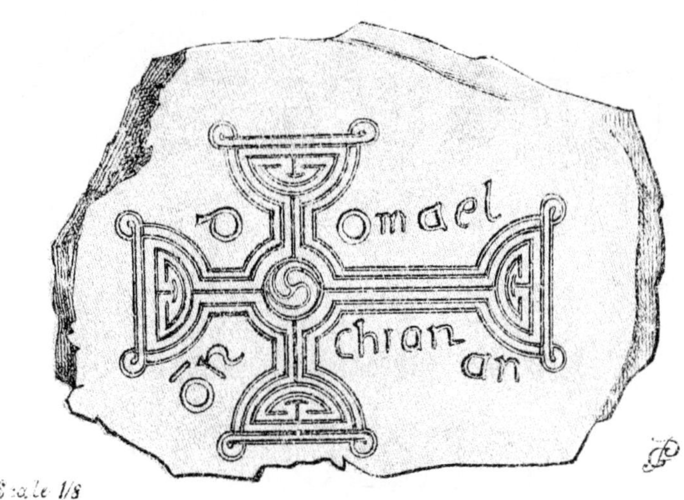

Scale 1/8

OR DO MAELCHIARAN

152

Scale 1/6

OR DO MAILMAIRE

Clonmacnois.

153

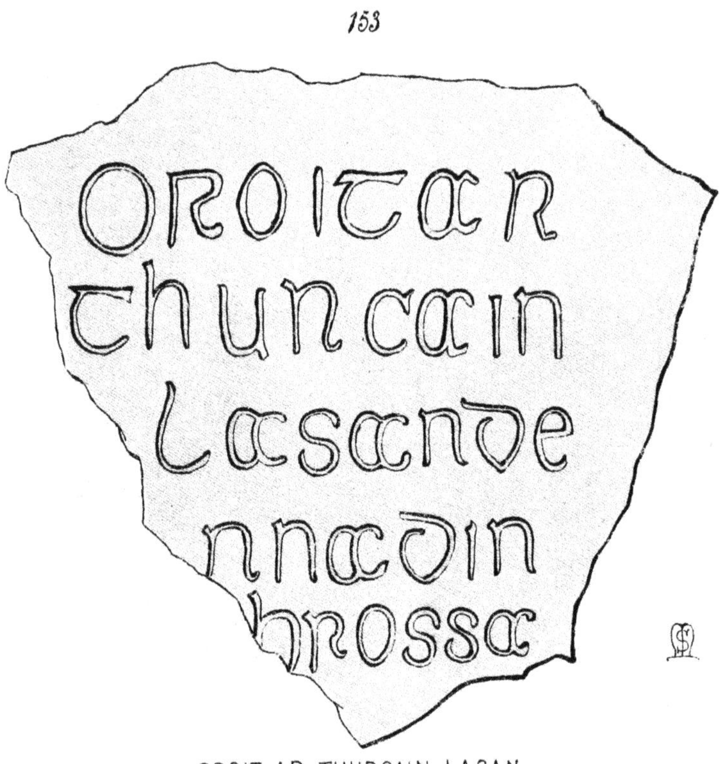

OROIT AR THURCAIN LASAN
DERNAD IN CHROSSA.

Scale 1/8

154

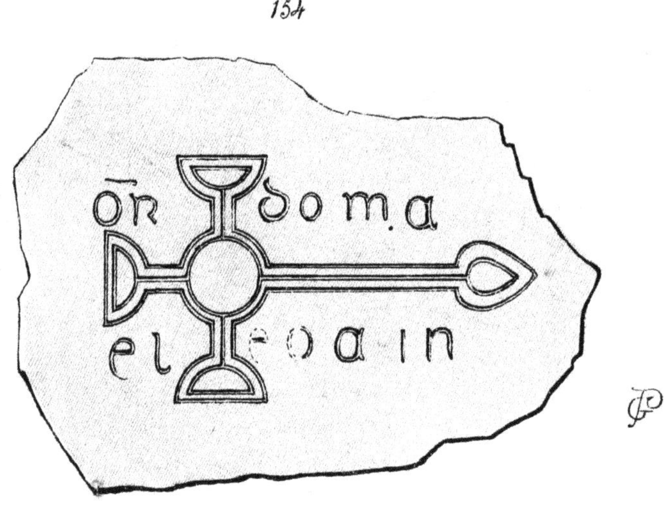

OR DO MAEL···A·IN.

Clonmacnois.

155

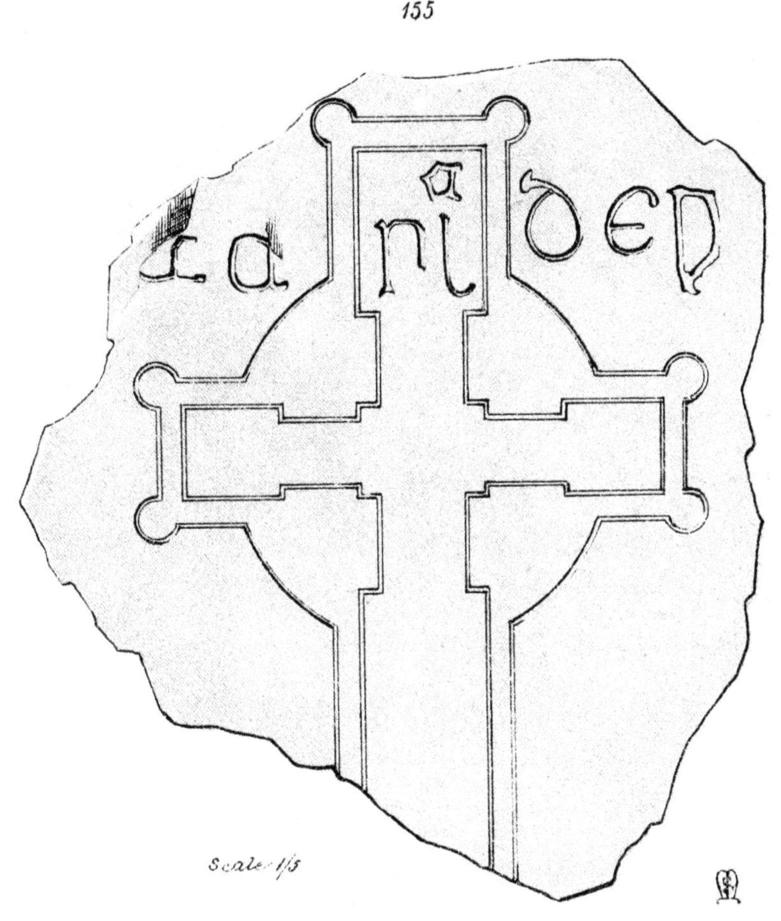

[HU] A R I A D E N

156

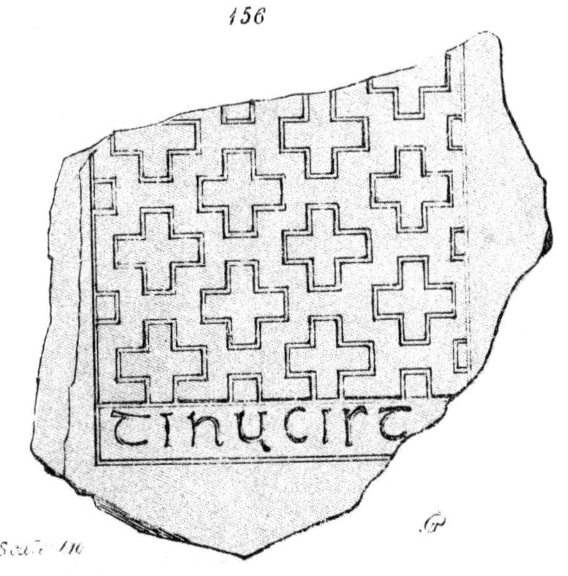

TIRUCIST

Clonmacnois

157

DO CHAINIG

158

Scale 1/6

OR DO MAELMHICHIL

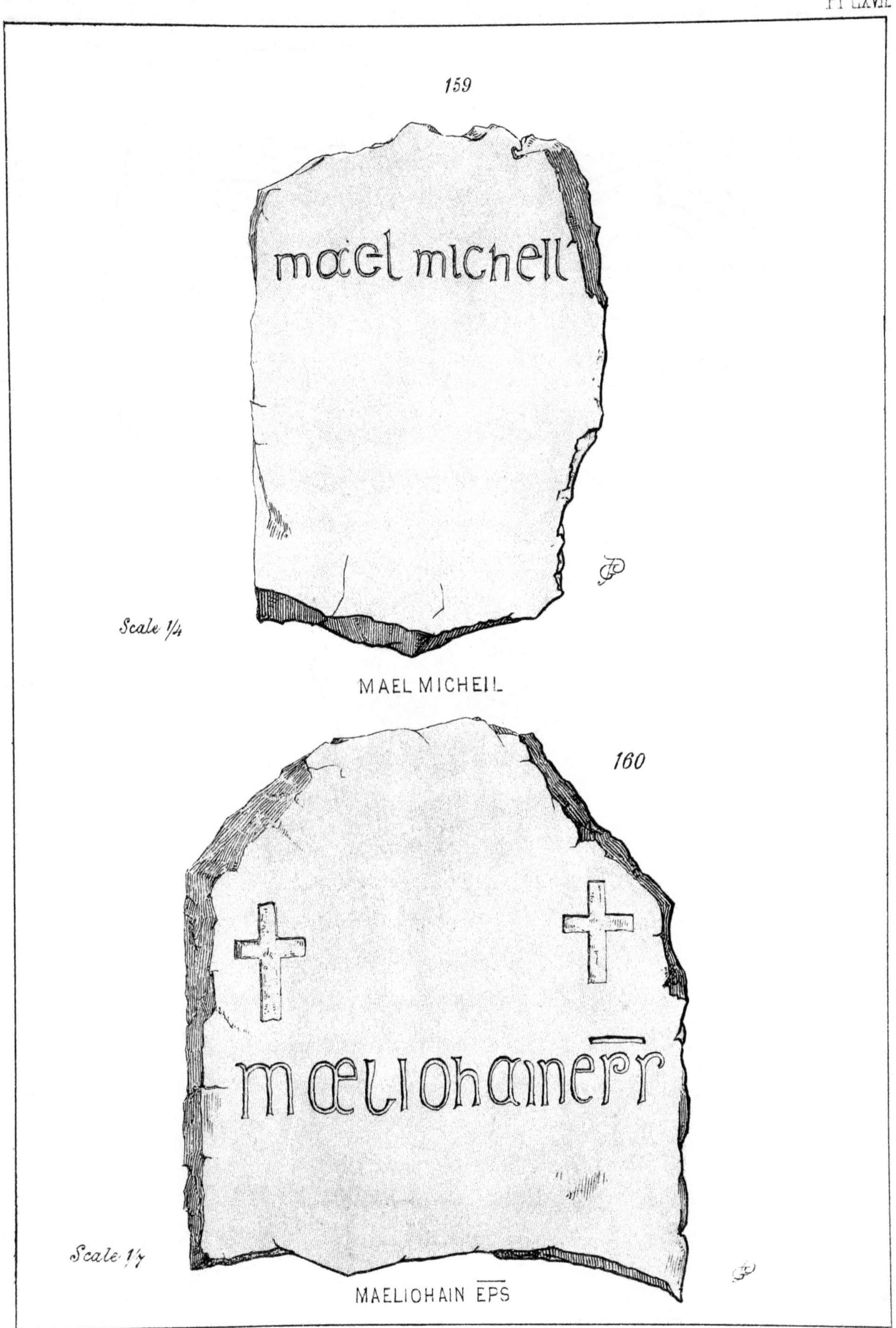

Clonmacnois.

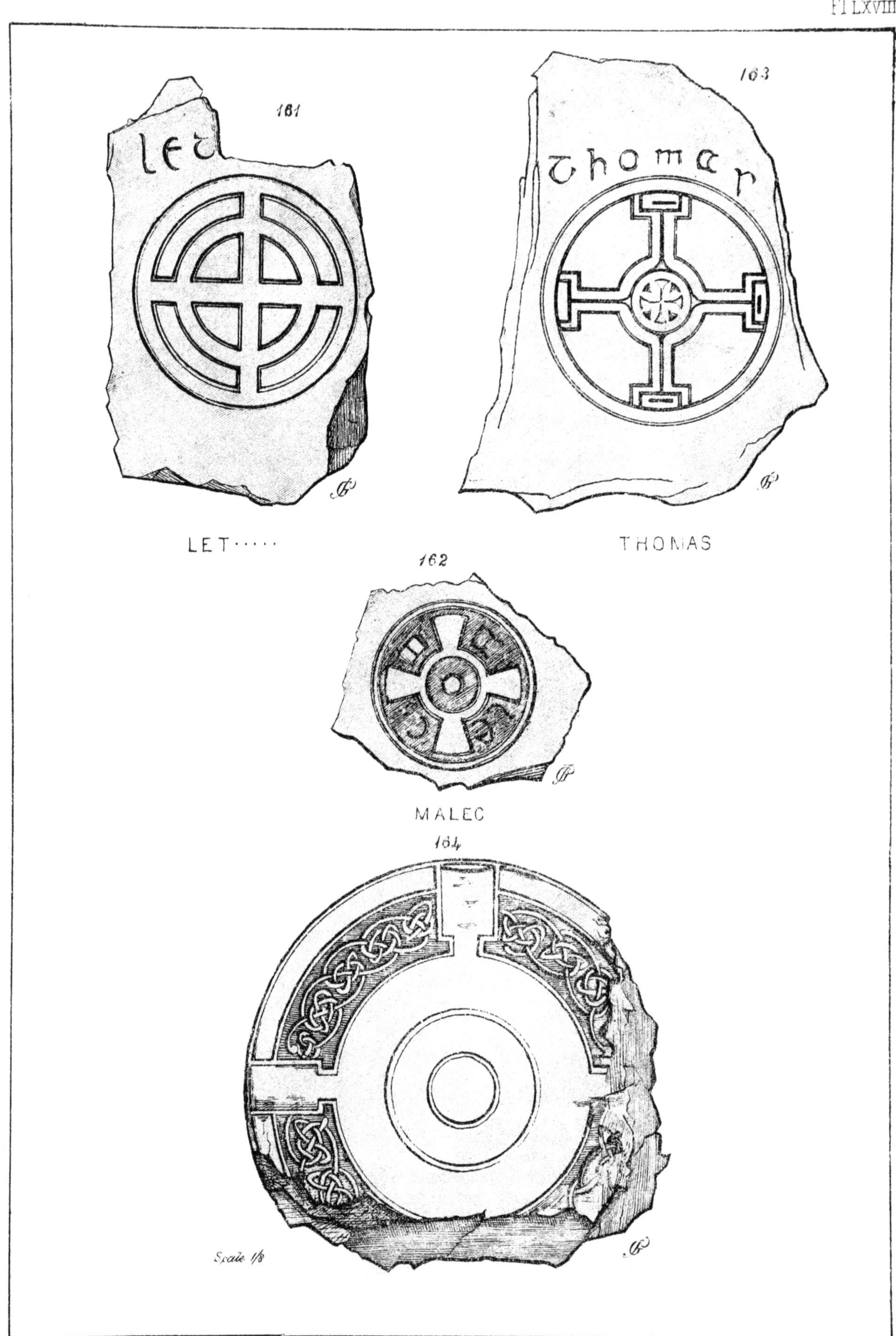

Clonmacnois

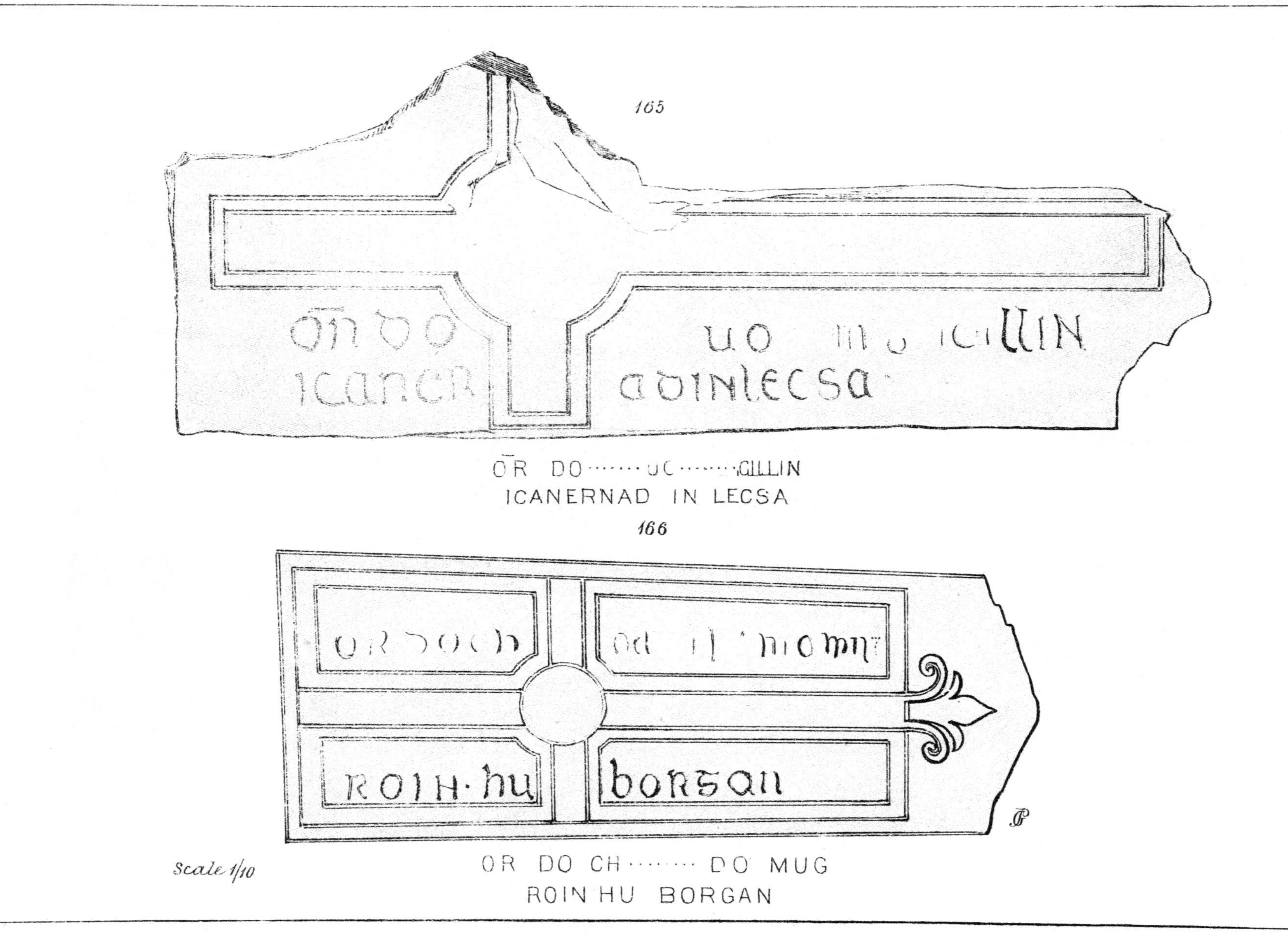

165

ŌR DO ...... UC ...... GILLIN
ICANERNAD IN LECSA

166

OR DO CH ...... DO MUG
ROIN HU BORGAN

scale 1/10

Clonmacnois

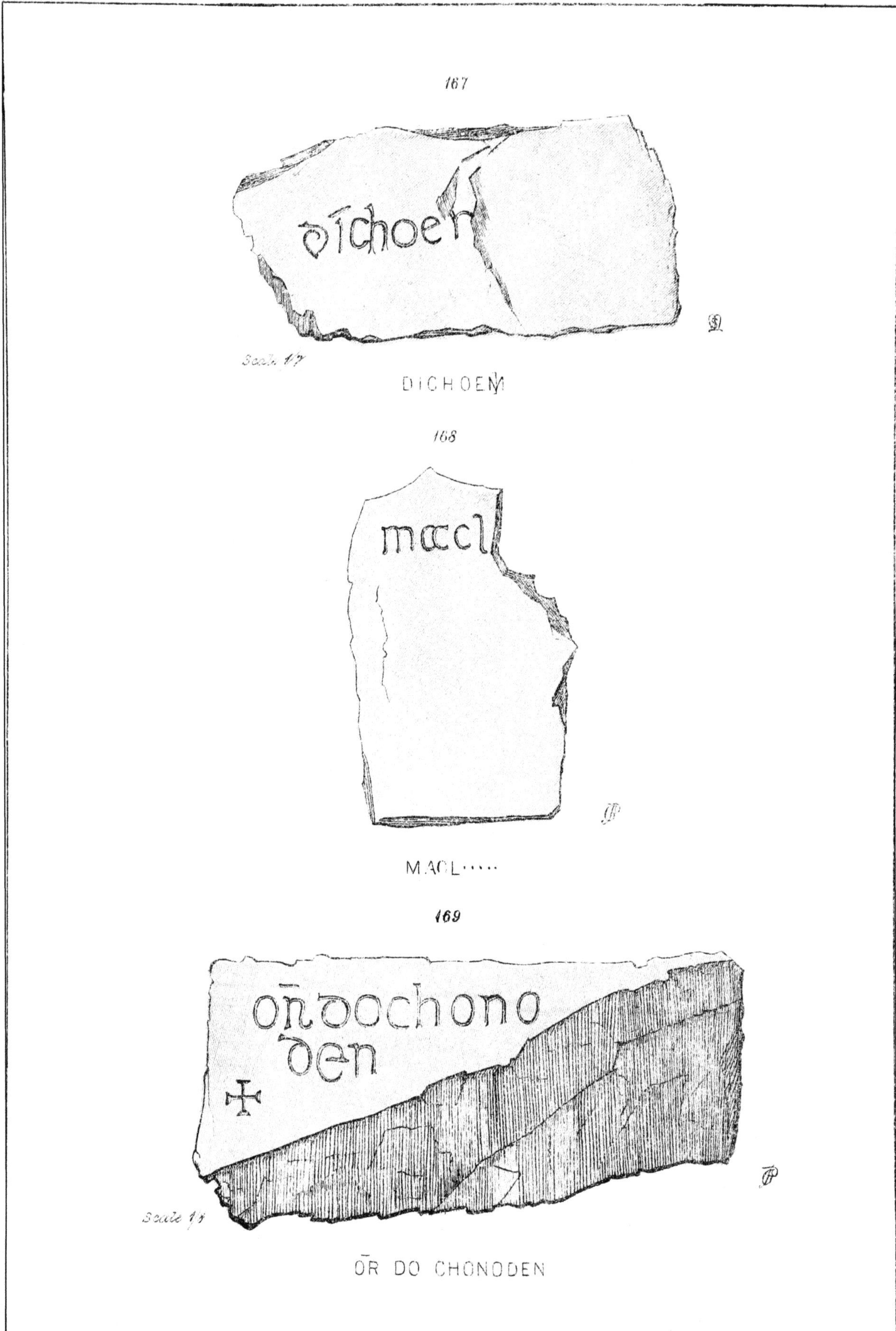

Clonmacnois

170

OR DO AED MAC······MAC TAIDG HUI CELLACH DO RIG HUMANE

Clonmacnois

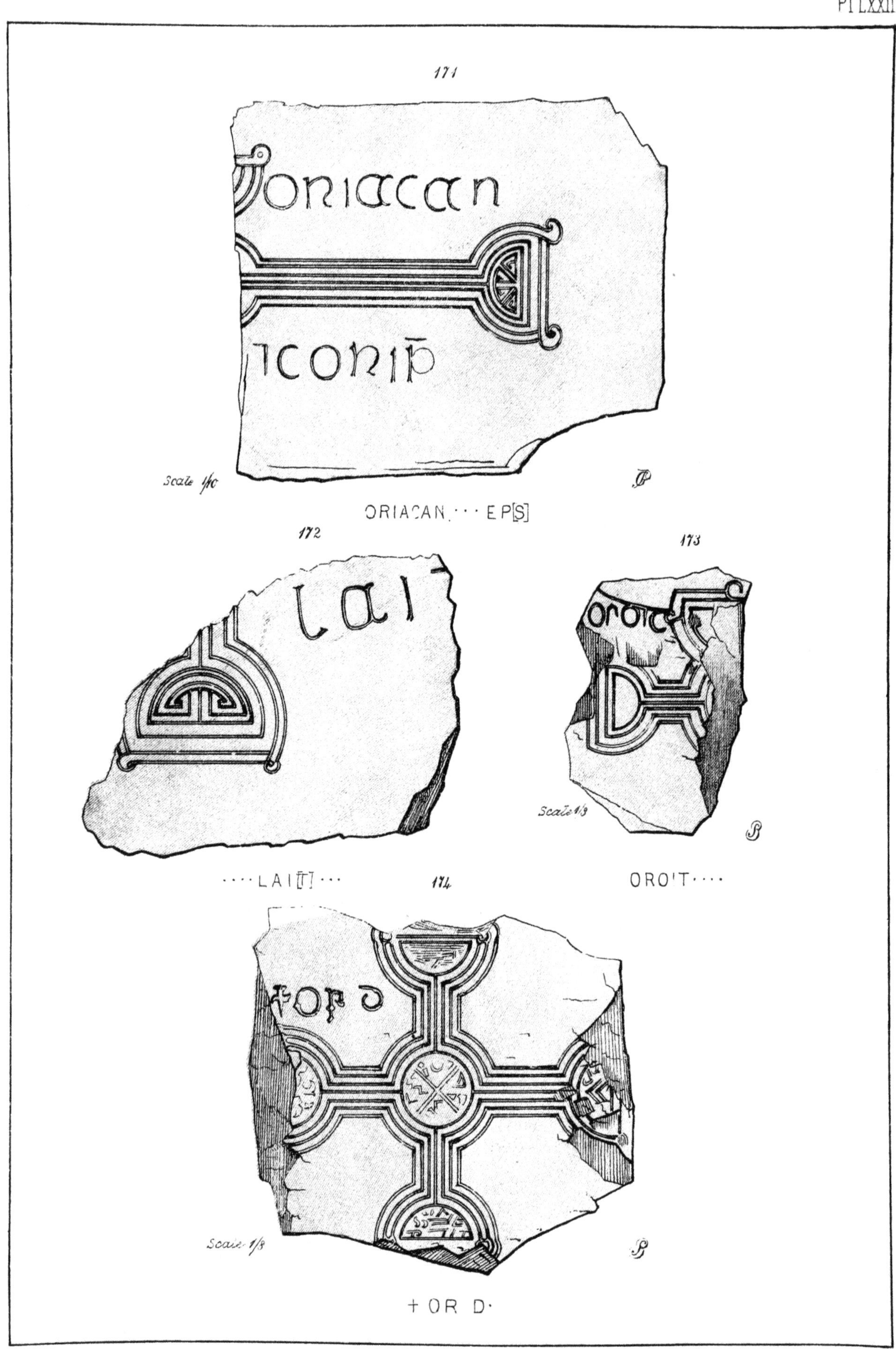

Clonmacnois

175

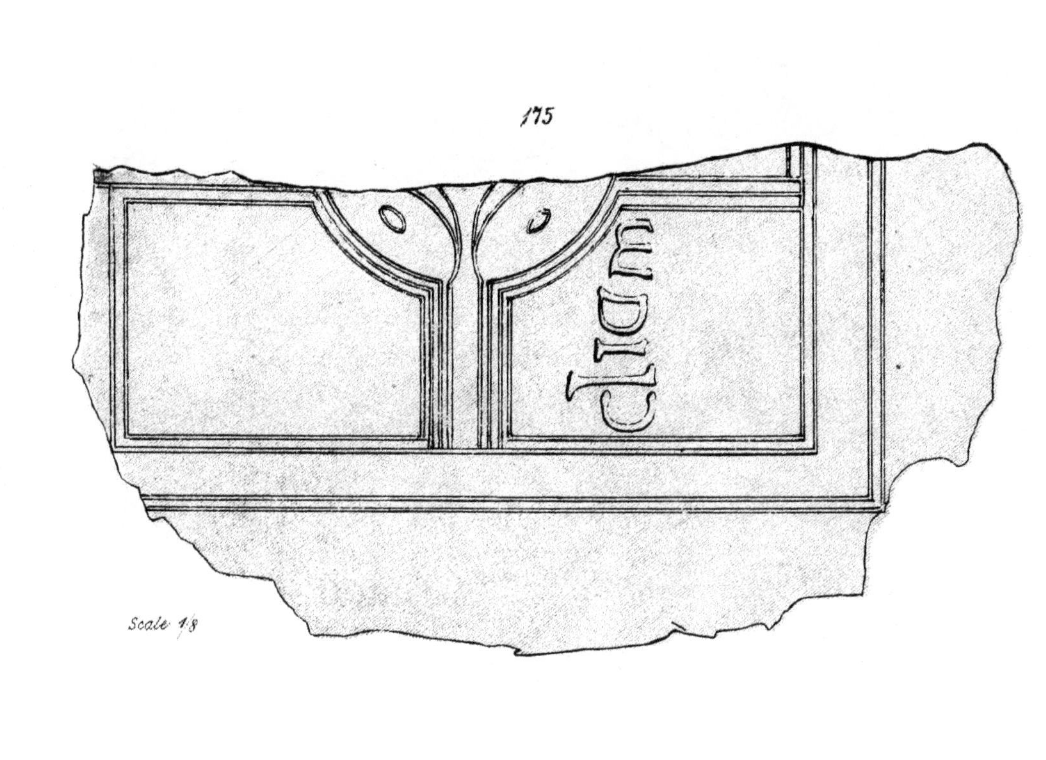

Scale 1/8

176

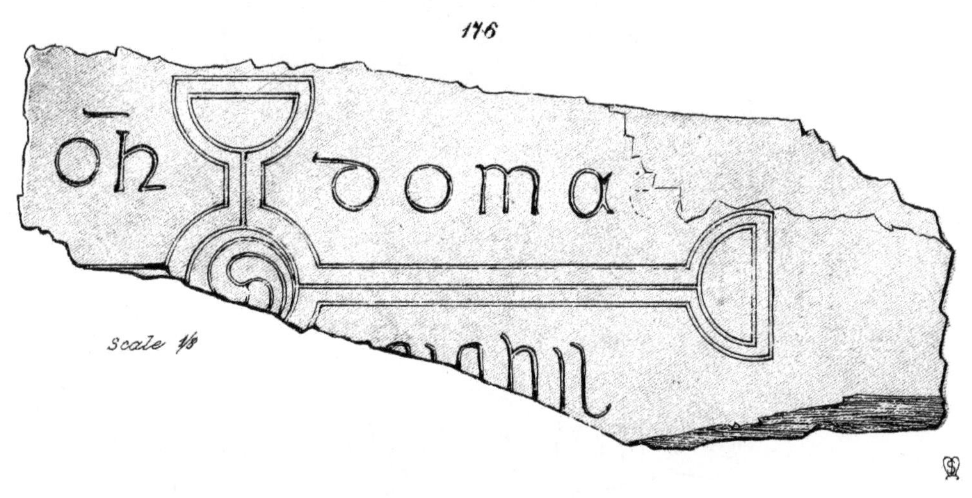

Scale 1/8

ŌR DO MA····ICH'IL

Clonmacnois

177

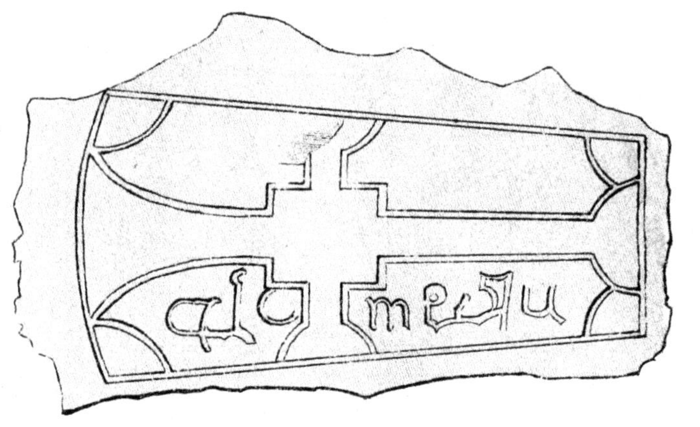

ARMEDA

178

+ DO CENNEDIG

179

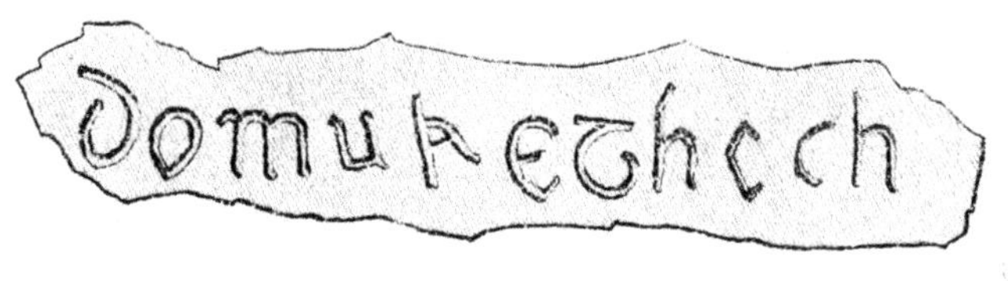

OR DO MURETHAGH

Clonmacnois.

For EU product safety concerns, contact us at Calle de José Abascal, 56–1°,
28003 Madrid, Spain or eugpsr@cambridge.org.

www.ingramcontent.com/pod-product-compliance
Ingram Content Group UK Ltd.
Pitfield, Milton Keynes, MK11 3LW, UK
UKHW051028150625
459647UK00023B/2857

* 9 7 8 1 1 0 8 0 8 0 1 3 2 *